FamilyCircle

Our Best Recipes

Meredith Consumer Marketing
Des Moines, Iowa

Family Circle. Our Best Recipes

Meredith. Consumer Marketing
Consumer Marketing Product Director: Heather Sorensen
Consumer Marketing Product Manager: Wendy Merical
Consumer Marketing Billing/Renewal Manager: Tami Beachem
Business Director: Ron Clingman
Senior Production Manager: Al Rodruck

Waterbury Publications, Inc.
Editorial Director: Lisa Kingsley
Associate Editor: Tricia Bergman
Associate Editor/Food Stylist: Annie Peterson
Assistant Food Stylist: Skyler Myers
Creative Director: Ken Carlson
Associate Design Director: Doug Samuelson
Production Assistant: Mindy Samuelson
Contributing Copy Editors: Terri Fredrickson, Gretchen Kauffman
Contributing Indexer: Mary Williams

Family Circle. Magazine
Editor in Chief: Linda Fears
Design Director: Lisa Kelsey
Food Director: Regina Ragone, M.S., R.D.
Executive Food Editor: Julie Miltenberger
Associate Food Editor: Michael Tyrrell
Associate Food Editor: Melissa Knific

Meredith National Media Group
President: Tom Harty

Meredith Corporation
Chairman and Chief Executive Officer: Stephen M. Lacy

In Memoriam: E.T. Meredith III (1933–2003)

Contents

HERE'S TO THE GOOD STUFF!

Since its beginning in the 1930s, the mission of *Family Circle* has been to help you, our readers, stay up to date on current news, trends, ideas and inspirations so that you can navigate the best and most meaningful part of your lives—your family. One of the most significant parts of creating a happy, healthy home is making mealtime as simple and pleasurable as possible. We pack the food section of every issue of the magazine with delicious, good-for-you recipes you can get on the table with minimal fuss.

We know that your family doesn't gather around the table simply to fuel up with nutritious food but also to spend time together—whether that's on a busy weeknight or to celebrate a special occasion. The recipes in this volume reflect both of those situations. *Family Circle Our Best Recipes* is packed with our favorites—more than 350 of the best recipes we've ever published. Our editors spent months combing through our collections to assemble the cream of the crop. The result: a balanced blend of beloved classics and new favorites.

There's something for everyone in these pages. The chapters cover everything from Appetizers to Desserts—and all courses and types of recipes in between. Throw a party and serve up nibbles such as elegant Crab Toasts (page 13), Salmon Sliders with Chipotle Mayonnaise (page 14), or fresh and light Vietnamese Vegetable Pinwheels (page 26). For a quick family dinner, try our speedy rendition of Chicken Cordon Bleu (page 60) or Panko Fried Fish and Smoky Chips (page 137). For a Meatless Monday, try slow-cooked Eggplant Parmesan (page 164). And for a special occasion, impress family and friends with Peppercorn-Crusted Beef Tenderloin (page 92) served with Scalloped Potatoes and Leeks with Manchego Cheese (page 222) and Mixed Lettuces with Pear and Blue Cheese (page 233). Follow it with Maple and Vanilla-Roasted Fruit (page 273)—or maybe Dark Chocolate Soufflé (page 271)!

Food and family are interconnected—this book will help you enjoy them both. We know there's a lot going on in your circle. We want to help you enjoy the ride and get to the good stuff every day.

—The Editors

CROSTINI,
RECIPES PAGE 10

Appetizers & Snacks

Throw a party or casual gathering with this collection of nibbles and drinks that makes entertaining easy.

CHERRY TOMATO
BRUSCHETTA

Cherry Tomato Bruschetta

MAKES 16 bruschettas **PREP** 20 minutes
GRILL 3 minutes

- 1 **loaf (10 oz) Italian bread, trimmed and cut into 16 pieces (each about ½ inch thick)**
- 3 **tbsp extra-virgin olive oil**
- 1 **cup ricotta cheese**
- ¼ **cup fresh basil leaves, chopped, plus small leaves for garnish**
- ½ **tsp lemon zest**
- ½ **tsp salt**
- ½ **tsp freshly ground black pepper**
- 2 **cloves garlic, halved lengthwise**
- 1½ **lb heirloom cherry tomatoes, sliced**
- 1 **tbsp lemon juice**

■ Heat grill or grill pan to medium-high. Brush bread slices on one side with 1 tbsp of the oil. Grill, oiled side down, for 1½ minutes. Brush with 1 tbsp oil and flip slices over. Grill another 1½ minutes or until toasted and lightly marked. Transfer to a platter.

■ In a medium bowl, stir together ricotta, 1 tbsp of the chopped basil, the lemon zest and ¼ tsp each of the salt and pepper.

■ Rub cut side of a garlic clove half on 4 of the bread slices. Repeat with remaining garlic clove halves and remaining grilled bread.

■ Gently toss cherry tomato slices with remaining 1 tbsp oil, remaining chopped basil, remaining ¼ tsp each salt and pepper and the lemon juice.

■ Spread 1 tbsp of the ricotta mixture on each grilled bread slice. Top with a spoonful of the tomato mixture and garnish with basil leaves.

PER BRUSCHETTA 106 **CAL**; 5 g **FAT** (2 g **SAT**); 4 g **PRO**; 11 g **CARB**; 1 g **FIBER**; 191 mg **SODIUM**; 8 mg **CHOL**

Pear, Goat Cheese and Hazelnut Crostini

MAKES 24 crostini **PREP** 15 minutes
BROIL 2 minutes

- 1 **French baguette (about ¾ lb)**
- 8 **oz semisoft goat cheese**
- 3 **tbsp heavy cream or milk**

PEAR, GOAT CHEESE AND HAZELNUT CROSTINI

1½ ripe pears
2 tbsp honey
⅓ cup toasted chopped hazelnuts
Freshly cracked black pepper

■ Slice French baguette on the bias into 24 slices. Using a hand mixer or spatula, combine goat cheese with heavy cream or milk until smooth. Spread 2 tsp of the goat cheese mixture on each crostino. Cut pears into twenty-four ¼-inch-thick slices; place 1 slice on top of each crostino. Drizzle honey over all the crostini. Broil on high for 2 minutes on the top rack. Top with hazelnuts and season with black pepper.

PER CROSTINO 110 CAL; 5 g FAT (3 g SAT); 4 g PRO; 12 g CARB; 1 g FIBER; 115 mg SODIUM; 10 mg CHOL

Egg Tartine

MAKES 1 tartine PREP 5 minutes

1 peeled hard-cooked egg (such as Eggland's Best), thinly sliced
1 slice black rye bread (such as Rubschlager)
2 tsp capers
2 tsp fresh dill, chopped
Olive oil, salt and freshly cracked black pepper

■ Layer egg slices on bread. Top with capers and chopped dill. Drizzle with olive oil and season with salt and pepper. Cut in half.

PER TARTINE 209 CAL; 10 g FAT (2 g SAT); 9 g PRO; 22 g CARB; 4 g FIBER; 402 mg SODIUM; 212 mg CHOL

RADISH-CRÈME FRAÎCHE TARTINE

RED PEPPER-HUMMUS TARTINE

EGG TARTINE

Radish-Crème Fraîche Tartine

MAKES 1 tartine PREP 5 minutes

1 tbsp crème fraîche
1 slice black rye bread (such as Rubschlager)
1 thinly sliced radish
1 tbsp sprouts
Sea salt and freshly cracked black pepper

■ Spread crème fraîche on bread. Layer on radish slices and scatter sprouts over tartine. Season with salt and pepper. Cut in half.

PER TARTINE 143 CAL; 6 g FAT (6 g SAT); 4 g PRO; 22 g CARB; 4 g FIBER; 178 mg SODIUM; 20 mg CHOL

Red Pepper–Hummus Tartine

MAKES 1 tartine PREP 5 minutes

4 tsp plain hummus
1 slice black rye bread (such as Rubschlager)
2 tbsp chopped roasted red pepper
1 tsp tahini
Harissa and fresh parsley

■ Spread hummus on bread. Scatter roasted red pepper on top, then drizzle with tahini. Garnish with harissa and parsley. Cut in half.

PER TARTINE 163 CAL; 5 g FAT (1 g SAT); 6 g PRO; 27 g CARB; 6 g FIBER; 354 mg SODIUM; 0 mg CHOL

GRILLED BRUSCHETTA CAPRESE

6   **tbsp extra-virgin olive oil, plus more for drizzling (optional)**
1   **tbsp lemon juice**
1   **tsp fresh chopped rosemary**
½   **tsp salt**
¼   **tsp black pepper**
24   **pieces crostini**

■ Heat oven to 400°. Place prosciutto on a baking sheet fitted with a rack. Bake at 400° for 15 to 18 minutes, until crispy. Roughly chop.

■ Set aside 1 cup beans. In a food processor, combine remaining beans, the oil, lemon juice, rosemary, salt and pepper. Stir in three-fourths of the prosciutto and the reserved beans. Spread 2 tbsp on each crostino. Garnish with remaining fourth of the prosciutto. Drizzle with more olive oil, if desired.

PER CROSTINO 107 **CAL**; 4 g **FAT** (1 g **SAT**); 4 g **PRO**; 13 g **CARB**; 2 g **FIBER**; 276 mg **SODIUM**; 2 mg **CHOL**

Roasted Grapes with Ricotta

MAKES 24 crostini   **PREP** 20 minutes
BAKE at 400° for 50 minutes

4   **cups red grapes**
1   **tbsp plus 1 tsp fresh thyme, plus more for garnish (optional)**
1   **tbsp olive oil**
¼   **tsp plus ⅛ tsp salt**
1   **container (15 oz) ricotta**
24   **pieces crostini**
1   **tbsp honey**

■ Heat oven to 400°. Toss grapes with 1 tbsp thyme, the olive oil and ⅛ tsp salt. Place on a rimmed baking sheet; roast at 400° for 40 to 50 minutes, shaking a few times, until wilted.

■ Mix ricotta and remaining 1 tsp thyme and ¼ tsp salt. Spread 1 generous tbsp on each crostino. Scatter grapes on top and garnish with more thyme, if desired. Drizzle with honey.

PER CROSTINO 103 **CAL**; 4 g **FAT** (2 g **SAT**); 4 g **PRO**; 14 g **CARB**; 0 g **FIBER**; 144 mg **SODIUM**; 9 mg **CHOL**

Grilled Bruschetta Caprese

MAKES 16 pieces   **PREP** 15 minutes
GRILL 2 minutes

1   **loaf sourdough bread (about 1 lb), cut into ½-inch-thick slices**
4   **garlic cloves, peeled**
2   **tbsp olive oil**
2   **tsp sea salt**
16   **large fresh basil leaves**
1   **lb fresh mozzarella, thinly sliced**
2   **heirloom tomatoes, thinly sliced**
  White balsamic vinegar

■ Heat a gas grill to medium-high or the coals in a charcoal grill to medium-hot.

■ Grill bread slices 1 minute per side, until toasted.

■ Rub one side of each slice with garlic, lightly brush with olive oil and sprinkle with a pinch of sea salt.

■ On each bruschetta, place a basil leaf, a slice of cheese and a tomato slice. Drizzle with balsamic vinegar and sprinkle with additional sea salt, if desired.

PER PIECE 192 **CAL**; 9 g **FAT** (5 g **SAT**); 10 g **PRO**; 18 g **CARB**; 1 g **FIBER**; 531 mg **SODIUM**; 20 mg **CHOL**

Crostini

Slice a 12-oz baguette into 24 pieces. Brush with 1 tbsp olive oil and bake at 400° for 8 to 10 minutes, until lightly toasted. Top with these three options.

Kale with Harissa

MAKES 24 crostini   **PREP** 20 minutes

8   **cups finely sliced kale, tough stems removed**
3   **tbsp light mayonnaise**
1   **tbsp harissa paste**
1   **tsp lemon juice**
⅛   **tsp salt**
24   **pieces crostini**

■ Toss kale with mayonnaise, harissa, lemon juice and salt. Set aside for 15 minutes. Mound on crostini.

PER CROSTINO 51 **CAL**; 1 g **FAT** (0 g **SAT**); 2 g **PRO**; 9 g **CARB**; 0 g **FIBER**; 125 mg **SODIUM**; 1 mg **CHOL**

White Bean and Prosciutto

MAKES 24 crostini   **PREP** 20 minutes
BAKE at 400° for 18 minutes

3   **oz prosciutto**
2   **cans cannellini beans, drained and rinsed**

WHITE BEAN AND
PROSCIUTTO

KALE WITH
HARISSA

ROASTED GRAPES
WITH RICOTTA

GREEK
FLATBREAD

CRAB TOASTS

CHEESY BROCCOLI AND
TOMATO FLATBREAD

Crab Toasts

MAKES 16 toasts **PREP** 15 minutes
BAKE at 400° for 12 minutes **COOK** 5 minutes

- 1 **French baguette (about 12 oz),
  cut on the bias into sixteen
  ½-inch-thick slices**
- 2 **tbsp olive oil**
- 2 **tbsp unsalted butter**
- 1 **cup cleaned and sliced leeks**
- ¼ **tsp crushed red pepper flakes**
- ¼ **cup light mayonnaise**
- ¼ **cup chopped fresh parsley, plus
  more for garnish**
- 1 **tbsp fresh lemon juice, plus 1 tsp
  zest**
- 1 **tsp Dijon mustard**
- ⅛ **tsp salt**
- 1 **lb lump crabmeat, drained**

■ Heat oven to 400°. Brush baguette slices on both sides with olive oil. Place on a baking sheet. Bake at 400° for 7 minutes; flip and bake another 5 minutes.

■ Melt butter in a skillet. Add leeks and red pepper flakes; sauté over medium heat for 5 minutes, until soft. Cool.

■ In a bowl, mix sautéed leeks with mayonnaise, parsley, lemon juice and zest, mustard and salt. Gently fold in crabmeat. Evenly spoon mixture onto toasts. Garnish with parsley. Chill in refrigerator until serving.

PER TOAST 134 **CAL**; 5 g **FAT** (2 g **SAT**); 8 g **PRO**; 13 g **CARB**; 1 g **FIBER**; 290 mg **SODIUM**; 30 mg **CHOL**

Greek Flatbread

MAKES 24 servings **PREP** 15 minutes
BAKE at 425° for 13 minutes

- 1 **cup artichoke tapenade**
- 8 **8-inch flatbreads (such as
  Toufayan lavash)**
- 1½ **cups shredded Fontina cheese**
- ¼ **cup halved, pitted Kalamata
  olives**
- ¼ **cup thinly sliced red onion**
- 2 **tbsp chopped fresh parsley**

■ Heat oven to 425°. Spread artichoke tapenade onto flatbreads. Top with cheese, Kalamata olives and red onion. Transfer to baking sheets and bake at 425° for 10 minutes. Carefully slide flatbreads from sheets directly to oven racks and bake for an additional 3 minutes, until crisp. Sprinkle with parsley and cut each square into 6 pieces.

PER SERVING 35 **CAL**; 6 g **FAT** (2 g **SAT**); 4 g **PRO**; 6 g **CARB**; 2 g **FIBER**; 178 mg **SODIUM**; 8 mg **CHOL**

Cheesy Broccoli and Tomato Flatbread

MAKES 6 servings **PREP** 10 minutes
COOK 7 minutes **BAKE** at 400° for 12 minutes

- 2 **tbsp olive oil**
- 3 **cups broccoli florets**
- 1 **cup sliced sweet onion**
- 3 **cloves garlic, sliced**
- ¼ **tsp salt**
- ¼ **tsp black pepper**
- 1 **flatbread multigrain pizza crust
  (10.5 oz)**
- 1½ **cups grated Fontina cheese**
- 1 **small tomato, thinly sliced**

■ Heat oven to 400°. Heat oil in a skillet over medium heat. Add broccoli and onion; sauté 5 minutes, until onion is soft. Add garlic; sauté 2 minutes. Stir in salt and pepper.

■ Place crust on a baking sheet. Scatter ¾ cup of the cheese on top. Distribute tomato slices and broccoli mixture on top, then scatter remaining ¾ cup cheese over it.

■ Bake at 400° for 12 minutes. Slice into 6 pieces.

PER SERVING 298 **CAL**; 15 g **FAT** (6 g **SAT**); 12 g **PRO**; 29 g **CARB**; 4 g **FIBER**; 574 mg **SODIUM**; 31 mg **CHOL**

CHEESE-STUFFED-CRUST PIZZA

SALMON SLIDERS WITH CHIPOTLE MAYONNAISE

Cheese-Stuffed-Crust Pizza

MAKES 16 squares   **PREP** 15 minutes
COOK 5 minutes   **BAKE** at 450° for 18 minutes

- 1 tbsp vegetable oil
- 1½ cups sliced mushrooms
- 1 yellow sweet pepper, seeded and sliced
- ½ red onion, sliced
- 1 refrigerated thin pizza crust
- 6 oz cheddar-mozzarella cheese sticks
- ½ cup marinara sauce
- ½ tsp dried oregano
- 1 cup reduced-fat shredded mozzarella cheese
- 1 oz sliced turkey pepperoni
- 1 cup grape tomatoes, halved

■ Heat oven to 450°. Heat oil in a large nonstick skillet over medium-high heat. Add mushrooms, yellow pepper and onion; cook for 5 minutes, stirring occasionally. Place on a plate and blot with a paper towel.

■ Meanwhile, unroll dough onto a baking sheet. With a floured rolling pin, roll into a 15 x 15-inch square. Place cheese sticks along the edges, cutting sticks as necessary. Roll 1 inch of dough over cheese and gently seal with a fork. Bake at 450° for 8 minutes. Remove from oven. Spread sauce evenly over pizza and sprinkle with oregano. Scatter mozzarella over pizza and top with vegetables, pepperoni and tomatoes. Bake at 450° for 8 to 10 minutes, until pizza is crisp and golden brown. Cool for 5 minutes. Cut into 16 squares.

PER SQUARE 143 **CAL**; 5 g **FAT** (3 g **SAT**); 9 g **PRO**; 16 g **CARB**; 1 g **FIBER**; 343 mg **SODIUM**; 15 mg **CHOL**

Salmon Sliders with Chipotle Mayonnaise

MAKES 16 sliders   **PREP** 15 minutes
COOK 6 minutes

- ½ cup plus 2 tbsp reduced-fat mayonnaise
- 1 tbsp adobo sauce, from canned chipotle in adobo
- 1½ lb salmon fillet, skin removed, cut into 1-inch pieces
- 1 red sweet pepper, cored, seeded and coarsely chopped
- 2 scallions coarsely chopped
- ½ cup panko bread crumbs
- 2 tbsp lemon juice
- ¼ tsp salt
- ¼ tsp black pepper
- 16 party-size potato rolls
  Lettuce (optional)

■ Combine ½ cup of the mayonnaise and the adobo. Cover and refrigerate.

■ In a food processor, add salmon, red pepper, scallions, panko, remaining 2 tbsp mayonnaise, the lemon juice, salt and black pepper. Pulse until just combined. Form into 16 patties (about scant ¼ cup each). Place on a greased baking sheet.

■ Heat a large nonstick skillet over medium-high heat and lightly coat with nonstick cooking spray. Cook patties in batches for 2 to 3 minutes per side, until browned and cooked through.

■ Place patties on rolls and spread about 1½ tsp chipotle mayonnaise over each. Add lettuce, if desired, and serve.

PER SLIDER 188 **CAL**; 8 g **FAT** (1 g **SAT**); 13 g **PRO**; 16 g **CARB**; 1 g **FIBER**; 280 mg **SODIUM**; 31 mg **CHOL**

Meatball Sliders

MAKES 12 sliders   **PREP** 15 minutes
BROIL 1 minute

- 1 pkg (12 oz) King's Hawaiian honey wheat rolls, split in half horizontally
- 1¼ cups marinara sauce
- 12 prepared Italian-style chicken meatballs
- 3 slices provolone cheese, sliced into quarters

■ Heat broiler to high. Place rolls on an aluminum foil-lined baking sheet.

■ In a small pot, heat marinara sauce. Stir in meatballs and heat until warmed through.

■ Place 1 meatball on each roll and spoon about 2 tbsp of the sauce over each. Top with a quarter slice of provolone.

■ Broil sliders for about 1 minute, until cheese melts and bread is lightly browned.

PER SLIDER 188 **CAL**; 8 g **FAT** (4 g **SAT**); 9 g **PRO**; 21 g **CARB**; 1 g **FIBER**; 434 mg **SODIUM**; 40 mg **CHOL**

Shrimp Salad Sliders

MAKES 12 sliders **PREP** 25 minutes
COOK 3 minutes

- ½ **lemon**
- 1 **lb peeled and cleaned shrimp**
- 2 **ribs celery, finely diced**
- ⅓ **cup light mayonnaise**
- 2 **tbsp minced shallot**
- 1 **tbsp chopped fresh dill**
- 1 **tbsp Dijon mustard**
- ¼ **tsp salt**
- **Pinch cayenne pepper**
- 12 **small soft dinner or slider rolls**
- 1 **cup packed arugula, chopped**

■ Bring a pot of water to a boil. Add juice from ½ lemon. Drop in shrimp and reduce heat to medium. Poach shrimp 2 to 3 minutes, until white. Drain and run under cold water until cool to the touch.

■ Finely chop shrimp and combine with celery, mayonnaise, shallot, dill, mustard, salt and cayenne. Cover and chill until serving.

■ Split rolls. Divide shrimp mixture evenly among them. Top each with chopped arugula.

PER SLIDER 179 **CAL**; 4 g **FAT** (0 g **SAT**); 12 g **PRO**; 24 g **CARB**; 1 g **FIBER**; 413 mg **SODIUM**; 63 mg **CHOL**

Chicken Tikka Masala Wings

MAKES 24 wings **PREP** 10 minutes
BAKE at 400° for 55 minutes

- 3 **lb drummettes and wings (about 24 pieces)**
- 2 **tbsp vegetable oil**
- 2 **tbsp unsalted butter plus 3 tbsp unsalted butter**
- 1 **tsp garam masala plus another ½ tsp garam masala**
- 1 **tsp salt**
- ⅓ **cup tomato sauce**
- **Fresh cilantro for garnish**

■ Coat a large rimmed baking sheet with nonstick cooking spray. In a bowl, toss drummettes and wings with 2 tbsp each vegetable oil and melted unsalted butter and 1 tsp each garam

CHICKEN TIKKA MASALA WINGS

masala and salt. Spread wings in a single layer on prepared sheet. Bake at 400° for 45 to 55 minutes, until crispy. Meanwhile, stir tomato sauce, 3 tbsp unsalted butter and ½ tsp garam masala in a small skillet over medium heat until simmering. Toss cooked wings with sauce in a clean bowl, transfer to a serving platter and garnish with chopped cilantro.

PER WING 90 **CAL**; 7 g **FAT** (3 g **SAT**); 5 g **PRO**; 0 g **CARB**; 0 g **FIBER**; 135 mg **SODIUM**; 35 mg **CHOL**

Korean-Style Fried Wings

MAKES 24 pieces **PREP** 20 minutes
FRY 36 minutes (12 minutes per batch)

- 6 **cups peanut oil**
- ¼ **cup cornstarch**
- 1 **tsp salt**
- ½ **tsp black pepper**
- ¼ **tsp cayenne pepper**
- ¾ **cup all-purpose flour**
- ¾ **cup cold water**
- 3 **cups panko bread crumbs, crushed**
- 24 **chicken wing pieces (3½ lb)**
- **Korean BBQ sauce, for dipping**

■ Place oil in a medium saucepan fitted with a deep-fry thermometer. Heat to 350°.

■ In a large bowl, whisk cornstarch, ½ tsp of the salt, the pepper and cayenne. In a second bowl, whisk flour and cold water. Place panko in a third bowl and season with remaining ½ tsp salt. Toss wing pieces in cornstarch mixture to coat.

■ Working in batches, dip wing pieces in flour batter, turning with tongs to coat completely. Lift from batter, allowing excess to drip back into bowl. Toss in panko and place on a wire rack set over a baking sheet.

■ Fry 8 wings at a time in hot oil for 6 minutes. Return to rack and repeat with remaining wings, allowing oil to return to 350° before adding next batch. Fry 6 more minutes per batch, until wings are golden, crispy and cooked through. Place on a paper towel-lined baking sheet. Serve with BBQ sauce on the side, for dipping.

PER PIECE 149 **CAL**; 8 g **FAT** (2 g **SAT**); 8 g **PRO**; 12 g **CARB**; 0 g **FIBER**; 143 mg **SODIUM**; 40 mg **CHOL**

SAUSAGE-BACON WRAPS

Sausage and Sage Arancini (Risotto Balls)

MAKES 24 arancini **PREP** 30 minutes
COOK 37 minutes **REFRIGERATE** 1 hour
FRY 3 minutes per batch

- 2 **links (about 6 oz) sweet Italian sausage, casings removed**
- ½ **cup diced onion**
- 2 **cloves garlic, minced**
- 2 **tbsp chopped fresh sage**
- 1 **cup Arborio rice**
- ½ **cup dry white wine**
- 2 **cups reduced-sodium chicken broth**
- ½ **tsp salt**
- ¼ **tsp black pepper**
- 8 **cups vegetable oil**
- 1 **egg, beaten**
- ¾ **cup plain bread crumbs**
- 24 **½-inch cubes Fontina cheese (about 3 oz)**

Marinara sauce (optional)

■ Heat a lidded pot over medium-high heat. Add sausage, breaking up with a spoon. Cook 6 minutes, until browned. Reduce heat to medium and stir in onion. Cook 3 to 5 minutes, until softened. Mix in garlic and sage; cook 1 minute. Stir in rice and wine. Cook until liquid evaporates. Pour in broth and 1½ cups water. Bring to a boil. Cover, reduce to a simmer and cook 25 minutes, until liquid is absorbed and rice is tender. Stir in salt and pepper. Spread rice on a rimmed baking sheet to cool 10 minutes, then refrigerate 1 hour.

■ Heat oil in a large, heavy-bottomed pot to 350° on a deep-fry thermometer. Scrape risotto into a bowl and mix with egg and ¼ cup of the bread crumbs. For each arancini, form a ball around a cube of cheese with 2 tbsp of the mixture. Roll in remaining bread crumbs.

■ Fry arancini in batches for 3 minutes each, maintaining temp around 350°. Place on a paper towel-lined plate; cool slightly. Serve hot with marinara on the side for dipping, if desired.

PER ARANCINO 100 **CAL**; 7 g **FAT** (2 g **SAT**); 3 g **PRO**; 6 g **CARB**; 0 g **FIBER**; 183 mg **SODIUM**; 15 mg **CHOL**

Honey Sesame Wings

MAKES 12 wings **PREP** 15 minutes
ROAST at 375° for 60 minutes

- ¼ **cup honey**
- 2 **tbsp sesame oil**
- 2 **tbsp reduced-sodium soy sauce**
- 1 **tbsp chopped fresh ginger**
- 2 **cloves garlic, chopped**
- 2½ **lb chicken wings (about 12)**
- 1 **tbsp sesame seeds**
- 3 **scallions, chopped**

■ Heat oven to 375°. Line a large shallow baking pan with nonstick foil.

■ In a small bowl, whisk together honey, sesame oil, soy sauce, ginger and garlic.

■ Place wings on prepared baking pan and roast at 375° for 45 minutes. Brush with half the honey-sesame mixture and roast an additional 10 minutes. Brush with remaining sauce and sprinkle with sesame seeds; roast 5 minutes. If desired, broil 1 to 2 minutes to crisp skin.

■ Garnish with chopped scallions.

PER WING 263 **CAL**; 18 g **FAT** (4 g **SAT**); 18 g **PRO**; 7 g **CARB**; 0 g **FIBER**; 173 mg **SODIUM**; 71 mg **CHOL**

Sausage-Bacon Wraps

MAKES 16 servings **PREP** 12 minutes
BAKE at 400° for 24 minutes
MICROWAVE 45 seconds

- 4 **center-cut bacon slices**
- 2 **tbsp apricot preserves plus another ⅓ cup**
- 1 **pkg (12 oz) spicy mango with jalapeño smoked chicken sausage**
- 1 **tbsp Dijon mustard**

■ Heat oven to 400°. Line a large baking sheet with parchment. Spread bacon slices on a cutting board, long edges touching. Spoon 2 tbsp apricot preserves into a small bowl. Spread about ½ tsp preserves over each slice of bacon. Cut slices in half. Cut smoked chicken sausage into 16 pieces (4 pieces per link). Roll up a sausage piece in a half slice of bacon. Secure with a toothpick and place, cut sides down, on prepared baking sheet. Repeat with 4 more bacon slices, remaining apricot preserves and remaining sausage. Bake at 400° for 12 minutes. Flip over and bake for another 12 minutes. Meanwhile, blend ⅓ cup apricot preserves with Dijon mustard. Microwave 45 seconds to heat. Serve with sausage-bacon wraps.

PER SERVING 81 **CAL**; 4 g **FAT** (1 g **SAT**); 4 g **PRO**; 9 g **CARB**; 0 g **FIBER**; 250 mg **SODIUM**; 21 mg **CHOL**

SAUSAGE AND
SAGE ARANCINI
(RISOTTO BALLS)

MEATBALL PARM
MUSHROOMS

KOREAN BEEF
SKEWERS

MINI CHICKEN
AND WAFFLES

Meatball Parm Mushrooms

MAKES 24 servings **PREP** 15 minutes
BAKE at 375° for 25 minutes

- 2 **pkg (14 oz) large stuffing mushrooms (about 24)**
- 12 **fully cooked Italian-style beef or chicken meatballs (thawed, if frozen)**
- 1½ **cups jarred spicy or traditional marinara sauce**
- ¾ **cup shredded Asiago cheese**
- ¼ **cup grated Parmesan**

■ Heat oven to 375°. Clean mushrooms and remove and discard stems. Place mushrooms, curved sides up, on a large rimmed baking sheet. Bake at 375° for 10 minutes. Remove tray from oven and carefully flip mushrooms over. Cut meatballs in half. Fit a meatball half into each mushroom cap and spoon 1 tbsp marinara sauce over each. Sprinkle mushrooms with Asiago cheese and grated Parmesan. Bake stuffed mushrooms at 375° for 15 minutes, until tops are lightly browned.

PER SERVING 57 **CAL**; 3 g **FAT** (1 g **SAT**); 5 g **PRO**; 4 g **CARB**; 4 g **FIBER**; 100 mg **SODIUM**; 0 mg **CHOL**

Korean Beef Skewers

MAKES 24 skewers **PREP** 15 minutes
BROIL 4 minutes

- 1 **lb shell steak (1½ to 2 inches thick)**
- ⅓ **cup Korean barbecue sauce (such as Sky Valley)**

  Sliced scallions (for garnish)

■ Slice steak on the bias into ¼-inch-thick slices. Toss with barbecue sauce. Thread on twenty-four 6-inch bamboo skewers (soaked in water) and place on a nonstick foil-lined baking sheet in a single layer. Broil on high for 2 minutes; flip and broil another 2 minutes. Garnish with sliced scallions.

PER SKEWER 35 **CAL**; 1 g **FAT** (1 g **SAT**); 4 g **PRO**; 1 g **CARB**; 0 g **FIBER**; 90 mg **SODIUM**; 10 mg **CHOL**

Mini Chicken and Waffles

MAKES 16 servings **PREP** 10 minutes
BAKE at 425° for 20 minutes **BROIL** 1 minute

- 16 **pieces popcorn chicken**
- 32 **mini Eggo waffles**
- 3 **tbsp peach preserves**
- 3 **tbsp honey mustard**

■ Heat oven to 425°. Spread popcorn chicken on a large rimmed baking sheet. Bake at 425° for 20 minutes, turning once. During the last 5 minutes, add mini Eggo waffles directly to oven rack. Remove chicken from oven and increase temperature to broil. Broil waffles 1 minute to toast until lightly browned. Spread ½ tsp peach preserves each on 16 of the waffles and ½ tsp honey mustard each on the 16 remaining waffles. Place each chicken piece between a preserves- and a mustard-coated waffle. Secure each with a toothpick.

PER SERVING 94 **CAL**; 4 g **FAT** (1 g **SAT**); 3 g **PRO**; 12 g **CARB**; 0 g **FIBER**; 180 mg **SODIUM**; 12 mg **CHOL**

CRAB-STUFFED MINI PEPPERS

MINI CRAB CAKES WITH DIJON THYME AÏOLI

Mini Crab Cakes with Dijon Thyme Aïoli

MAKES 24 pieces **PREP** 30 minutes
REFRIGERATE 30 minutes **COOK** 12 minutes

AÏOLI

- ½ **cup mayonnaise**
- 1 **tbsp Dijon mustard**
- 1 **tbsp olive oil**
- 1 **tsp fresh thyme leaves**

CRAB CAKES

- 1 **lb crabmeat**
- ½ **cup plain dry bread crumbs**
- 1 **egg, lightly beaten**
- 2 **tbsp lemon juice**
- 1 **tbsp mayonnaise**
- 1 **tbsp Dijon mustard**
- 2 **tsp Old Bay seasoning**
- 2 **scallions, chopped**
- ¼ **cup canola oil**

■ **Aïoli.** In a small bowl, combine mayonnaise, mustard, olive oil and thyme. Cover and refrigerate until ready to serve.

■ **Crab Cakes.** In a large bowl, combine crabmeat, bread crumbs, egg, lemon juice, mayonnaise, mustard, Old Bay and scallions. Gently mix. Form into 24 small patties, about 2 heaping tbsp each. Place on a large wax paper-lined baking sheet and refrigerate 30 minutes.

■ In a large nonstick skillet, heat 2 tbsp of the oil over medium-high heat. Cook half the crab cakes 2 to 3 minutes per side, until nicely browned. Remove to a plate and repeat with remaining oil and crab cakes. Serve crab cakes with aïoli.

PER PIECE 74 **CAL**; 5 g **FAT** (1 g **SAT**); 4 g **PRO**; 2 g **CARB**; 0 g **FIBER**; 177 mg **SODIUM**; 24 mg **CHOL**

Crab-Stuffed Mini Peppers

MAKES 24 pieces **PREP** 15 minutes
BAKE at 300° for 15 minutes

- 12 **oz lump crabmeat**
- 2 **tbsp mayonnaise**
- 2 **tbsp finely chopped sweet red pepper**
- 2 **tbsp Dijon mustard**
- ¼ **cup snipped dill plus additional for garnish (if desired)**
- 2 **tbsp olive oil**
- ¼ **tsp salt**
- ¼ **tsp black pepper**
- 12 **mini sweet peppers**

■ Heat oven to 300°. Combine crabmeat, mayonnaise, red pepper, Dijon mustard, dill, olive oil, salt and black pepper. Slice sweet peppers in half horizontally and fill with crab mixture. Place on a baking sheet and bake at 300° for 15 minutes. Garnish with additional fresh dill, if desired.

PER PIECE 27 **CAL**; 1 g **FAT** (0 g **SAT**); 3 g **PRO**; 0 g **CARB**; 0 g **FIBER**; 175 mg **SODIUM**; 10 mg **CHOL**

Shrimp Dumplings with Miso Dipping Sauce

MAKES 8 servings (48 dumplings)
PREP 1 hour **COOK** 12 minutes

- 2 **tbsp white miso paste**
- 2 **tsp rice vinegar**
- 6 **large scallions, sliced**
- 1 **tsp wasabi**
- 1 **tbsp low-sodium soy sauce**
- 1 **lb uncooked peeled and deveined shrimp, finely chopped**
- 1 **can (8 oz) water chestnuts, drained and finely chopped**
- 4 **tsp grated fresh ginger**
- 1 **pkg (12 oz) wonton wrappers**
- 2 **egg whites, lightly beaten**

■ In a small bowl, whisk together miso paste, rice vinegar and ½ cup water until smooth. Stir in 2 of the sliced scallions. Cover; set aside until serving.

■ In a separate bowl, whisk together wasabi and soy sauce until smooth. Stir in remaining scallions, the shrimp, water chestnuts and ginger. Bring a large pot of lightly salted water to a boil. Place 1 wonton wrapper on a dry surface. Add 2 tsp filling to center and brush edges with egg whites. Bring together corners and press firmly to seal (see folding instructions on package). Repeat with remaining wrappers. (Cover wrappers and dumplings with damp towels while prepping.)

■ Add 12 dumplings to boiling water. Cook for 3 minutes; dumplings will float to surface. Repeat 3 more times, until all dumplings are cooked. Serve hot with miso dipping sauce.

PER SERVING 207 **CAL**; 2 g **FAT** (0 g **SAT**); 18 g **PRO**; 29 g **CARB**; 3 g **FIBER**; 559 mg **SODIUM**; 93 mg **CHOL**

**GRILLED PEPPERS,
SHRIMP AND CHORIZO**

Grilled Peppers, Shrimp and Chorizo

MAKES 8 appetizer servings **PREP** 20 minutes
GRILL 28 minutes

- **2 tbsp olive oil, plus more for coating peppers**
- **1 tbsp white wine vinegar**
- **½ tsp smoked paprika**
- **¼ tsp garlic powder**
- **¼ tsp plus ⅛ tsp salt**
- **½ lb large peeled and deveined shrimp**
- **4 sweet peppers (combination of red, orange and yellow)**
- **2 fully cooked chorizo sausages (3 oz each), split lengthwise**
-    **Fresh parsley, chopped (optional)**

■ Heat grill or grill pan to medium-high heat. In a bowl, whisk together oil, vinegar, paprika, garlic powder and salt. Toss 2 tsp of the vinaigrette with shrimp. Thread shrimp onto 2 skewers. Set aside remaining vinaigrette.

■ Lightly coat peppers with oil. Grill over medium-high heat for 20 minutes, turning every 5 minutes. Transfer to a bowl and cover with plastic wrap to cool slightly. Peel and discard skins (it's okay to leave a little on). Quarter peeled peppers, discarding stems and cores. Toss with remaining vinaigrette.

■ Grill the 4 chorizo halves 3 to 4 minutes per side. Slice into half-moons. Grill shrimp skewers 2 minutes per side, until cooked through.

■ Arrange pepper quarters on a large platter. Scatter chorizo and shrimp on top; drizzle with any residual vinaigrette. Garnish with chopped parsley, if desired.

PER SERVING 139 **CAL**; 9 g **FAT** (2 g **SAT**); 9 g **PRO**; 6 g **CARB**; 2 g **FIBER**; 295 mg **SODIUM**; 56 mg **CHOL**

Buffalo Deviled Eggs

MAKES 18 servings **PREP** 10 minutes
COOK 10 minutes **STAND** 10 minutes

- **9 large eggs**
- **2 tbsp bottled blue cheese dressing**

WEDGE SALAD STACKS

- **2 tbsp light mayonnaise**
- **2 tbsp Frank's hot sauce, plus more for drizzling**
- **1 celery rib, finely diced**
- **2 tbsp crumbled blue cheese**
- **2 tbsp celery leaves, chopped (optional)**

■ Place eggs in a medium saucepan. Add cold water to cover by 1 inch. Bring to a boil, then reduce heat to medium and simmer 10 minutes. Drain and run under cool water. Let stand in cool water 10 minutes.

■ Peel eggs and cut in half lengthwise. If making ahead, refrigerate peeled eggs in a resealable plastic bag overnight. Place yolks in a medium bowl and whites on a platter. Add dressing, mayonnaise and hot sauce to yolks and mash with a fork until smooth. Stir in celery and blue cheese; transfer to a quart-size resealable plastic bag. Snip off a ¾-inch corner and pipe mixture into egg whites. Garnish with chopped celery leaves, if desired, and drizzle with more hot sauce.

PER EGG HALF 56 **CAL**; 4 g **FAT** (1 g **SAT**); 3 g **PRO**; 1 g **CARB**; 0 g **FIBER**; 120 mg **SODIUM**; 95 mg **CHOL**

Wedge Salad Stacks

MAKES 16 stacks **PREP** 15 minutes
MICROWAVE 3 minutes

- **8 thick-cut bacon slices, cut into quarters (32 pieces total)**
- **1 head of iceberg lettuce**
- **8 grape or cherry tomatoes**
-    **Bottled blue cheese salad dressing**
- **¼ cup crumbled blue cheese (optional)**

■ Cut bacon slices into quarters (32 pieces total). Stack on layers of paper towels and microwave 3 minutes until cooked but still pliable. Cut a 1-inch slice from a head of iceberg lettuce. Cut slice crosswise into 1-inch squares (you'll need a total of 16 squares, so you may have to cut another slice from the head of lettuce). Using 6-inch bamboo skewers, begin making stacks: On each skewer, slide 1 lettuce square, 2 bacon pieces and half a grape or cherry tomato. Place on a platter and drizzle stacks with a few tbsp bottled blue cheese salad dressing. Sprinkle with crumbled blue cheese (if desired). Serve ⅓ cup additional dressing for dipping.

PER STACK 80 **CAL**; 7 g **FAT** (2 g **SAT**); 3 g **PRO**; 1 g **CARB**; 0 g **FIBER**; 202 mg **SODIUM**; 9 mg **CHOL**

VIETNAMESE
VEGETABLE
PINWHEELS

Vietnamese Vegetable Pinwheels

MAKES 24 pieces **PREP** 20 minutes
REFRIGERATE 2 to 4 hours

- **4 burrito-size flour tortillas**
- **4 large leaves red leaf lettuce, tough ribs removed**
- **4 tbsp sesame-soy salad dressing, plus more for dipping (optional)**
- **1⅓ cups shredded cabbage**
- **½ cup shredded carrot**
- **1 cucumber, peeled, cut into 2-inch matchsticks**
- **4 tsp rice vinegar**
- **1 cup fresh cilantro leaves**
- **1 cup fresh mint leaves**

■ Place a tortilla on a flat work surface. On one side place a lettuce leaf and drizzle with 1 tbsp of the dressing. Layer with ⅓ cup cabbage, 2 tbsp carrot and 12 cucumber sticks. Drizzle with 1 tsp vinegar and top with some of the cilantro and mint. Roll up tightly and wrap in plastic wrap. Twist ends of wrap to secure tightly. Repeat with remaining ingredients. Refrigerate 2 to 4 hours.

■ To serve, unwrap rolls and cut each on the bias into 6 pieces. If desired, serve with additional dressing for dipping.

PER PIECE 36 **CAL**; 1 g **FAT** (0 g **SAT**); 0 g **PRO**; 7 g **CARB**; 1 g **FIBER**; 85 mg **SODIUM**; 0 mg **CHOL**

GAZPACHO

Gazpacho

MAKES 6 servings **PREP** 15 minutes
STAND 15 minutes **CHILL** 1 hour

3	slices white bread
2	lb tomatoes, stemmed and roughly chopped
1	red sweet pepper, cored, seeded and roughly chopped
1¼	cups diced cucumber
1	cup diced white onion
1	large clove garlic
⅓	cup extra-virgin olive oil, plus more for drizzling (optional)
3	tbsp sherry vinegar, plus more for drizzling (optional)
1¼	tsp salt
¼	tsp black pepper

■ In a bowl, cover bread slices with cold water; let stand 15 minutes. Drain and squeeze water from bread.

■ In a food processor, combine tomatoes, sweet pepper, 1 cup of the cucumber, the onion, garlic and ½ cup cold water. Process until very finely chopped. Add bread, oil, vinegar, salt and black pepper. Process until smooth.

■ Transfer to a resealable container and chill for 1 hour. Garnish gazpacho with remaining ¼ cup cucumber and, if desired, drizzle with additional olive oil and vinegar.

PER SERVING 194 **CAL**; 13 g **FAT** (2 g **SAT**); 3 g **PRO**; 19 g **CARB**; 3 g **FIBER**; 597 mg **SODIUM**; 0 mg **CHOL**

SPANAKOPITA CUPS

Spanakopita Cups

MAKES 30 mini cups **PREP** 15 minutes
BAKE at 350° for 15 minutes

1	pkg (10 oz) thawed frozen spinach (squeezed dry)
1	large chopped scallion
1	tbsp olive oil
1	tsp dry minced onion
½	tsp garlic powder
1	cup crumbled herb-flavor feta
2	eggs
30	mini phyllo shells (two 1.9-oz pkg)

■ Heat oven to 350°. In a large skillet, cook spinach and scallion in olive oil 4 minutes. Stir in onion and garlic powder. In a large bowl, combine spinach mixture with feta and lightly beaten eggs. Spoon mixture into shells. Place on a baking sheet and bake at 350° for 15 minutes.

PER MINI CUP 39 **CAL**; 2 g **FAT** (1 g **SAT**); 2 g **PRO**; 3 g **CARB**; 0 g **FIBER**; 78 mg **SODIUM**; 16 mg **CHOL**

FRIED GREEN TOMATOES WITH RED PEPPER AÏOLI

Fried Mac and Cheese Bites

MAKES 30 bites **PREP** 30 minutes
COOK 7 minutes **REFRIGERATE** overnight
FRY 4 minutes per batch

12	oz (about 4 cups) elbow macaroni
2	tbsp unsalted butter
2	tbsp all-purpose flour
1½	cups milk
½	tsp salt
¼	tsp black pepper
	Pinch cayenne pepper
2	cups shredded cheddar
4	oz thinly sliced deli American cheese, cut into thin strips
1	cup shredded mozzarella
2	large eggs
1	box (8 oz) Italian seasoned panko bread crumbs
6	cups peanut or vegetable oil, for frying

■ Bring a large pot of lightly salted water to a boil. Add macaroni and cook per package directions; drain.

■ Meanwhile, melt butter in a saucepan over medium heat. Whisk in flour, cooking until bubbly. While whisking, add 1¼ cups of the milk in a thin stream. Season with salt, black pepper and cayenne. Bring to a simmer and cook 2 minutes. Remove from heat and mix in 1 cup of the cheddar and the American cheese. Fold into macaroni. Let cool slightly, then stir in mozzarella and remaining 1 cup cheddar. Spread onto a rimmed sheet. Cover with plastic and refrigerate overnight.

■ Use a scoop to spoon out about ¼ cup of the mixture at a time; shape into 2- to 3-inch balls, compressing slightly.

■ Whisk eggs with remaining ¼ cup milk. Dip balls in egg mixture, then coat in panko.

■ Heat oil in a deep 4-qt pot to 360° on a deep-fry thermometer. Fry 6 or 7 mac and cheese bites at a time for 3 to 4 minutes per batch, until golden. Serve immediately.

PER BITE 200 **CAL**; 14 g **FAT** (5 g **SAT**); 6 g **PRO**; 13 g **CARB**; 0 g **FIBER**; 255 mg **SODIUM**; 31 mg **CHOL**

Fried Green Tomatoes with Red Pepper Aïoli

MAKES 9 servings **PREP** 25 minutes
COOK 4 minutes per batch
KEEP WARM in 200° oven

RED PEPPER AÏOLI

½	cup light mayonnaise
¼	cup roasted red peppers, drained
1	large clove garlic, coarsely chopped

TOMATOES

2	lb firm green tomatoes
½	tsp salt
⅓	cup all-purpose flour
2	large eggs
⅔	cup yellow cornmeal
2	tbsp grated Parmesan cheese
⅛	tsp black pepper
	Pinch cayenne pepper
7	tbsp vegetable or canola oil, for frying

■ **Aïoli.** Combine mayonnaise, red peppers and garlic in a mini chopper. Process until well combined and fairly smooth, scraping down sides of chopper halfway through. Transfer to a small bowl. Refrigerate until serving.

■ **Tomatoes.** Core tomatoes and cut a thin slice from top and bottom of each. Cut each tomato into three or four ¼-inch-thick slices and dry slightly on paper towels. Sprinkle with ⅛ tsp of the salt.

■ Combine flour and ⅛ tsp of the salt in a shallow dish. Lightly beat eggs in a second shallow dish; whisk together cornmeal, Parmesan, remaining ¼ tsp salt, the black pepper and cayenne in a third shallow dish.

■ Coat 6 of the tomato slices in seasoned flour, followed by eggs, then cornmeal mixture. Heat oven to 200°.

■ Heat 3 tbsp of the oil in a large nonstick skillet over medium-high heat. Add the 6 coated tomato slices and fry for 2 minutes. Carefully flip over slices and fry an additional 2 minutes. Transfer to a baking sheet fitted with a wire rack and keep warm in oven. Repeat, coating all tomato slices with seasoned flour, egg and cornmeal mixture.

■ Add 2 tbsp of the oil to skillet before frying each consecutive batch (you should have 2 more batches to fry). Serve tomatoes warm with aïoli on the side.

PER SERVING 216 **CAL**; 17 g **FAT** (2 g **SAT**); 4 g **PRO**; 13 g **CARB**; 1 g **FIBER**; 299 mg **SODIUM**; 53 mg **CHOL**

**FRIED MAC AND
CHEESE BITES**

BUTTERNUT SQUASH-GOAT
CHEESE BITES

BUFFALO CHICKEN SALAD

Butternut Squash-Goat Cheese Bites

MAKES 30 bites **PREP** 20 minutes
BAKE at 350° for 10 minutes **FRY** 30 seconds

1	cup frozen cooked winter squash puree, thawed (such as Birds Eye, from a 12-oz pkg)
2	tbsp heavy cream
4	oz soft goat cheese, at room temperature
1	egg yolk
¾	tsp salt
⅛	tsp ground white pepper
2	boxes (1.9 oz each) Athens Mini Fillo Shells
⅓	cup canola oil
30	fresh sage leaves

■ Heat oven to 350°. In a small pot, whisk together squash and heavy cream over medium-low heat. When hot, whisk in goat cheese until melted. Remove from heat and stir in egg yolk, ½ tsp of the salt and the pepper. Cool slightly.

■ Place pastry shells on a baking sheet. Transfer squash mixture into a resealable plastic bag; snip corner. Pipe into pastry shells. Bake at 350° for 8 to 10 minutes, until set.

■ In a small skillet, heat canola oil until shimmering. Fry sage leaves (in 2 batches) for 30 seconds, until crisp. Remove to a paper towel and sprinkle with remaining ¼ tsp salt. Garnish bites with fried sage leaves.

PER BITE 37 **CAL**; 2 g **FAT** (1 g **SAT**); 1 g **PRO**; 3 g **CARB**; 0 g **FIBER**; 81 mg **SODIUM**; 10 mg **CHOL**

POMEGRANATE GUACAMOLE

Buffalo Chicken Salad

MAKES 4 servings **PREP** 15 minutes
COOK 10 minutes

1½	lb boneless, skinless chicken breasts
2	large ribs celery, diced, plus more, cut into sticks, for dipping
¼	cup buttermilk
¼	cup light mayonnaise
¼	cup mild Buffalo sauce
¼	cup chopped chives
2	tbsp chopped dill
	Carrot sticks, for dipping

■ Bring a large, lidded pot of water to a low simmer. Add chicken breasts; cover and poach 10 minutes or until cooked through. Cool slightly. Dice and place in a large bowl with diced celery.

■ In a separate bowl, whisk together buttermilk, light mayo, Buffalo sauce, chives and dill. Pour into bowl with

chicken. Mix well. Serve with celery and carrot sticks.

PER SERVING 216 **CAL**; 7 g **FAT** (1 g **SAT**); 34 g **PRO**; 3 g **CARB**; 0 g **FIBER**; 244 mg **SODIUM**; 88 mg **CHOL**

Pomegranate Guacamole

MAKES 12 servings **PREP** 10 minutes

3	peeled and pitted avocados
¾	cup pomegranate seeds
½	cup chopped cilantro
2	tbsp lime juice
½	tsp salt
	Sliced jicama or tortilla chips

■ In a bowl, mash avocados. Stir in pomegranate seeds, chopped cilantro, lime juice and salt. Serve with sliced jicama or tortilla chips.

PER SERVING 100 **CAL**; 8 g **FAT** (1 g **SAT**); 1 g **PRO**; 9 g **CARB**; 6 g **FIBER**; 354 mg **SODIUM**; 3 mg **CHOL**

BLACK BEAN AND AVOCADO DIP

WARM BLACK BEAN DIP

Black Bean and Avocado Dip

MAKES 20 (¼-cup) servings **PREP** 20 minutes

- 1 can (15.5 oz) black beans, drained and rinsed
- ½ seedless cucumber, peeled and diced
- 1 orange, peeled, sections cut into ½-inch pieces
- ¼ cup chopped scallions
- 2 firm-ripe avocados, peeled, pitted and diced
- 2 tbsp white wine vinegar
- 2 tbsp olive oil
- ½ tsp salt
  Black pepper
  Pita chips

■ In a medium bowl, toss black beans, cucumber, orange and scallions. If making in advance, do not cut up avocados until just before serving.

■ Add diced avocados to bowl and drizzle with vinegar and oil. Season with salt and pepper and gently stir, trying to keep avocados from getting smashed. Serve with chips.

PER ¼ CUP 120 **CAL**; 6 g **FAT** (1 g **SAT**); 3 g **PRO**; 14 g **CARB**; 4 g **FIBER**; 254 mg **SODIUM**; 0 mg **CHOL**

Warm Black Bean Dip

MAKES 8 servings **PREP** 10 minutes
BAKE at 350° for 25 minutes

- 2 cans (15 oz each) black beans, drained and rinsed
- ½ red onion, chopped
- ⅓ cup cilantro leaves
- 2 tbsp red wine vinegar
- 2 tbsp olive oil
- 2 cloves garlic
- ¾ tsp ground cumin
- ½ tsp salt
- ¼ tsp black pepper
- 1 cup (4 oz) shredded Monterey Jack
- 1 bag (12 oz) baked tortilla chips
  Lime wedges and cilantro, for garnish (optional)

■ Heat oven to 350°. Coat a 1-qt baking dish with nonstick cooking spray.

■ In a food processor, combine 1 can of the beans, the onion, cilantro, vinegar, olive oil, garlic, cumin, salt and pepper. Process until smooth. Remove to a medium bowl and stir in remaining can of black beans and ¾ cup of the Monterey Jack.

■ Spoon mixture into prepared baking dish, top with remaining ¼ cup cheese and bake at 350° for 25 minutes or until bubbly.

■ Serve with chips. Garnish with lime and cilantro, if desired.

PER ½ CUP DIP PLUS CHIPS 383 **CAL**; 14 g **FAT** (4 g **SAT**); 13 g **PRO**; 50 g **CARB**; 10 g **FIBER**; 848 mg **SODIUM**; 15 mg **CHOL**

Deviled Crab Dip

MAKES 24 (¼-cup) servings
PREP 15 minutes **BAKE** at 375° for 30 minutes
BROIL 2 minutes

- 1 cup light mayonnaise
- 2 eggs
- ¼ cup fresh lemon juice
- ¼ cup milk
- 1 tbsp seafood seasoning (such as J.O. Spice Company or Old Bay)
- 1 tsp dry mustard
- 1 lb crab claw meat
- 1 red sweet pepper, diced
- ½ cup diced onion
- 2 ribs celery, diced
- 1 cup plus 2 tbsp plain bread crumbs
- 2 tbsp olive oil

■ Heat oven to 375°. In a large bowl, whisk together mayonnaise, eggs, lemon juice, milk, seafood seasoning and dry mustard. Carefully fold in crab, pepper, onion, celery and 1 cup of the bread crumbs.

■ Transfer mixture to a shallow 1½-qt oven-safe baking dish. Sprinkle remaining 2 tbsp bread crumbs on top and drizzle with oil. Bake at 375° for 30 minutes. Broil on high for 2 minutes or until browned. Serve with crackers.

PER SERVING 96 **CAL**; 5 g **FAT** (1 g **SAT**); 6 g **PRO**; 6 g **CARB**; 0 g **FIBER**; 282 mg **SODIUM**; 43 mg **CHOL**

SPINACH-PARMESAN DIP

Spinach-Parmesan Dip

MAKES 16 servings **PREP** 10 minutes
SLOW COOK on HIGH for 1½ hours or LOW
for 2½ hours

- Nonstick cooking spray
- 2 pkg (10 oz each) frozen chopped spinach, thawed
- 1 can (14 oz) quartered artichoke hearts, drained and coarsely chopped
- 1 cup chopped onion (1 large)
- 1 tbsp Dijon mustard
- 4 cloves garlic, minced
- ½ tsp dried oregano, crushed
- ¼ tsp cayenne pepper
- ½ cup light mayonnaise or salad dressing
- ½ cup fat-free sour cream
- ¼ cup shredded Parmesan cheese (1 oz)
- ¼ cup shredded Italian cheese blend (1 oz)
- 1 tbsp lemon juice

■ Coat a 3½- or 4-qt slow cooker with cooking spray; set aside. Squeeze spinach dry, reserving ⅓ cup spinach liquid. In prepared cooker combine spinach, the ⅓ cup liquid, the artichokes, onion, mustard, garlic, oregano and cayenne pepper.

■ Cover and cook on HIGH for 1½ hours or LOW for 2½ to 3 hours. Turn off cooker; stir in mayonnaise, sour cream, Parmesan cheese, Italian cheese blend and lemon juice.

PER SERVING 66 **CAL**; 4 g **FAT** (1 g **SAT**); 3 g **PRO**; 6 g **CARB**; 2 g **FIBER**; 229 mg **SODIUM**; 5 mg **CHOL**

Za'atar Nut Mix

MAKES 5 cups **PREP** 10 minutes
BAKE at 300° for 15 minutes

- 2 cups shelled pistachios
- 2 cups cashews
- 1 cup golden raisins
- 1 tbsp olive oil
- 2 tbsp Za'atar seasoning
- ½ tsp salt
- ¼ tsp black pepper

CHAI TEA BASE

■ Heat oven to 300°. In a large bowl, combine shelled pistachios, cashews, raisins, olive oil, Za'atar seasoning, salt and pepper. Spread mixture on a rimmed baking pan and bake at 300° for 15 minutes.

PER ¼ CUP 176 **CAL**; 13 g **FAT** (2 g **SAT**); 5 g **PRO**; 14 g **CARB**; 2 g **FIBER**; 62 mg **SODIUM**; 0 mg **CHOL**

Chai Tea Base

MAKES 14 servings **PREP** 15 minutes
STAND 10 minutes **SLOW COOK** on HIGH for
3 hours or LOW for 6 hours

- 8 cups water
- ⅔ cup honey
- 4 2- to 3-inch sticks cinnamon
- 2 inches fresh ginger, thinly sliced
- ½ tsp whole cardamom seeds (without pods)
- 16 whole cloves
- 16 whole black peppercorns
- ¼ tsp ground nutmeg
- 12 black tea bags
- 7 cups low-fat milk

■ In a 3½- or 4-qt slow cooker, stir together the water and honey until dissolved. Add stick cinnamon, ginger, cardamom seeds, cloves, peppercorns and nutmeg.

■ Cover and cook on HIGH for 3 to 4 hours or LOW for 6 to 8 hours. Add tea bags. Cover and let stand for 10 minutes. Strain the mixture through a fine-mesh sieve lined with a double thickness of 100-percent-cotton cheesecloth. Store in the refrigerator for up to 2 weeks.

■ For each serving, use ½ cup Chai Tea Base and ½ cup low-fat milk. Heat in a saucepan until steaming.

Iced Chai Prepare as directed, except serve over ice.

PER SERVING 104 **CAL**; 1 g **FAT** (1 g **SAT**); 4 g **PRO**; 20 g **CARB**; 0 g **FIBER**; 59 mg **SODIUM**; 6 mg **CHOL**

SOUTHERN SWEET TEA

STRAWBERRY
AGUA FRESCA

Southern Sweet Tea

MAKES 12 servings **PREP** 5 minutes
STEEP 30 minutes

- **10** black tea bags (such as Lipton)
- **¾** cup sugar
- **1** lemon, sliced, plus more slices for garnish (optional)

■ Secure tea bags around the handle of a small lidded pot filled with 4 cups water. Bring to a boil. Turn off heat, stir in sugar and cover. Let steep for 30 minutes. Cool completely.

■ Pour cooled tea into a pitcher with 4 cups cold water. Add lemon slices and enough ice to fill pitcher. Serve over ice in tall glasses. Garnish with more lemon slices, if desired.

PER SERVING 31 **CAL**; 0 g **FAT** (0 g **SAT**); 0 g **PRO**; 9 g **CARB**; 0 g **FIBER**; 0 mg **SODIUM**; 0 mg **CHOL**

Strawberry Agua Fresca

MAKES 5 cups **PREP** 10 minutes

- **2** to 3 cups cut-up strawberries
- **2** cups water; more as desired
- **1** to 2 cups ice
- **1** to 2 tbsp fresh mint leaves
  Sugar (optional)
  Juice of 1 lime (optional)

■ Put strawberries, water, ice and mint in a blender and blend until smooth (you don't want chips of ice). Taste and add sugar or lime juice as desired and blend again. If seeds will bother you, strain through a sieve. Serve in a pitcher with additional ice. Thin with more water for a very light drink, if desired.

Cucumber-Lime Agua Fresca

MAKES 8 servings **PREP** 10 minutes

- **1** lb cucumbers, cut into large chunks, plus slices for garnish
- **⅓** cup fresh lime juice, plus wedges for garnish
- **3** tbsp sugar
- **⅛** tsp salt

■ In a blender, combine cucumbers, lime juice, sugar, salt and 4 cups cold water. Blend until smooth. Pour mixture into a mesh strainer placed over a pitcher, pressing pulp to release as much liquid as possible. Discard pulp. Add enough ice to fill pitcher. Garnish agua fresca and glasses with cucumber slices and lime wedges.

PER SERVING 16 **CAL**; 0 g **FAT** (0 g **SAT**); 0 g **PRO**; 5 g **CARB**; 0 g **FIBER**; 37 mg **SODIUM**; 0 mg **CHOL**

CUCUMBER-LIME AGUA FRESCA

ROSEMARY
GIN FIZZ

HOLIDAY GLOGG

MAPLE OLD-
FASHIONED

Maple Old-Fashioned

MAKES 1 serving **PREP** 5 minutes

- ½ **oz maple syrup**
- 2 **maraschino cherries**
- 2 to 3 dashes **Angostura bitters**
- 2 **oz rye or bourbon**
- **Orange peel**

■ In a rocks glass, add maple syrup, cherries and bitters. Pour in rye, then add ice. Stir 1 minute. Run orange peel around rim of glass then add to drink.

PER SERVING 206 **CAL**; 0 g **FAT** (0 g **SAT**); 0 g **PRO**; 20 g **CARB**; 0 g **FIBER**; 2 mg **SODIUM**; 0 mg **CHOL**

Rosemary Gin Fizz

MAKES 1 serving **PREP** 5 minutes

- 2 **oz gin**
- ½ **oz lemon juice**
- ½ **oz Rosemary Simple Syrup (recipe follows)**
- 2 **oz seltzer**
- **Fresh rosemary sprig**

■ Fill a cocktail shaker with ice. Pour in gin, lemon juice and Rosemary Simple Syrup. Shake 1 minute. Pour into a highball glass over ice. Stir 1 minute. Top with seltzer and garnish with rosemary.

PER SERVING 169 **CAL**; 0 g **FAT** (0 g **SAT**); 0 g **PRO**; 11 g **CARB**; 0 g **FIBER**; 2 mg **SODIUM**; 0 mg **CHOL**

Rosemary Simple Syrup

■ Combine 1 cup sugar, 1 cup water and 1 sprig rosemary in a small pot. Bring to a boil and simmer until sugar is dissolved. Cover, remove from heat and steep at least 15 minutes. Let cool before using.

Holiday Glogg

MAKES 14 servings **PREP** 10 minutes
STEEP 1 hour

- 2 **bottles (750 ml each) fruity, full-bodied wine (such as Zinfandel)**
- 1 **bottle (750 ml) port**
- 1 **cup brandy**
- 1 **cup raisins**
- 1 **cup blanched slivered almonds**
- ½ **orange, sliced into half-moons**
- ¼ **cup sugar**
- 4 **cloves**
- 1 **cinnamon stick**
- 1 **bay leaf**

■ Combine all ingredients in a large pot. Heat until steam rises from liquid, but don't bring to a simmer (it will cook off the alcohol). Cover and steep on lowest heat setting for 1 hour. Serve warm.

PER SERVING 283 **CAL**; 5 g **FAT** (0 g **SAT**); 3 g **PRO**; 20 g **CARB**; 2 g **FIBER**; 9 mg **SODIUM**; 0 mg **CHOL**

WATERMELON MARGARITAS

PEACH BELLINI

Watermelon Margaritas

MAKES 8 servings **PREP** 10 minutes

- **5 cups cubed watermelon**
- **3 cups ice**
- **12 oz (1½ cups) silver (blanco) tequila**
- **⅓ cup fresh lime juice**
- **2 tbsp agave syrup**
- **½ tsp kosher salt**
- **Salt and lime wedges, for garnish (optional)**

■ In a blender, combine watermelon, ice, tequila, lime juice, agave and kosher salt. Blend until smooth. Serve over ice in, if desired, salt-rimmed glasses with lime wedges.

PER SERVING 140 **CAL**; 0 g **FAT** (0 g **SAT**); 1 g **PRO**; 12 g **CARB**; 0 g **FIBER**; 120 mg **SODIUM**; 0 mg **CHOL**

Cranberry-Hibiscus Spritzer

MAKES 8 servings **PREP** 5 minutes **STEEP** 4 minutes

- **¼ cup plus 2 tbsp sugar**
- **2 hibiscus tea bags**
- **1 cup chilled unsweetened cranberry juice (such as R.W. Knudsen Just Cranberry)**
- **1 bottle (750 ml) dry sparkling wine, chilled**
- **2 cups ice**
- **1 cup frozen cranberries (for garnish and to keep punch cold)**

■ In a small, lidded pot, bring 2½ cups water and sugar to a boil. Turn off heat. Add tea bags; cover and steep 4 minutes. Cool.

■ In a medium punch bowl, combine cooled tea, cranberry juice, sparkling wine and ice. Stir. Pour in frozen cranberries. Serve cold.

PER SERVING 107 **CAL**; 0 g **FAT**; 0 g **PRO**; 11 g **CARB**; 0 g **FIBER**; 1 mg **SODIUM**; 0 mg **CHOL**

Peach Bellini

MAKES 12 servings **PREP** 10 minutes

- **3 ripe peaches (or 1 lb frozen peaches, thawed), peeled, pitted and cut into wedges**
- **1 tbsp sugar**
- **2 bottles chilled Prosecco**
- **Thin peach slices for garnish**

■ Blend peaches and sugar in a blender.

■ For each Bellini, spoon 2 tbsp of the peach puree into the bottom of a champagne flute. Carefully pour in 4 oz Prosecco. Stir gently. Garnish with a thin peach slice. Serve immediately.

PER SERVING 117 **CAL**; 0 g **FAT** (0 g **SAT**); 0 g **PRO**; 7 g **CARB**; 0 g **FIBER**; 0 mg **SODIUM**; 0 mg **CHOL**

LEMON CAPER CHICKEN,
RECIPE PAGE 53

Poultry

From family-friendly weeknight fare to company-special dinners, these chicken and turkey recipes offer a variety of flavors to please any palate.

Chicken Cacciatore

MAKES 6 servings PREP 20 minutes
COOK 41 minutes

- 2 **tbsp olive oil**
- 1 **whole cut-up chicken (8 pieces; about 5 lb), skin removed (reserve wings for another use)**
- 1½ **tsp salt**
- ¼ **tsp black pepper**
- 1 **large onion, diced**
- 1 **large green sweet pepper, seeded and diced**
- 2 **fresh hot cherry peppers, seeded and sliced**
- 4 **cloves garlic, sliced**
- 2 **cups quartered mixed mushrooms, such as button, baby bella and shiitake**
- 3 **tbsp tomato paste**
- 1 **cup chicken broth**
- 6 **cups diced, seeded plum tomatoes (about 2½ lb)**
- 2 **sprigs fresh oregano**
- 2 **sprigs fresh thyme**
- ½ **cup fresh basil leaves**
  Polenta (optional)

■ Heat 1 tbsp of the oil in a large Dutch oven over medium-high heat. Season chicken with ½ tsp of the salt and ⅛ tsp of the black pepper. Cook, skinned sides down, 5 minutes; turn and cook 3 minutes.

■ Add remaining 1 tbsp olive oil; stir in onion, peppers and garlic. Cook 5 minutes, stirring occasionally. Add mushrooms and tomato paste; cook 3 minutes. Stir in broth and tomatoes, scraping any browned bits from bottom of pan. Bring to a boil and simmer, with lid ajar, 10 minutes.

■ Stir in remaining 1 tsp salt, remaining ⅛ tsp black pepper, and the oregano and thyme. Place chicken pieces into sauce and add any accumulated juices from plate. Simmer, with lid ajar, 15 minutes. Stir in basil. Serve with polenta, if desired.

PER SERVING 382 CAL; 8 g FAT (2 g SAT); 60 g PRO; 16 g CARB; 4 g FIBER; 1,128 mg SODIUM; 140 mg CHOL

Roasted Chicken with Truffled Mushroom Sauce

MAKES 8 servings PREP 30 minutes
ROAST at 400° for 45 minutes
COOK 6 minutes

- 2 **whole chickens (about 3 lb each), cut into 8 pieces each (breasts halved; about 4 lb after discarding wings and backs)**
- 3 **tbsp olive oil**
- 1½ **tsp salt**
- ¼ **tsp black pepper**
- 1 **lb wild mushrooms, halved or quartered**
- 1 **tbsp unsalted butter**
- 2 **tbsp finely diced shallots**
- 1 **tbsp all-purpose flour**
- 1 **cup unsalted chicken stock**
- ½ **cup heavy cream**
- 1 **tsp chopped fresh thyme**
- 1 **tsp truffle oil, plus more (if desired) for drizzling**
  Freshly cracked black pepper (optional)

■ Heat oven to 400°. Place chicken pieces on a rimmed baking sheet and drizzle with 1 tbsp of the olive oil, then season with 1 tsp of the salt and ⅛ tsp of the pepper. On a separate rimmed baking sheet, toss mushrooms in remaining 2 tbsp oil, ¼ tsp of the salt and remaining ⅛ tsp pepper. Roast chicken and mushrooms at 400° for 35 minutes, until golden. Remove mushrooms. Roast chicken 10 minutes more, until cooked.

■ In a large skillet, melt butter over medium heat. Stir in shallots and cook 2 minutes. Stir in flour and cook 1 minute. Whisk in stock, cream and mushrooms. Bring to a boil and cook 3 minutes, until thickened. Stir in thyme, truffle oil, remaining ¼ tsp salt and, if using, freshly cracked pepper.

■ Place chicken on a platter and pour truffled mushroom sauce over top. If desired, drizzle with additional truffle oil.

PER SERVING 299 CAL; 14 g FAT (6 g SAT); 37 g PRO; 4 g CARB; 0 g FIBER; 558 mg SODIUM; 110 mg CHOL

ROASTED CHICKEN WITH
TRUFFLED MUSHROOM SAUCE

CHICKEN TAGINE WITH
OLIVES AND FIGS

Chicken Tagine with Olives and Figs

MAKES 8 servings **PREP** 20 minutes
COOK 40 minutes

- **3 tbsp vegetable oil**
- **1 large broiler-fryer chicken (about 4 lb), cut into 8 pieces**
- **1 tsp salt**
- **½ tsp black pepper**
- **1 large onion, chopped**
- **3 cloves garlic, sliced**
- **2 tbsp fresh ginger, chopped**
- **½ tsp ground cumin**
- **½ tsp cinnamon**
- **1 cup reduced-sodium chicken broth**
- **½ cup chopped dried figs**
- **½ cup pitted green cocktail olives**
- **1 lemon, cut into wedges**
- **2 cups Israeli couscous, cooked following pkg directions**
- **2 tbsp sliced almonds**

■ In a large Dutch oven, heat oil over medium-high heat. Season chicken with ¾ tsp of the salt and ¼ tsp of the pepper. Cook chicken about 5 minutes per side or until browned. Remove to a plate. Add onion, garlic, ginger, cumin, cinnamon and remaining ¼ tsp each salt and pepper; cook 5 minutes, stirring occasionally.

■ Add back chicken, skin sides up, and spoon some of the onion mixture on top. Add broth and simmer, covered, for 15 minutes over medium heat. Stir in figs, olives and half the lemon wedges; simmer, covered, for an additional 10 minutes or until temperature of chicken reaches 165°.

■ To serve, spoon couscous onto a large serving platter and place chicken over top. Spoon liquid from pot over chicken and garnish with almonds and remaining lemon.

PER SERVING 513 CAL; 24 g FAT (5 g SAT); 33 g PRO; 39 g CARB; 3 g FIBER; 675 mg SODIUM; 89 mg CHOL

Roasted Chicken and Greek-Style Potatoes

MAKES 8 servings **PREP** 15 minutes
ROAST at 425° for 70 minutes

- **6 tbsp olive oil**
- **3 tbsp lemon juice**
- **1 large shallot**
- **2 cloves garlic**
- **¼ cup fresh parsley leaves**
- **2 tbsp fresh oregano leaves**
- **¾ tsp salt**
- **½ tsp black pepper**
- **1 whole chicken (about 4 lb)**
- **2½ lb russet potatoes, cut into thin wedges**

■ Heat oven to 425°.

■ Add olive oil, lemon juice, shallot, garlic, parsley, oregano, ½ tsp of the salt and ¼ tsp of the pepper to a blender; blend until combined. Liberally season chicken with half the mixture and place on a rack in a large

ROASTED CHICKEN AND
GREEK-STYLE POTATOES

PANKO HONEY-FRIED
CHICKEN AND NAPA SLAW

roasting pan. Season with ⅛ tsp each of the salt and pepper. Roast at 425° for 60 to 70 minutes or until internal temperature reaches 165°.

■ Meanwhile, toss potatoes with remaining olive oil mixture. Place on a baking sheet and roast with chicken for 40 to 45 minutes, until browned and fork-tender. Season with remaining ⅛ tsp each salt and pepper.

■ Slice chicken and serve with potatoes.

PER SERVING 461 CAL; 26 g FAT (6 g SAT); 31 g PRO; 26 g CARB; 2 g FIBER; 305 mg SODIUM; 89 mg CHOL

Panko Honey-Fried Chicken and Napa Slaw

MAKES 4 servings PREP 25 minutes
REFRIGERATE 1 hour COOK 8 minutes

NAPA SLAW

- 6 cups shredded napa cabbage
- 2 cups sliced snow peas
- 2 thinly sliced carrots
- 1 cup shredded red cabbage
- 1 container (7 oz) Greek 2% plain yogurt
- 2 tbsp milk
- 1 tbsp honey
- 1 tbsp lemon juice
- 1 tsp spicy brown mustard
- ½ tsp salt
- ⅛ tsp black pepper
- 2 tbsp chopped parsley

FRIED CHICKEN

- 1 lb uncooked chicken tenders (fillets)

- ¼ cup honey combined with 2 tbsp warm water
- 1½ cups panko bread crumbs
- 5 tbsp canola oil
- ½ tsp salt
- ⅛ tsp black pepper

■ Napa Slaw. In a large bowl, combine napa cabbage, snow peas, carrots and red cabbage. Whisk yogurt, milk, honey, lemon juice, mustard, salt and pepper. Stir in parsley. Fold mixture into slaw. Cover and refrigerate 1 hour.

■ Fried Chicken. Dip chicken in honey mixture. Coat with panko.

■ In a large skillet, heat 3 tbsp of the oil over medium-high heat. Season chicken with ¼ tsp of the salt and the pepper. Add half to pan; cook 1 to 2 minutes per side or until internal temperature reaches 160°. Add remaining 2 tbsp oil; cook second batch. Remove to a plate and season with remaining ¼ tsp salt. Serve chicken topped with slaw.

PER SERVING 523 CAL; 21 g FAT (2 g SAT); 29 g PRO; 57 g CARB; 6 g FIBER; 746 mg SODIUM; 66 mg CHOL

SHAWARMA
CHICKEN POT PIE

Shawarma Chicken Pot Pie

MAKES 4 servings **PREP** 20 minutes
COOK 13 minutes **BAKE** at 400° for 25 minutes

- 2 tbsp canola oil
- 1½ lb boneless, skinless chicken breast, cut into 1-inch pieces
- 1 medium onion, chopped
- ½ green sweet pepper, cored, seeded and chopped
- 4 oz white mushrooms, stems removed, quartered
- 2 carrots, diced
- 1 rib celery, diced
- ⅓ cup all-purpose flour
- 2 tbsp shawarma seasoning (see Tip)
- ½ tsp salt
- ¼ tsp black pepper
- 1½ cups reduced-sodium chicken broth
- 1 cup fat-free milk
- 1 cup frozen green peas, thawed
- 2 sheets frozen puff pastry (from a 17.3 oz pkg), thawed
- 1 egg, lightly beaten

■ Heat oven to 400°. Coat four 1½-cup ramekins with nonstick cooking spray (see Tip).

■ Heat 1 tbsp of the oil in a large nonstick skillet over medium-high heat. Add chicken and cook 5 minutes, turning once. Remove and place on a plate.

■ Add remaining 1 tbsp oil, the onion, sweet pepper, mushrooms, carrots and celery. Cook 5 minutes, stirring occasionally. Add flour, shawarma seasoning, salt and black pepper. Cook 1 minute. Gradually stir in broth and milk; simmer until thickened, about 2 minutes. Return chicken to skillet and add peas. Stir to combine.

■ Spoon a generous 1½ cups of the mixture into each prepared ramekin.

■ Unroll pastry sheets and cut two 5-inch circles from each (½ inch wider than ramekin). Place a piece of pastry over each ramekin, tuck under and flute. Brush each with egg. Make a vent in center of each with a small knife.

CHICKEN IN DIJON CREAM

■ Place on a baking sheet and bake at 400° for 25 minutes. Cool slightly.

PER SERVING 487 **CAL**; 19 g **FAT** (4 g **SAT**); 45 g **PRO**; 34 g **CARB**; 6 g **FIBER**; 752 mg **SODIUM**; 148 mg **CHOL**

Tip: Look for shawarma seasoning in your supermarket's international foods aisle or in a specialty store.

Tip: For one large pie, spoon chicken mixture into an 11 x 8-inch baking dish. Fit pastry over top, vent in a few places and brush with egg. Bake at 400° for 30 to 35 minutes, until browned and bubbly.

Chicken in Dijon Cream

MAKES 4 servings **PREP** 20 minutes
COOK 11 minutes

- 4 boneless, skinless chicken breast halves (about 2 lb)
- ½ tsp plus ⅛ tsp kosher salt
- 1 tbsp extra-virgin olive oil
- ½ tbsp unsalted butter
- ½ small onion, minced
- ¼ cup dry white wine
- 1 cup chicken stock
- 1 tbsp Dijon mustard
- ¼ cup heavy cream
- 1½ tsp chopped fresh thyme
- 1½ tsp chopped fresh tarragon

■ On a large cutting board, place chicken between sheets of wax paper. Pound with a meat mallet, rolling pin or heavy skillet until meat is an even ½ inch in thickness. Season chicken with ½ tsp salt (¼ tsp on each side).

■ Heat a large skillet over medium-high heat. Coat with oil, then add butter. When butter is foamy but not brown, add half the chicken. Cook until browned, about 3 minutes. Flip chicken and cook until browned but not cooked through, about 2 additional minutes. Transfer to a plate. Repeat with remaining chicken.

■ Add onion to skillet. Cook 1 minute, scraping browned bits from pan. Add wine and cook until reduced by half, about 1 minute, then add stock. Simmer 1 minute.

■ Whisk in mustard and cook 1 minute. Stir in cream and remaining ⅛ tsp salt. Bring to a boil; reduce heat to a simmer, then add chicken back to pan with its juices. Simmer until chicken is cooked through, about 2 minutes. Stir in thyme and tarragon.

PER SERVING 390 **CAL**; 17 g **FAT** (6 g **SAT**); 52 g **PRO**; 2 g **CARB**; 0 g **FIBER**; 730 mg **SODIUM**; 190 mg **CHOL**

chopped peanuts. Serve each bowl with a lime wedge.

PER SERVING 468 CAL; 16 g FAT (3 g SAT); 32 g PRO; 51 g CARB; 4 g FIBER; 763 mg SODIUM; 49 mg CHOL

Tip: To save time, buy precooked chicken from the deli counter, slice and serve over noodle mixture. Swap a reduced-calorie bottled Asian sesame salad dressing or peanut sauce for the dressing made here.

Chicken and Tortellini

MAKES 6 servings   PREP 3 minutes
COOK 15 minutes

- 1 **pkg (9 oz) refrigerated spinach tortellini**
- 1 **pkg (9 oz) refrigerated cheese tortellini**
- 1½ **lb boneless, skinless chicken breasts**
- 2 **tbsp olive oil**
- ⅛ **tsp plus ½ tsp salt**
- 1 **bag (5 oz) baby spinach**
- 1 **pint grape or cherry tomatoes, halved (2 cups)**
- ⅓ **cup heavy cream**
- 2 **tbsp grated Parmesan**
  Freshly ground black pepper

■ Bring a large pot of lightly salted water to a boil. Add tortellini and cook 7 minutes (or as per pkg directions).

■ Meanwhile, dice chicken into 1-inch pieces. Drain tortellini, reserving ¼ cup of the cooking water.

■ Heat oil in a large skillet over medium-high heat. Sprinkle chicken with ⅛ tsp of the salt. Add to skillet and brown on all sides, 5 minutes. Stir in spinach, tomatoes, heavy cream and remaining ½ tsp salt. Simmer 1 minute. Add tortellini and reserved pasta water, if needed; cook 2 minutes. Remove from heat and toss with Parmesan. Grind pepper over top.

PER SERVING 492 CAL; 17 g FAT (7 g SAT); 40 g PRO; 45 g CARB; 4 g FIBER; 784 mg SODIUM; 123 mg CHOL

Thai Rice Noodle Bowl

MAKES 4 servings   PREP 16 minutes
COOK 2 minutes   GRILL OR BROIL 6 minutes

- 7 **oz (half a 14-oz box) thin stir-fry rice noodles**
- ⅓ **cup rice vinegar**
- 3 **tbsp low-sodium soy sauce**
- 3 **tbsp creamy peanut butter**
- 2 **tbsp fish sauce**
- 2 **tbsp warm water**
- 1 **tbsp plus 1 tsp sugar**
- ¼ **tsp red pepper flakes**
- ½ **seedless cucumber**
- ¾ **lb small chicken breast halves, boneless pork chops or steak (see Tip)**
- ¾ **tsp cornstarch**
- 1 **cup sweet pepper strips**
- ½ **cup shredded carrot**
- 3 **scallions, trimmed and sliced**
- ⅓ **cup fresh cilantro leaves, sliced, plus more for serving**
- ½ **cup chopped peanuts**
  Lime wedges

■ Bring a large saucepan of water to a boil. Add noodles, turn off heat and let soak 6 to 8 minutes.

■ Meanwhile, in a small bowl, whisk vinegar, soy sauce, peanut butter, fish sauce, warm water, sugar and red pepper flakes until smooth. Peel, halve and slice cucumber into half-moons.

■ Heat grill pan or broiler. Place chicken in a resealable plastic bag or a glass dish. Add 3 tbsp of the dressing, turning to coat.

■ Place remaining dressing in a small saucepan with cornstarch. Bring to a boil; boil 2 minutes. Remove from heat. Set aside.

■ Grill or broil chicken 6 minutes, turning once, until cooked through.

■ Drain and rinse noodles and transfer to a large bowl. Add sweet pepper, shredded carrot, cucumber, scallions and sliced cilantro. Drizzle dressing into bowl and toss to combine. Divide among 4 bowls. Slice chicken and divide among bowls. Sprinkle with cilantro leaves and

CHICKEN AND TORTELLINI

Couscous with Summer Pesto

MAKES 6 servings **PREP** 20 minutes
COOK 10 minutes

- 1¾ **cups pearl couscous**
- 2 **cups packed basil leaves**
- 2 **tbsp pine nuts, toasted**
- 1 **clove garlic, halved**
- 1 **tbsp lemon juice**
- ⅓ **cup extra-virgin olive oil**
- 2 **tbsp grated Parmesan**
- ¾ **tsp salt**
- 4 **cups shredded chicken breast**
- 1 **pkg (10.5 oz) cherry tomatoes, halved**
- 4 **oz smoked mozzarella, cubed**

■ In a medium pot, bring 2½ cups water to a boil. Add couscous, cover and cook 10 minutes. Drain and rinse under cold water.

■ Meanwhile, make pesto. In a blender or food processor, combine basil, pine nuts, garlic and lemon juice. Process, slowly streaming in oil until smooth. Remove to a large bowl and stir in Parmesan and ¼ tsp of the salt.

■ Mix couscous, chicken, tomatoes, mozzarella and remaining ½ tsp salt into pesto. Stir well to combine.

PER SERVING 500 **CAL**; 22 g **FAT** (5 g **SAT**); 39 g **PRO**; 36 g **CARB**; 3 g **FIBER**; 520 mg **SODIUM**; 95 mg **CHOL**

Tagliatelle with Heirloom Tomatoes, Mushrooms and Chicken

MAKES 6 servings **PREP** 15 minutes
COOK 8 minutes

- 2 **tbsp olive oil**
- ½ **lb mixed mushrooms**
- 1 **lb boneless, skinless chicken breasts, cut into 1-inch pieces**
- 3 **cloves garlic, chopped**
- 1 **tsp salt**
- ¼ **tsp black pepper**
- 1½ **lb heirloom tomatoes, cut into 1-inch pieces**
- 1 **lb tagliatelle pasta**
- 1 **8-oz burrata cheese**

Freshly cracked black pepper
Basil, for garnish

■ In a large nonstick skillet, heat oil over medium-high heat. Add mushrooms and cook 1 minute, stirring frequently. Add chicken, garlic, ½ tsp of the salt and ¼ tsp pepper; cook 5 minutes, stirring occasionally. Add tomatoes and cook 1 minute to heat through.

■ Meanwhile, cook pasta following package directions, about 8 minutes. Drain and reserve ½ cup pasta cooking water.

■ In a large serving bowl, toss cooked pasta with chicken and tomato mixture. Add pasta water, if needed to create a sauce. Season with remaining ½ tsp salt.

■ Place burrata on top of pasta and cut into large pieces with 2 knives. Toss, season with freshly cracked pepper and garnish with basil.

PER SERVING 544 **CAL**; 16 g **FAT** (7 g **SAT**); 35 g **PRO**; 65 g **CARB**; 2 g **FIBER**; 473 mg **SODIUM**; 81 mg **CHOL**

TAGLIATELLE WITH HEIRLOOM TOMATOES, MUSHROOMS AND CHICKEN

COCONUT CHICKEN
SOBA NOODLES

Coconut Chicken Soba Noodles

MAKES 6 servings PREP 15 minutes
GRILL 22 minutes COOK 11 minutes

- 2 tbsp packed light brown sugar
- ½ tsp salt
- ¼ tsp cayenne
- 1½ lb boneless, skinless chicken breasts
- 1 lb mini sweet peppers
- 4 scallions
- 2 tsp vegetable oil
- 1 box (12 oz) soba noodles (such as Annie Chun's)
- ¼ cup unsweetened flaked coconut
- 3 cloves garlic, minced
- 1 tbsp grated ginger
- 1 can (13.5 oz) light coconut milk
- 2 tbsp lime juice
- 1 tbsp fish sauce
- 1 tsp cornstarch
  Cilantro, for garnish

■ Heat a grill or grill pan to medium-high and brush grate with oil. In a small bowl, combine 1 tbsp of the brown sugar, ¼ tsp of the salt and ⅛ tsp of the cayenne. Rub onto chicken breasts. Grill chicken over medium-high heat 5 to 6 minutes per side, until cooked through.

■ Toss peppers and scallions in 1 tsp of the vegetable oil. Skewer peppers and grill 4 minutes; flip and grill

another 4 minutes. Grill scallions 2 minutes per side. Thinly slice chicken on the bias. Cut peppers into rings, discarding stems, and chop scallions.

■ Bring a pot of lightly salted water to a boil. Add soba and cook 4 to 5 minutes, until tender. Drain and rinse immediately under cold water.

■ Heat a skillet over medium heat. Toast coconut 2 to 3 minutes, stirring frequently. Remove to a plate. Add remaining 1 tsp oil to skillet. Add garlic and ginger to skillet; sauté 1 minute. Pour in coconut milk, lime juice, fish sauce, remaining 1 tbsp brown sugar, remaining ¼ tsp salt and remaining ⅛ tsp cayenne. Bring to a simmer. Mix cornstarch with 1 tsp cold

RIGATONI WITH GORGONZOLA SAUCE AND CHICKEN

water. Add to mixture and simmer 2 minutes, until thickened.

■ In a large bowl, toss sauce with chicken, peppers, scallions and soba. Divide among 6 bowls and garnish with coconut and cilantro.

PER SERVING 440 **CAL**; 10 g **FAT** (4.5 g **SAT**); 35 g **PRO**; 52 g **CARB**; 5 g **FIBER**; 880 mg **SODIUM**; 85 mg **CHOL**

Rigatoni with Gorgonzola Sauce and Chicken

MAKES 8 servings **PREP** 10 minutes
COOK 6 minutes **STAND** 5 minutes

- **2 tbsp vegetable oil**
- **1½ lb boneless, skinless chicken breasts, cut into 1½-inch pieces**
- **¼ tsp salt**
- **⅛ tsp black pepper**
- **2 cloves garlic, sliced**
- **⅓ cup white wine**
- **½ cup chicken broth**
- **½ cup heavy cream**
- **1½ cups crumbled Gorgonzola cheese**
- **1 cup shredded Parmesan cheese**
- **1 lb rigatoni, cooked following pkg directions**
- **½ cup fresh basil leaves, sliced**
- **½ cup toasted walnuts, coarsely chopped**
- **Freshly cracked black pepper (optional)**

■ Heat oil in a large skillet over medium-high heat. Season chicken with ⅛ tsp of the salt and the ⅛ tsp pepper. Cook chicken 4 minutes, turning once. Remove to a plate.

LEMON CAPER CHICKEN

■ Add garlic and wine to skillet and cook 1 minute. Stir in broth and cream; add back chicken and simmer 1 minute. Take off heat and stir in Gorgonzola and ½ cup of the Parmesan. Add pasta and toss to coat with sauce. Allow to stand 5 minutes.

■ To serve, spoon into a large bowl; stir in basil, walnuts, remaining ⅛ tsp salt and remaining ½ cup Parmesan cheese. Sprinkle with freshly cracked pepper, if desired.

PER SERVING 552 **CAL**; 26 g **FAT** (11 g **SAT**); 35 g **PRO**; 44 g **CARB**; 3 g **FIBER**; 636 mg **SODIUM**; 9 mg **CHOL**

Lemon Caper Chicken

MAKES 3 servings **PREP** 15 minutes
COOK 9 minutes

- **1 tsp kosher salt**
- **1 tsp black pepper**
- **1 tsp lemon pepper**
- **4 tbsp all-purpose flour**
- **3 chicken cutlets**
- **Zest and juice of 1 lemon**
- **2 tbsp olive oil**
- **1 cup chicken broth**
- **2 tbsp capers**
- **3 cloves garlic, finely minced**
- **Splash half-and-half (optional)**
- **Parsley, for garnish (optional)**

■ On a flat dish, combine kosher salt, black pepper, lemon pepper and 2 tbsp of the flour. Coat chicken cutlets in flour mixture and place on a plate. Sprinkle half of the lemon zest over cutlets.

■ Heat oil in a large skillet over medium heat. Brown chicken until cooked through, about 7 minutes, turning once. Transfer to a fresh plate.

■ In a bowl, whisk lemon juice, chicken broth, capers, garlic and remaining zest. Pour into skillet with drippings and whisk until combined. Add half-and-half, if desired. Return chicken to pan and heat through, 2 minutes. To serve, spoon sauce over cutlets and, if desired, garnish with parsley.

CHICKEN FAJITAS

Chicken Korma

MAKES 4 servings PREP 15 minutes
STAND 15 minutes COOK 13 minutes

- ¼ cup unsalted cashews
- 2 tbsp canola oil
- 1 large onion, sliced
- 1 tbsp fresh ginger, chopped
- 2 cloves garlic, chopped
- 2 tsp curry powder
- 1 tsp turmeric
- 1¼ lb boneless, skinless chicken breasts, cut into 1-inch pieces
- ½ cup reduced-sodium chicken broth
- ¼ cup tomato sauce
- ¾ tsp salt
- ½ cup low-fat plain Greek yogurt
- 2 tsp cornstarch
- 3 cups cooked basmati rice
  Naan (optional)
  Crispy Green Beans (optional; recipe follows)

■ Place cashews in a small bowl and add ¼ cup boiling water. Let stand for 15 minutes.

■ Heat oil in a large nonstick skillet over medium-high heat. Add onion, ginger and garlic; cook for 3 minutes, stirring occasionally. Stir in curry and turmeric and cook for 30 seconds. Add chicken and cook for 3 minutes. Stir in broth, tomato sauce and salt; simmer for 3 minutes.

■ Meanwhile, in a food processor, blend cashews with soaking water and yogurt until smooth. Add to skillet and simmer for 2 minutes. Blend cornstarch with 1 tbsp water and stir into skillet. Cook for 1 minute, until thickened.

■ Serve chicken with cooked rice and, if desired, naan and Crispy Green Beans.

PER SERVING 496 CAL; 16 g FAT (3 g SAT); 36 g PRO; 53 g CARB; 2 g FIBER; 669 mg SODIUM; 80 mg CHOL

Crispy Green Beans Microwave 1 pkg (12 oz) steam-in-bag fresh green beans for 3 minutes. Heat 1 tbsp canola oil in a large nonstick skillet over medium-high heat. Add green beans, 1 tbsp chopped garlic and ⅛ tsp salt. Cook, stirring frequently, for 5 minutes or until dark and crisp.

Chicken Fajitas

MAKES 4 servings PREP 20 minutes
BROIL 6 minutes COOK 10 minutes

- 4 thin-cut boneless, skinless chicken breasts (about 4 oz each)
- 2 tbsp McCormick Perfect Pinch Mexican seasoning
- 1 tbsp canola oil
- 1 large sweet onion, cut into ¼-inch slices
- 1 green sweet pepper, seeded and cut into ¼-inch slices
- 1 small zucchini, cut into matchsticks
- 1 small yellow squash, cut into matchsticks
- ½ tsp salt
- 8 corn tortillas
- 1 pouch Minute Rice Multigrain Medley, cooked per pkg directions
- ½ cup reduced-fat sour cream
- 1 lime, cut into wedges

■ Heat broiler. Coat broiler pan with nonstick cooking spray.

■ Season chicken on both sides with 4 tsp of the Mexican seasoning. Broil 3 minutes, turn and broil 3 minutes more or until internal temperature reaches 165°. Place chicken on a cutting board and keep warm.

■ Meanwhile, heat oil in a large nonstick skillet over medium-high heat. Add onion; cook for 5 minutes, stirring occasionally. Stir in sweet pepper, zucchini, summer squash, salt and remaining 2 tsp of the Mexican seasoning; cook an additional 5 minutes, stirring occasionally.

■ Slice chicken breasts and wrap in tortillas with vegetables. Serve with rice, sour cream and lime wedges for squeezing over fajitas.

PER SERVING 438 CAL; 12 g FAT (3 g SAT); 31 g PRO; 51 g CARB; 6 g FIBER; 712 mg SODIUM; 78 mg CHOL

CHICKEN KORMA

POMEGRANATE CHICKEN

Pomegranate Chicken

MAKES 4 servings **PREP** 15 minutes
COOK 15 minutes

- **1** cup wheat berries (quick-cooking)
- **3** cups low-sodium chicken broth
- **¾** cup pomegranate seeds (about 1 pomegranate)
- **¼** cup chopped fresh parsley
- **1** tsp salt
- **½** tsp pepper
- **1¼** lb boneless, skinless chicken breasts (4 breasts)
- **1** tbsp olive oil
- **1½** cups plus 2 tsp pomegranate juice
- **2** tsp cornstarch
- **1** tbsp unsalted butter

■ In a medium pot, combine wheat berries and 2½ cups of the chicken broth. Cover and bring to a boil. Reduce heat to a simmer and cook 15 minutes. Drain and return to pot. Stir in pomegranate seeds, 3 tbsp of the parsley, ¼ tsp plus ⅛ tsp of the salt and ¼ tsp of the pepper. Cover and set aside.

■ Meanwhile, season chicken with ½ tsp of the salt and ¼ tsp of the pepper. Heat oil in a large sauté pan over medium-high heat. Add chicken and cook 4 to 5 minutes per side or until cooked through. Remove to a plate and set aside.

■ In same pan, add the 1½ cups pomegranate juice and remaining ½ cup chicken broth. Bring to a boil. In a small bowl, stir together remaining 2 tsp pomegranate juice and the cornstarch. Whisk into boiling pomegranate mixture; cook 4 minutes until thickened. Remove from heat; stir in butter and remaining ⅛ tsp salt. Return chicken to pan; toss to coat. Serve chicken over wheat berries. Drizzle with extra pomegranate sauce and garnish with remaining 1 tbsp parsley.

PER SERVING 479 **CAL**; 9 g **FAT** (3 g **SAT**); 42 g **PRO**; 55 g **CARB**; 5 g **FIBER**; 742 mg **SODIUM**; 89 mg **CHOL**

OVEN SWEET-AND-SOUR CHICKEN WITH RED QUINOA

Oven Sweet-and-Sour Chicken with Red Quinoa

MAKES 4 servings **PREP** 20 minutes
BAKE at 400° for 25 minutes **COOK** 15 minutes

- **3** tbsp apricot preserves
- **2** tbsp ketchup
- **1** tbsp reduced-sodium soy sauce
- **1** tbsp rice vinegar
- **½** tsp ground ginger
- **1** lb boneless, skinless chicken breasts, cut into 2-inch pieces
- **1** large green sweet pepper, cored, seeded and cut into 1-inch pieces
- **1** large red sweet pepper, cored, seeded and cut into 1-inch pieces
- **1** large carrot, peeled and cut into thick coins
- **6** scallions, trimmed and cut into 2-inch pieces
- **1** cup red quinoa
- **1** can (14.5 oz) reduced-sodium chicken broth
- **⅛** tsp salt
- **⅛** tsp black pepper
- **½** lb Brussels sprouts, trimmed and shredded
- **2** tbsp sliced almonds

■ Heat oven to 400°. Coat a 13 x 9 x 2-inch baking dish with nonstick cooking spray.

■ In a medium bowl, whisk apricot preserves, ketchup, soy sauce, vinegar, ginger and 1 tbsp water. Toss chicken with 3 tbsp of the apricot mixture and place in prepared baking dish. Toss peppers, carrot and scallions with remaining mixture and spoon over chicken. Loosely tent with foil, venting at one end.

■ Bake at 400° for 25 minutes or until chicken reaches 160° and vegetables are tender.

■ Meanwhile, place quinoa, broth, salt and black pepper in a medium saucepan. Bring to a boil over high heat; reduce heat to medium-low and simmer, covered, for 15 minutes or until tender. Stir in Brussels sprouts during last minute of cooking.

■ Sprinkle almonds over quinoa. Serve with chicken and vegetables.

PER SERVING 395 **CAL**; 7 g **FAT** (1 g **SAT**); 32 g **PRO**; 51 g **CARB**; 6 g **FIBER**; 790 mg **SODIUM**; 63 mg **CHOL**

CHICKEN-FRIED CHICKEN
AND TOMATO GRAVY

Chicken-Fried Chicken and Tomato Gravy

MAKES 4 servings **PREP** 15 minutes
COOK 20 minutes

- 1½ **lb plum tomatoes, seeded, cut into 1-inch pieces**
- 3 **tbsp unsalted butter**
- ¼ **tsp salt**
- ⅛ **tsp plus ½ tsp black pepper**
- 4 **boneless, skinless chicken breasts (about 6 oz each)**
- 1 **tsp seasoned salt**
- ¾ **cup all-purpose flour**
- 2 **tbsp cornstarch**
- ½ **cup vegetable oil**
  Dirty Rice (optional; recipe follows)

■ In a medium saucepan, combine tomatoes, butter, salt and ⅛ tsp of the pepper. Cover and simmer 20 minutes, stirring occasionally.

■ Meanwhile, season chicken with seasoned salt and remaining ½ tsp black pepper. Combine flour and cornstarch in a bowl; dredge chicken in mixture.

■ In a large nonstick skillet, heat oil over medium-high heat. Add chicken and sauté for 4 minutes per side or until internal temperature reaches 165°.

■ Serve chicken with tomato gravy and, if desired, Dirty Rice.

PER SERVING 446 **CAL**; 27 g **FAT** (8 g **SAT**); 37 g **PRO**; 14 g **CARB**; 2 g **FIBER**; 587 mg **SODIUM**; 117 mg **CHOL**

Dirty Rice

In a medium saucepan, heat 1 tbsp vegetable oil over medium-high heat. Add 2 sweet Italian sausages, casings removed, and 2 oz chicken livers; cook 2 minutes. Add 1 cup chopped onion, ½ chopped red sweet pepper, 1 rib chopped celery and 4 cloves garlic, minced. Cook 6 minutes, stirring occasionally. Add 1½ cups RiceSelect Royal Blend, 2¼ cups water, ¼ cup salt and ⅛ tsp cayenne pepper. Bring to a boil; simmer, covered, over medium-low 20 to 24 minutes or until tender. Garnish with chopped scallions.

Shredded Chicken

MAKES 8 sandwiches **PREP** 5 minutes
SLOW COOK on HIGH for 6 hours or
LOW for 8 hours **COOK** 3 minutes
STAND 10 minutes
BAKE at 350° for 3 minutes

- 1½ **lb boneless, skinless chicken breasts**
- 1½ **lbs boneless, skinless chicken thighs, trimmed of excess fat**
- 1 **tsp dried oregano**
- ½ **tsp ground cumin**
- 1 **cup Dr Pepper soda**
- 1 **can (8 oz) tomato sauce**
- 2 **chipotle peppers in adobo, seeded and diced**
- ¼ **cup sugar**
- 2 **tbsp cornstarch**
- ½ **tsp salt**
- 3 **tbsp balsamic vinegar**
- 8 **slices white cheddar or pepper Jack cheese**
- 8 **soft egg buns**
- **Pickle slices**
- **Sliced red onion (optional)**

- Place chicken in a 4- to 5-qt slow cooker. Season with oregano and cumin. In a bowl, stir together soda, tomato sauce and chipotles. Pour into slow cooker, cover and cook on HIGH for 6 hours or LOW for 8 hours.

- Heat oven to 350°. Remove chicken to a bowl and pour liquid from slow cooker into a saucepan. In a small bowl, blend sugar, cornstarch and salt. Stir into a saucepan along with vinegar. Place over medium-high heat and bring to a boil.

- Reduce heat to medium and simmer 3 minutes, until thickened and clear. Shred chicken with 2 forks. Pour sauce over chicken and stir to combine. Let stand, covered, for 10 minutes.

- Make sandwiches: Place a slice of cheese on each bun. Bake at 350° for 2 to 3 minutes or until cheese melts. Divide chicken among buns. Add pickle slices and, if desired, red onion.

PER SERVING 474 **CAL**; 15 g **FAT** (6 g **SAT**); 46 g **PRO**; 38 g **CARB**; 2 g **FIBER**; 858 mg **SODIUM**; 152 mg **CHOL**

CHICKEN POT PIE

Chicken Pot Pie

MAKES 6 servings **PREP** 15 minutes
COOK 15 minutes **BAKE** at 400° for 35 minutes
COOL 10 minutes

CRUST

- 2 **cups all-purpose flour**
- ½ **tsp salt**
- ¾ **cup solid vegetable shortening**

FILLING

- 1 **tbsp olive oil**
- 1 **potato (6 oz), peeled and diced**
- 1 **small onion, chopped**
- 2 **ribs celery, chopped**
- 2 **large carrots, peeled and sliced**
- 1½ **cups chicken broth**
- 2 **tbsp all-purpose flour**
- 2 **tsp fresh thyme leaves, chopped**
- ¼ **tsp each salt and black pepper**
- 2 **cups cubed cooked chicken breast**

- Heat oven to 400°. **Crust.** Combine flour and salt in a food processor. Drop in pieces of shortening and process in on-and-off bursts until combined. Drizzle with 3 to 4 tbsp ice water; process until crust comes together in a ball. Divide in two, with one portion just slightly larger.

- With a floured rolling pin, roll larger dough into a 12-inch circle on a floured sheet of wax paper. Invert into a 10½-inch cast-iron skillet, patching any cracks. Roll remaining dough into an 11-inch circle. Refrigerate while making filling.

- **Filling.** Heat oil in a large nonstick skillet over medium heat. Add potato, onion, celery and carrots. Cook, stirring, 5 minutes.

- Blend broth and flour; add to skillet along with thyme, salt and pepper. Simmer 10 minutes. Stir in chicken; remove from heat.

- Pour filling into bottom crust. Top with remaining crust. Pinch edge together and tuck down slightly into pan. Cut slits into top crust.

- Bake at 400° for 35 minutes, until lightly browned and bubbly. Cool 10 minutes.

PER SERVING 512 **CAL**; 28 g **FAT** (7 g **SAT**); 19 g **PRO**; 42 g **CARB**; 3 g **FIBER**; 585 mg **SODIUM**; 36 mg **CHOL**

ASIAN CHICKEN NOODLE BOWL

Asian Chicken Noodle Bowl

MAKES 6 servings **PREP** 15 minutes
SLOW COOK on HIGH for 4 hours or
LOW for 6 hours

- 1 **large onion, sliced**
- 2 **large carrots, peeled and cut into ¼-inch coins**
- 3 **cloves garlic, sliced**
- 2½ **lb boneless, skinless chicken thighs, cut into 1-inch pieces**
- 1 **can (20 oz) pineapple chunks in juice**
- 3 **tbsp cornstarch**
- ¼ **cup sugar**
- ¼ **cup cider vinegar**
- ¼ **cup ketchup**
- 3 **tbsp reduced-sodium soy sauce**
- 1 **large red sweet pepper, seeded and sliced**
- ¼ **lb snow peas, trimmed and thinly sliced lengthwise**
- ½ **teaspoon salt**
- 4 **cups cooked rice noodles**
- ⅓ **cup toasted almonds**

■ Coat a 3½- or 4-qt slow cooker with nonstick cooking spray.

■ Place onion, carrots and garlic in slow cooker. Add chicken evenly over top. Drain pineapple and set aside, reserving ¼ cup of the juice in a bowl. Whisk together juice, cornstarch, sugar, vinegar, ketchup and soy sauce; pour over chicken.

■ Cover and cook on HIGH for 4 hours or LOW for 6 hours.

■ Stir in pepper, snow peas, salt and pineapple during last 30 minutes.

■ Serve with rice noodles and almonds.

PER SERVING 484 **CAL**; 11 g **FAT** (2 g **SAT**); 37 g **PRO**; 61 g **CARB**; 7 g **FIBER**; 758 mg **SODIUM**; 147 mg **CHOL**

Chicken Cordon Bleu

MAKES 4 servings **PREP** 20 minutes
BAKE at 375° for 30 minutes

- 4 **boneless, skinless chicken breasts (about 4 oz each)**
- ⅛ **tsp salt**
- ⅛ **tsp black pepper**
- 8 **thin slices (about 4 oz) reduced-fat Swiss cheese**
- 4 **thin slices (about 4 oz) reduced-sodium smoked ham**
- 2 **egg whites, lightly beaten**
- 1 **tbsp Dijon mustard**
- 1 **cup seasoned panko bread crumbs**
- 1 **envelope (0.9 oz) hollandaise sauce**
- 1 **cup 2% milk**
- 2 **tbsp Brummel & Brown yogurt spread**

Orzo and Broccoli Pilaf (recipe follows) (optional)

■ Heat oven to 375°. Place a rack in a baking pan; coat rack with nonstick cooking spray.

■ On a flat work surface, place chicken between sheets of plastic wrap and pound to ¼-inch thickness. Remove top sheet of plastic wrap and season top of chicken with salt and pepper. Place an equal amount of cheese and ham on each breast and roll up tightly from a short end.

■ Place egg whites and mustard in a shallow dish and whisk to combine. Place panko in a second shallow dish. Roll chicken in egg mixture and then in panko, covering all sides. Place on prepared rack, seam sides down, and spritz with nonstick cooking spray. Bake at 375° for 30 minutes or until chicken is cooked through.

■ Prepare hollandaise mix following package directions, using 2% milk and yogurt spread in place of butter.

■ Serve chicken with sauce and, if desired, Orzo and Broccoli Pilaf.

PER SERVING 471 **CAL**; 16 g **FAT** (7 g **SAT**); 42 g **PRO**; 38 g **CARB**; 1 g **FIBER**; 781 mg **SODIUM**; 104 mg **CHOL**

Orzo and Broccoli Pilaf In a saucepan, cook ½ small chopped onion in 1 tbsp olive oil for 2 minutes. Stir in 1 cup RiceSelect whole wheat orzo, 2 cups reduced-sodium chicken stock and ¼ tsp salt; simmer, covered, about 8 minutes or until broth is absorbed. Stir in 2 cups steamed broccoli florets.

CHICKEN CORDON BLEU

Maple-Mustard Chicken with Fingerlings and Brussels Sprouts

MAKES 4 servings **PREP** 20 minutes
ROAST 35 minutes at 450°

- 3 **tbsp canola oil**
- 1 **tsp salt**
- 1 **tsp dried thyme**
- ¼ **tsp black pepper**
- 1½ **lb fingerling potatoes**
- 1 **lb Brussels sprouts**
- 3 **tbsp maple syrup**
- 1 **tbsp coarse-grain mustard**
- 8 **small chicken thighs (5 oz each)**

■ Line a 13 x 9-inch rimmed sheet pan with nonstick foil. Combine canola oil, salt, thyme and black pepper. In prepared sheet pan, combine fingerling potatoes and Brussels sprouts with 2 tbsp of the oil mixture. Combine remaining oil mixture, maple syrup and coarse-grain mustard; spoon over chicken thighs. Place on sheet pan and roast at 450° for 35 minutes.

Red Wine Braised Chicken

MAKES 6 servings **PREP** 15 minutes
SLOW COOK on HIGH for 6 hours or LOW for 8 hours

- ½ **large onion, chopped**
- 3 **lb bone-in skinless chicken thighs**
- 1 **envelope (1.3 oz) McCormick Slow Cookers Red Wine Braised Roast Seasoning mix**
- 1 **cup small peeled baby carrots, halved**
- 10 **oz white button mushrooms, quartered**
- 1 **bag (14.4 oz) frozen pearl onions, thawed**
- ½ **cup dry red wine**
- ½ **cup fresh parsley, chopped**
  Mashed potatoes and green peas (optional)

■ Coat a 5- to 6-qt slow cooker with nonstick cooking spray.

■ Place chopped onion in slow cooker; season chicken with seasoning mix and place on top of

CHICKEN WITH FIGS AND BLUE CHEESE

onion. Add carrots, mushrooms and pearl onions. Pour red wine and ½ cup water over top.

■ Cover and cook on HIGH for 6 hours or LOW for 8 hours.

■ Stir in parsley and, if desired, serve with mashed potatoes and peas.

PER SERVING 343 **CAL**; 9 g **FAT** (2 g **SAT**); 47 g **PRO**; 12 g **CARB**; 3 g **FIBER**; 832 mg **SODIUM**; 188 mg **CHOL**

Chicken with Figs and Blue Cheese

MAKES 6 servings **PREP** 20 minutes
COOK 13 minutes
SLOW COOK on LOW for 5 hours

- 1½ **cups low-sodium chicken broth**
- ¼ **cup balsamic vinegar**
- 1 **tbsp grated orange zest**
- ¾ **tsp salt**
- ½ **tsp black pepper**
- 1 **pkg (8 oz) dried Mission figs, stems removed**
- 2 **tbsp vegetable oil**
- 2 **lb boneless, skinless chicken thighs**
- 1 **large onion, thinly sliced**
- 2 **tbsp flour**
- 1 **tube (16 oz) prepared polenta**
- ⅔ **cup crumbled blue cheese**

■ In a small bowl, stir together broth, vinegar, orange zest and ¼ tsp each salt and pepper; set aside. Coarsely chop figs.

■ Heat oil in a large nonstick skillet over medium-high heat. Add chicken to skillet and cook 5 minutes per side or until browned. Remove chicken to slow cooker and add onion to skillet. Sprinkle with ¼ tsp each salt and pepper and cook, stirring often, for 2 minutes. Stir in flour and cook for 1 minute. Pour in broth mixture and bring to a boil. Pour skillet contents into a 4-qt slow cooker and add figs.

■ Cover and cook on LOW for 5 hours.

■ Meanwhile, prepare polenta following package directions. Sprinkle remaining ¼ tsp salt into chicken mixture. Serve polenta with chicken and fig mixture; divide blue cheese among servings.

PER SERVING 459 **CAL**; 17 g **FAT** (5 g **SAT**); 37 g **PRO**; 42 g **CARB**; 5 g **FIBER**; 997 mg **SODIUM**; 160 mg **CHOL**

CHICKEN AND
GOAT CHEESE
CREPES

Chicken and Goat Cheese Crepes

MAKES 4 servings (2½ crepes per serving)
PREP 15 minutes

- 5 cups packed arugula
- 1 cup fresh basil leaves
- 1 tsp extra-virgin olive oil
- 1 tsp fresh lemon juice
- Pinch salt
- Freshly cracked black pepper
- 1 container (5.3 oz) Chavrie sweet basil goat cheese
- 1 pkg (5 oz) Melissa's ready-to-use crepes
- 2½ cups shredded rotisserie chicken

■ In a bowl, gently toss arugula, basil, oil, lemon juice, salt and pepper.

■ Spread 1 tbsp of the goat cheese on each crepe. Add ¼ cup of the shredded chicken, then top with ½ cup of the greens. Fold or roll and serve.

PER SERVING 390 **CAL**; 16 g **FAT** (6 g **SAT**); 33 g **PRO**; 24 g **CARB**; 1 g **FIBER**; 427 mg **SODIUM**; 118 mg **CHOL**

Chicken Tikka Masala

MAKES 4 servings **PREP** 20 minutes
BROIL 12 minutes **COOK** 24 minutes

- 2 tbsp chopped fresh ginger
- 2½ tsp garam masala
- 3 cloves garlic, chopped
- ½ tsp salt
- ¼ tsp cayenne pepper
- 1 cup plain low-fat yogurt
- 8 small boneless, skinless chicken thighs (about 1¾ lb)
- 1 tbsp vegetable oil
- 1 large onion, thinly sliced
- 1 can (28 oz) whole, peeled tomatoes
- ¼ cup heavy cream
- ¼ cup fresh cilantro leaves
- 1 cup basmati rice, cooked following pkg directions, substituting chicken broth for water
- Naan (optional)

■ Heat broiler to high. Line broiler pan with nonstick foil.

■ In a small bowl, combine ginger, garam masala, garlic, salt and cayenne. In a large bowl, combine 1 tbsp of the ginger mixture and ½ cup of the yogurt. Add chicken and toss to coat. Place on prepared broiler pan and broil 6 inches from heat for 6 minutes per side.

■ Meanwhile, heat oil in a large nonstick skillet over medium-high heat. Add onion and cook 5 minutes; stir in remaining ginger mixture and cook 1 minute. Stir in tomatoes, cream and remaining ½ cup yogurt. Simmer, covered, for 10 minutes, breaking up tomatoes with a wooden spoon. Add chicken to skillet; simmer, covered with lid slightly ajar, for 6 to 8 minutes or until internal temperature reaches 165°.

■ Garnish with cilantro. Serve with rice and, if desired, naan.

PER SERVING 611 **CAL**; 22 g **FAT** (8 g **SAT**); 49 g **PRO**; 59 g **CARB**; 4 g **FIBER**; 995 mg **SODIUM**; 217 mg **CHOL**

Easiest-Ever One-Dish Chicken Tamales

MAKES 8 servings **PREP** 15 minutes
BAKE at 400° for 40 minutes
COOL 10 minutes

- 1 pkg (8.5 oz) corn muffin mix
- 1 can (14.75 oz) cream-style corn
- 2 eggs, lightly beaten
- ½ cup milk
- 1 tsp chili powder
- ½ tsp ground cumin
- 1 pkg (8 oz) shredded taco cheese blend
- 1 can (10 oz) hot enchilada sauce
- 3 cups shredded cooked chicken, from rotisserie chicken
- 1 cup sour cream (optional)
- Lime wedges (optional)

■ Heat oven to 400°. Coat a 13 x 9 x 2-inch baking dish with nonstick cooking spray.

■ In a large bowl, combine muffin mix, corn, eggs, milk, chili powder, cumin and 1 cup of the cheese. Spoon into prepared baking dish. Bake at 400° for 20 minutes.

■ Pierce casserole with a small knife in about 12 places and spread enchilada sauce over top. Scatter chicken and remaining 1 cup cheese over casserole; bake for an additional 20 minutes.

■ Allow to cool for 10 minutes and cut into 8 squares. If desired, serve with sour cream and lime wedges.

PER SERVING 415 **CAL**; 20 g **FAT** (9 g **SAT**); 27 g **PRO**; 36 g **CARB**; 1 g **FIBER**; 780 mg **SODIUM**; 128 mg **CHOL**

CHILAQUILES

CHEESY CHICKEN
ENCHILADAS

Chilaquiles

MAKES 6 servings **PREP** 15 minutes
COOK 8 minutes

- 1   **cup canola oil**
- 8   **corn tortillas, cut into ¾-inch strips**
- ¼   **tsp plus ⅛ tsp salt**
- 6   **eggs, beaten**
- 2   **cups shredded cooked chicken**
- 1   **cup salsa verde**
     Shredded queso fresco, sliced scallions and chopped fresh cilantro (optional)

■ Heat oil in a large heavy-bottomed skillet over medium-high heat until shimmering, about 350° to 375° on a deep-fry thermometer. Fry tortilla strips in 3 batches until golden brown, 1 to 2 minutes each, gently moving around in oil with a slotted spoon. Remove with spoon to a paper towel-lined plate. Season strips with ¼ tsp of the salt.

■ Carefully discard all but 1 tbsp of the oil. Add eggs and cook over medium heat until scrambled, about 2 minutes. Season with remaining ⅛ tsp salt. Meanwhile, heat the shredded chicken and salsa verde in a medium pan.

■ Arrange tortilla strips on a large platter. Spoon chicken mixture on top, then scatter eggs on the chicken. Garnish with shredded queso fresco, sliced scallions and chopped cilantro, if desired.

PER SERVING 320 **CAL**; 17 g **FAT** (3 g **SAT**); 23 g **PRO**; 19 g **CARB**; 2 g **FIBER**; 392 mg **SODIUM**; 251 mg **CHOL**

Cheesy Chicken Enchiladas

MAKES 8 servings **PREP** 20 minutes
BAKE at 375° for 20 minutes and at 400° for 5 minutes

- 1   **can (19 oz) mild enchilada sauce**
- 4   **cups shredded chicken (from a large rotisserie chicken) or 1¼ lb poached chicken breast**
- 1   **bag (8 oz) shredded Mexican cheese blend**
- ⅔   **cup Neufchâtel (⅓-less-fat cream cheese)**
- 16 **small flour tortillas**
     Sliced fresh jalapeño peppers, fresh cilantro leaves and diced fresh tomato for garnish (optional)

■ Heat oven to 375°. Coat one 4-qt or two 2-qt baking dishes with nonstick cooking spray. If using 1 dish, spread ⅓ cup of the enchilada sauce in bottom. If using 2 dishes, spread 3 tbsp of the enchilada sauce in bottom of each dish.

■ In a bowl, combine chicken, 1 cup of the shredded cheese and ¾ cup of the enchilada sauce.

■ Spread 2 tsp Neufchâtel on a tortilla. Spoon 2 to 3 tbsp chicken mixture in a strip in center of tortilla. Roll up tightly to enclose filling; transfer to prepared dish(es). Repeat with remaining tortillas, cream cheese and chicken mixture to make 16 enchiladas total.

■ Pour remaining sauce over enchiladas, dividing evenly between dishes (if using 2). Top with remaining cheese. Bake at 375° for 20 minutes. Increase temperature to 400° and bake an additional 5 minutes, until cheese begins to brown slightly. Garnish with jalapeño slices, cilantro and tomato, if desired.

PER SERVING 415 **CAL**; 20 g **FAT** (10 g **SAT**); 25 g **PRO**; 30 g **CARB**; 0 g **FIBER**; 930 mg **SODIUM**; 77 mg **CHOL**

Triple-Cheese Chicken Enchiladas

MAKES 10 servings   **PREP** 20 minutes
COOK 10 minutes
SLOW COOK on LOW for 4 hours
COOL 30 minutes

- 2   **tbsp olive oil**
- 1½ **lb ground chicken**
- 1   **cup chopped onion**
- 2   **Cubanelle peppers, seeded and chopped**
- 3   **cloves garlic, chopped**
- 1   **can (8 oz) tomato sauce**
- 1   **can (15 oz) kidney beans, drained and rinsed**
- 1   **can (15 oz) pinto beans, drained and rinsed**
- 2   **tsp chili powder**
- ½   **tsp ground cumin**
- ½   **tsp salt**
- 2   **cups shredded Monterey Jack**
- 2   **cups shredded cheddar**
- 1   **cup shredded Swiss cheese**
- 13 **corn tortillas**

■ Heat oil in a large skillet over medium-high heat. Add chicken, onion, peppers and garlic. Cook 8 minutes, stirring occasionally.

■ Stir in tomato sauce, beans, chili powder, cumin and salt. Simmer 2 minutes. In a large bowl, combine cheeses.

■ Line a round 4-qt slow cooker with a slow cooker liner. Coat liner with nonstick cooking spray.

■ Fit 2½ tortillas into bottom of slow cooker; top with 1½ cups of the chicken mixture and ¾ cup of the cheese mixture. Repeat layering 3 times. For the final layer, fit 3 tortillas into slow cooker. Top with remaining chicken mixture and cheese.

■ Cook on LOW for 4 hours. Let cool at least 30 minutes before cutting into wedges.

PER SERVING 468 **CAL**; 26 g **FAT** (11 g **SAT**); 30 g **PRO**; 30 g **CARB**; 7 g **FIBER**; 1,002 mg **SODIUM**; 94 mg **CHOL**

**CRISPY CHICKEN
LETTUCE WRAPS**

Crispy Chicken Lettuce Wraps

MAKES 4 servings **PREP** 20 minutes
COOK 12 minutes

- 2 **tbsp canola oil**
- 1 **lb boneless, skinless chicken thighs, cut into ½-inch pieces**
- 8 **oz cremini mushrooms, chopped**
- 1 **red sweet pepper, seeded and chopped**
- 3 **scallions, chopped**
- 2 **cloves garlic, chopped**
- ½ **tsp Chinese five-spice powder**
- ¼ **tsp red pepper flakes**
- 1 **can (8 oz) chopped water chestnuts, drained**
- ¼ **cup chicken broth**
- 2 **tbsp reduced-sodium soy sauce**
- 1 **tbsp hoisin sauce**
- 1 **head Boston lettuce, separated into 16 leaves**
- ½ **cup crispy rice noodles**
  Duck sauce (optional)

■ Heat oil in a large skillet over medium-high heat. Add chicken and stir-fry for 6 minutes; remove to a plate.

■ Add mushrooms, red sweet pepper, scallions, garlic, five-spice powder and red pepper flakes. Stir-fry for 3 minutes or until mushrooms and peppers are tender. Stir in water chestnuts, broth, soy sauce and hoisin sauce. Bring to a simmer; add chicken and cook for 3 minutes, stirring occasionally.

■ To serve, spoon chicken mixture into lettuce leaves and sprinkle with some rice noodles. If desired, serve with duck sauce for dipping.

PER SERVING 374 **CAL**; 16 g **FAT** (3 g **SAT**); 30 g **PRO**; 30 g **CARB**; 5 g **FIBER**; 769 mg **SODIUM**; 110 mg **CHOL**

Chicken-and-Egg Burgers

MAKES 4 servings **PREP** 15 minutes
COOK 15 minutes

- 1 **lb ground chicken breast**
- 3 **cups packed spinach, chopped**
- 1 **large shallot, grated**
- 1 **clove garlic, grated**
- 1 **tbsp Dijon mustard**
- ½ **tsp salt**
- ¼ **tsp plus ⅛ tsp black pepper**
- 1 **tbsp vegetable oil**
- 4 **oz thinly sliced sharp cheddar**
- 1 **tbsp unsalted butter**
- 4 **eggs**
- 4 **whole wheat hamburger buns, split**
- 1 **tsp white wine vinegar**

■ In a bowl, combine chicken, 2 cups of the spinach, the shallot, garlic, mustard, salt and ¼ tsp of the pepper. Form into 4 patties.

■ Heat oil in a large nonstick skillet over medium heat. Cook burgers 6 minutes per side or until cooked through, adding cheese after flipping. (To help cheese melt, cover with a lid or tent loosely with aluminum foil.) Set burgers on a plate.

■ Add butter to skillet. Fry eggs 2 minutes, until cooked, and sprinkle with remaining ⅛ tsp pepper. Top each burger with an egg. Add buns to pan, cut sides down; toast 1 minute. Transfer burgers to bottom halves of buns. Toss remaining 1 cup spinach with vinegar. Top each burger with some spinach mixture and remaining bun halves.

PER SERVING 438 **CAL**; 21 g **FAT** (7 g **SAT**); 37 g **PRO**; 27 g **CARB**; 4 g **FIBER**; 833 mg **SODIUM**; 297 mg **CHOL**

CHICKEN-AND-EGG BURGERS

SAUSAGE AND
PEPPER BAKE

Sausage and Pepper Bake

MAKES 6 servings **PREP** 25 minutes
REFRIGERATE overnight
BAKE at 375° for 30 minutes and at 350° for
30 minutes

- 2 **pkg (10 oz each) microwave-ready frozen brown rice**
- 2 **tbsp chopped fresh parsley**
- 1 **tsp chopped fresh rosemary**
- 1 **tsp chopped fresh oregano**
- 1 **bag (8 oz) 2% Italian cheese blend**
- 1 **red sweet pepper, sliced**
- 1 **green sweet pepper, sliced**
- 1 **pkg (8 oz) sliced mushrooms**
- 2 **plum tomatoes, cored and diced**
- 1 **pkg (12 oz) fully cooked sweet pepper and Asiago chicken sausage, cut into coins**
- 2 **tbsp balsamic vinegar**
- 1 **tbsp olive oil**
- ¼ **tsp salt**
- ¼ **tsp black pepper**
- 2 **tbsp grated Parmesan cheese**

■ Toss frozen rice with herbs and spread into bottom of a 3-qt baking dish. Top with 1 cup of the Italian cheese blend.

■ Combine peppers, mushrooms, tomatoes and sausage in a large bowl. Whisk together vinegar, oil, salt and black pepper in a small bowl. Toss with sausage mixture. Add to baking dish on top of rice. Cover and refrigerate overnight.

■ To bake, remove casserole from refrigerator. Heat oven to 375°. Remove plastic from casserole; sprinkle dish with remaining Italian cheese blend and the Parmesan. Bake at 375° for 30 minutes. Reduce heat to 350°. Cover with foil and bake 30 minutes more.

PER SERVING 362 **CAL**; 16 g **FAT** (6 g **SAT**); 24 g **PRO**; 9 g **CARB**; 3 g **FIBER**; 762 mg **SODIUM**; 68 mg **CHOL**

APPLE, SAUSAGE AND WALNUT PASTA

Apple, Sausage and Walnut Pasta

MAKES 6 servings **PREP** 10 minutes
COOK 15 minutes

- 1 lb whole wheat penne
- ½ cup walnuts
- 3 links (3 oz each) Italian chicken sausage, removed from casings
- 1 tbsp all-purpose flour
- 1 cup low-sodium chicken broth
- 2 apples, diced into ½-inch pieces
- 1 bag (6 oz) baby spinach
- ½ cup grated Asiago cheese
- ½ tsp salt
- ¼ tsp pepper

■ Bring a large pot of lightly salted water to a boil. Cook pasta according to package directions. Drain.

■ Meanwhile, add walnuts to a large nonstick sauté pan over medium heat; toast 5 minutes, stirring occasionally. Remove to a cutting board to cool, then roughly chop.

■ In same pan, add chicken sausage. Cook over medium heat 5 to 7 minutes, breaking apart with a wooden spoon, until browned. Stir in flour; cook 1 minute. Add broth and bring to a simmer over medium-high heat. Mix in apples and cook 2 minutes. Stir in spinach until wilted. Mix in walnuts, Asiago, salt and pepper. Transfer to a bowl with pasta; stir to combine.

PER SERVING 464 **CAL**; 15 g **FAT** (3 g **SAT**); 16 g **PRO**; 67 g **CARB**; 5 g **FIBER**; 644 mg **SODIUM**; 41 mg **CHOL**

QUINOA WITH SUMMER VEGETABLES AND SAUSAGE

Quinoa with Summer Vegetables and Sausage

MAKES 4 servings **PREP** 15 minutes
MICROWAVE 8 minutes

- 2 tbsp extra-virgin olive oil
- 2 tbsp white balsamic vinegar
- 1 tbsp Dijon mustard
- ¼ tsp salt
- ¼ tsp black pepper
- 16 oz (about 3 cups) cooked plain quinoa
- 1 pkg (12 oz) Al Fresco roasted garlic chicken sausage
- 2 cups frozen fire-roasted corn
- 2 cups grape tomatoes, halved
- 1 cup roasted red peppers, sliced
- 1 tbsp chopped fresh thyme

■ In a large bowl, whisk together oil, vinegar, mustard, salt and black pepper. Set aside.

■ Heat quinoa in microwave 3 to 4 minutes or per package directions. Place sausage on a plate; microwave 2 minutes. Allow sausage to rest while heating corn in a microwave-safe bowl with 1 tbsp water for 2 minutes. Slice sausage into coins.

■ Toss quinoa, sausage, corn, tomatoes, roasted red peppers and thyme in bowl with dressing.

PER SERVING 459 **CAL**; 17 g **FAT** (3 g **SAT**); 23 g **PRO**; 54 g **CARB**; 6 g **FIBER**; 782 mg **SODIUM**; 65 mg **CHOL**

SAUSAGE AND VEGGIE LASAGNA

Squash and Farro Salad

MAKES 6 servings **PREP** 25 minutes
ROAST at 450° for 20 minutes
REFRIGERATE overnight **COOK** 16 minutes
MICROWAVE 2 minutes

- 1½ **lb diced fresh butternut squash**
- 4 **tbsp olive oil**
- 1 **tsp salt**
- ½ **tsp black pepper**
- 1 **small rotisserie chicken**
- 1½ **cups parboiled farro**
- ½ **cup sweetened dried cranberries**
- ½ **tsp ground cumin**
- ½ **tsp ground ginger**
- ½ **tsp ground cinnamon**
- ¼ **cup cider vinegar**
- 2 **tsp Dijon mustard**
- 1 **tsp honey**
- 2 **cups mixed baby kale, shredded**
- ½ **cup crumbled goat cheese**
- ⅓ **cup toasted walnuts, chopped**

■ Heat oven to 450°. Toss diced squash with 2 tbsp of the oil and ¼ tsp each of the salt and pepper; spread onto a large baking pan. Roast at 450° for 20 minutes, stirring halfway through; cool.

■ Meanwhile, remove and discard skin from chicken. Shred meat (you need 3 cups), discarding bones. Refrigerate squash and chicken overnight.

■ The next day, combine farro, ½ tsp of the salt and 4½ cups water in a large pot. Boil for 10 minutes, then stir in dried cranberries. Boil for 5 minutes; drain and rinse.

■ In a small skillet, combine remaining ¼ tsp each salt and pepper, the cumin, ginger and cinnamon. Toast over medium heat for 1 minute.

■ In a bowl, whisk together vinegar, mustard, honey and remaining 2 tbsp oil. Whisk into skillet with seasonings. Remove from heat. Reheat squash and chicken. Combine farro, squash, chicken and kale in a bowl. Drizzle with dressing, then toss and sprinkle with goat cheese and walnuts.

PER SERVING 479 **CAL**; 18 g **FAT** (3 g **SAT**); 24 g **PRO**; 59 g **CARB**; 9 g **FIBER**; 673 mg **SODIUM**; 38 mg **CHOL**

Sausage and Veggie Lasagna

MAKES 8 servings **PREP** 25 minutes
COOK 6 minutes
SLOW COOK on LOW for 4 hours
COOL 30 minutes

- 1 **lb chicken sausage, casings removed**
- 1 **pkg (8 oz) sliced mushrooms**
- 2 **large carrots, peeled and grated**
- 1 **zucchini (8 oz), trimmed and grated**
- 1 **jar (24 oz) marinara sauce**
- 1 **container (15 oz) part-skim ricotta cheese**
- 1 **bag (7 oz) 2% shredded Italian cheese blend**
- ⅓ **cup fresh basil, chopped**
- 12 **traditional lasagna noodles (not no-boil)**

■ Line a 5-qt slow cooker with a slow cooker liner. Coat liner with nonstick cooking spray. Crumble sausage into a nonstick skillet and cook over medium to medium-high heat for 6 minutes, breaking apart with a wooden spoon.

■ Meanwhile, in a large bowl, combine mushrooms, carrots, zucchini and 1 cup of the marinara sauce. Stir remaining sauce into the sausage.

■ In a medium bowl, stir together ricotta, 1 cup of the shredded cheese and the basil.

■ Begin layering: Break 3 noodles into thirds and spread on bottom of slow cooker. Top with half the vegetable mixture, spreading level, and 3 more noodles, broken into thirds. Spread noodles with sausage mixture and top with 3 more noodles, broken into thirds. Spread noodles with ricotta mixture and remaining 3 noodles (in thirds). Top noodles with remaining vegetable mixture and remaining shredded cheese. Cover and cook on LOW for 4 hours.

■ Remove crock insert from slow cooker and cool for 30 minutes. Uncover and use liner bag to lift lasagna from crock. Remove liner and cut lasagna into pieces.

PER SERVING 487 **CAL**; 20 g **FAT** (9 g **SAT**); 33 g **PRO**; 45 g **CARB**; 4 g **FIBER**; 1,083 mg **SODIUM**; 91 mg **CHOL**

SPINACH, ORANGE AND
CHICKEN SALAD

Spinach, Orange and Chicken Salad

MAKES 6 servings **PREP** 25 minutes
MICROWAVE 40 seconds **MARINATE** 15 minutes
GRILL 14 minutes

- 6 small juice oranges
- 2 tbsp red wine vinegar
- 1 tsp grainy mustard
- ½ tsp sugar
- ½ tsp salt
- ¼ tsp black pepper
- ⅛ tsp ground cumin
- ⅓ cup olive oil
- 1½ lb boneless, skinless chicken breasts
- 1 pkg (5 oz) baby spinach
- 1 head green leaf lettuce, trimmed, cleaned and torn into bite-size pieces
- ½ red onion, thinly sliced
- 1 pkg (3.5 oz) crumbled goat cheese

■ Cut off peel and slice sections from 5 of the oranges. Place in a bowl. Juice remaining orange (you will need ¼ cup juice).

■ In a small bowl, whisk orange juice, vinegar, mustard, sugar, ¼ tsp of the salt and ⅛ tsp of the pepper. Microwave cumin in a small bowl for 40 seconds or until fragrant. Whisk into orange juice mixture. While whisking, add oil in a thin stream.

■ Place chicken in a resealable plastic bag and add ⅓ cup of the dressing. Marinate 15 minutes.

■ Meanwhile, heat grill or grill pan. Remove chicken from marinade and discard any remaining marinade. Grill for 14 minutes, turning once, or until chicken registers 160° on an instant-read thermometer.

■ In a very large bowl, toss spinach, lettuce, orange sections (and any juice in bowl), red onion slices, goat cheese and remaining dressing. Slice chicken and fan over top of salad. Sprinkle with remaining ¼ tsp salt and ⅛ tsp pepper and serve.

PER SERVING 528 **CAL**; 16 g **FAT** (4 g **SAT**); 29 g **PRO**; 65 g **CARB**; 4 g **FIBER**; 661 mg **SODIUM**; 72 mg **CHOL**

Buffalo Turkey Chopped Salad

MAKES 4 servings **PREP** 30 minutes
COOK 2 minutes

- 1 lb fresh turkey cutlets
- 3 tbsp Frank's Original Hot Sauce
- 2 tbsp red wine vinegar
- ⅛ tsp salt
- ⅛ tsp black pepper
- 1 tsp Dijon mustard
- 3 tbsp olive oil
- 1 head red leafy lettuce, torn into bite-size pieces
- 2 large carrots, diced
- 1 large zucchini, diced
- 1 cup diced radishes
- ½ English cucumber, diced
- 2 ribs celery, diced
- 1 avocado, peeled, pitted and sliced into 16 thin wedges
- ¼ cup blue cheese crumbles

■ Place turkey cutlets in a lidded skillet and add water to cover by at least 1 inch. Cover and bring to a simmer. Gently simmer 2 minutes or until cooked through. Remove to a cutting board and slice or dice into pieces. Place turkey pieces in a medium bowl and toss with hot sauce. Set aside.

■ In a large bowl, whisk vinegar, salt, pepper and mustard. Gradually whisk in olive oil. Add red leafy lettuce, carrots, zucchini, radishes, cucumber and celery. Toss to combine and coat all ingredients with dressing.

■ Divide salad among 4 plates. Top each with 4 avocado slices, turkey and blue cheese crumbles.

PER SERVING 383 **CAL**; 22 g **FAT** (4 g **SAT**); 33 g **PRO**; 16 g **CARB**; 7 g **FIBER**; 703 mg **SODIUM**; 71 mg **CHOL**

BUFFALO TURKEY CHOPPED SALAD

Chicken and Rice Soup

MAKES 6 servings **PREP** 25 minutes
SLOW COOK on LOW for 6 hours

- 1   cup peeled and sliced carrots
- 1   cup sliced celery
- 1   cup diced onion
- 2   sprigs fresh thyme
- 4   whole cloves
- 1   tsp whole black peppercorns
- 1   whole chicken, quartered
- 4   cups unsalted chicken stock
- ½   cup fresh dill, chopped
- 1½ tsp salt
- 1   pkg (8.8 oz) Uncle Ben's whole grain brown Ready Rice

  Freshly cracked pepper

■ Place carrots, celery, onion, thyme, cloves and peppercorns in a 4- to 5-qt slow cooker. Arrange chicken, including back and wings, on top. Pour in chicken stock and 1 cup water. Cook on LOW for 6 hours.

■ Remove chicken from slow cooker. Shred, discarding bones and skin. Return meat to slow cooker and stir in dill, salt and rice. Serve with freshly cracked pepper.

PER SERVING 372 **CAL**; 7 g **FAT** (2 g **SAT**); 55 g **PRO**; 17 g **CARB**; 2 g **FIBER**; 820 mg **SODIUM**; 135 mg **CHOL**

Crystal-Clear Chicken Soup with Julienned Vegetables and Angel Hair

MAKES 6 quarts; 24 servings **PREP** 15 minutes
COOK 4 hours **REFRIGERATE** overnight

STOCK BASE

- 1   chicken (about 3½ lb), cut into 8 pieces
- 2   bone-in chicken breasts (about 1½ lb)
- 4   or 5 beef marrow bones (about 2 lb)
- 5   medium carrots, quartered
- 2   large parsnips, quartered
- 2   small turnips, quartered
- 2   medium parsley roots, quartered, or use a combo of more parsnips and turnips

1 large green sweet pepper, halved, ribs and seeds removed

1 large onion

3 tbsp kosher salt

20 fresh parsley sprigs

½ head cauliflower, broken into florets

7 cloves garlic

20 black or white peppercorns

4 whole allspice

SOUP

1 large zucchini, cut into ⅛-inch julienne

1 large carrot, peeled, cut into ⅛-inch julienne

1 large daikon radish, peeled, cut into ⅛-inch julienne

1 lb Passover noodles, cooked and drained, at room temperature

■ **Stock base.** Place chicken, marrow bones, carrots, parsnips, turnips, parsley roots, sweet pepper, onion and 1 tbsp of the salt in a 12-qt stockpot. Cover with 6 qt cold water and bring to a boil over high heat. Skim and discard foam that forms at the top when it comes to a boil.

■ Add remaining 2 tbsp salt, the parsley, cauliflower, garlic, peppercorns and allspice and return to a boil. Simmer, covered, over low heat for 1 hour. Remove the 4 chicken breasts and allow them to cool slightly. Remove meat from bones. Shred or chop meat and store it in fridge to serve in soup or for another use. Return bones to pot. Continue simmering, covered, over low heat, for at least 2 hours more.

■ Strain entire contents of pot through a colander lined with cheesecloth. Discard all solids or save them for another use. Chill broth overnight.

■ **Soup.** Remove surface fat and pour broth into a large pot. Bring to a simmer over low heat and cook until warm, 10 to 15 minutes. Add zucchini, carrot, daikon and, if desired, reserved chicken. Simmer 5 minutes to cook vegetables and heat chicken. Be careful to keep soup over low heat; bringing soup to a boil can make it cloudy. Season to taste with salt.

AFRICAN CHICKEN AND PEANUT STEW

■ Place ¼ cup Passover noodles in each soup bowl and ladle hot soup over pasta. Serve immediately.

■ This soup can be frozen after surface fat is removed. You can freeze breast meat separately if you want to use it for other dishes.

African Chicken and Peanut Stew

MAKES 8 servings **PREP** 15 minutes
SLOW COOK on HIGH for 4 hours or LOW for 6 hours

2¼ lb bone-in chicken thighs, skin removed

2 lb sweet potatoes, peeled and diced

1 3-inch piece ginger, peeled and chopped

2 cloves garlic, chopped

1½ cups unsalted chicken stock

½ cup natural chunky peanut butter

1 can (14 oz) diced tomatoes

1 tsp ground coriander

¾ tsp salt

½ tsp black pepper

1 tsp cider vinegar

Cilantro and peanuts (optional)

■ Place chicken, sweet potatoes, ginger and garlic in a 5- to 6-qt slow cooker. In a bowl, whisk stock and peanut butter until blended. Stir in tomatoes, coriander, ½ tsp of the salt and the pepper. Pour into slow cooker. Press down until chicken and potatoes are mostly submerged. Cover and cook on HIGH for 4 hours or LOW for 6 hours.

■ Carefully remove chicken to a cutting board. Shred chicken, discarding bones. Stir vinegar and remaining ¼ tsp salt into liquid. Stir in shredded chicken.

■ Ladle into bowls. Garnish with cilantro and peanuts, if desired.

PER SERVING 320 **CAL**; 14 g **FAT** (3 g **SAT**); 24 g **PRO**; 22 g **CARB**; 4 g **FIBER**; 520 mg **SODIUM**; 100 mg **CHOL**

CAJUN CHICKEN AND DUMPLINGS

Sausage and Bean Tortilla Soup

MAKES 6 servings PREP 5 minutes
COOK 15 minutes

- 2 **tbsp canola oil**
- 2 **cups frozen chopped onions and peppers, thawed**
- 2 **fully cooked jalapeño chicken sausages (such as Aidells spicy mango with jalapeño), sliced**
- 1 **can (14.5 oz) reduced-sodium stewed tomatoes**
- 1 **can (14.5 oz) reduced-sodium chicken broth**
- 1 **can (15 oz) pinto beans, drained and rinsed**
- 1 **can (15 oz) black beans, drained and rinsed**
- 1 **cup frozen corn, thawed**
- 1 **tsp ancho chile powder**
- 1 **tsp dried oregano**
- ⅛ **tsp salt**
- 2 **oz baked tortilla chips**
- ¼ **cup sliced scallion**
- 1 **avocado, diced**

■ Heat oil in a large pot over medium-high heat. Add onions and peppers; cook for 2 minutes, stirring occasionally. Add sausages; cook for 3 minutes.

■ Stir in tomatoes, breaking up with a spoon. Add chicken broth, pinto beans, black beans, corn, chile powder, oregano and salt. Bring to a boil; lower heat and simmer, covered, for 10 minutes.

■ To serve, spoon into soup bowls; crush tortilla chips over each serving and top with scallion and avocado.

PER SERVING 382 CAL; 13 g FAT (2 g SAT); 17 g PRO; 54 g CARB; 14 g FIBER; 780 mg SODIUM; 17 mg CHOL

Cajun Chicken and Dumplings

MAKES 8 servings PREP 20 minutes
SLOW COOK on HIGH for 5 hours or LOW for 7 hours, plus 1 hour

- 1 **large onion, thinly sliced**
- 2½ **lb boneless, skinless chicken thighs, cut into 1½-inch pieces**
- 2 **tbsp salt-free Cajun seasoning**
- 4 **cloves garlic, finely chopped**
- ¼ **tsp salt**
- 7 **oz light kielbasa (from a 14-oz pkg, sliced**
- 1 **can (14.5 oz) fire-roasted diced tomatoes**
- 1 **cup reduced-sodium chicken broth**
- 2 **tbsp all-purpose flour**
- 1 **green sweet pepper, seeded and cut into ½-inch slices**
- 2 **ribs celery, cut into ½-inch slices**
- 1 **can (15 oz) pinto beans, drained and rinsed**
- 2 **cups biscuit baking mix**
- ⅔ **cup milk**
- 2 **tbsp chopped fresh cilantro**

■ Coat a 5- to 6-qt slow cooker with nonstick cooking spray.

■ Place onion in slow cooker. Season chicken with Cajun seasoning, garlic and salt; distribute evenly over onion. Add kielbasa and tomatoes. Combine broth and flour; pour over tomatoes. Scatter sweet pepper and celery over top.

■ Cover and cook on HIGH for 5 hours or LOW for 7 hours.

■ Add beans. Combine biscuit mix and milk; spoon heaping tablespoonfuls over top and cover again. Cook 1 hour more (on either HIGH or LOW).

■ Spoon into individual bowls and sprinkle with cilantro.

PER SERVING 432 CAL; 17 g FAT (5 g SAT); 39 g PRO; 34 g CARB; 5 g FIBER; 956 mg SODIUM; 156 mg CHOL

**SAUSAGE AND BEAN
TORTILLA SOUP**

BUFFALO CHICKEN CHILI

Buffalo Chicken Chili

MAKES 6 servings **PREP** 15 minutes
COOK 5 minutes **SLOW COOK** on HIGH for
4 hours or LOW for 6 hours

- 1½ **lb ground chicken or turkey**
- 1 **large onion, chopped**
- 2 **large carrots, peeled and chopped**
- 2 **ribs celery, chopped**
- 4 **cloves garlic, chopped**
- 1 **can (28 oz) fire-roasted diced tomatoes**
- 2 **tbsp chili powder**
- 1 **tsp ground cumin**
- 1 **tsp dried oregano**
- ¼ **tsp cayenne pepper**
- 1 **can (15 oz) black beans, drained and rinsed**
- ½ **cup crumbled blue cheese**
- 3 **tbsp white vinegar**
- ¼ **tsp salt**
  Celery and carrot sticks (optional)

■ Coat a 3½- or 4-qt slow cooker with nonstick cooking spray.

■ Heat a large nonstick skillet over medium-high heat; add chicken and cook 5 minutes, stirring occasionally, until browned. Drain excess fat and spoon chicken into slow cooker. Stir in onion, carrots, celery, garlic, tomatoes, chili powder, cumin, oregano and cayenne pepper.

■ Cover and cook on HIGH for 4 hours or LOW for 6 hours. Add beans during last 30 minutes.

■ Stir in blue cheese, vinegar and salt. Serve chili with celery and carrot sticks, if desired.

PER SERVING 343 **CAL**; 17 g **FAT** (6 g **SAT**); 28 g **PRO**; 23 g **CARB**; 7 g **FIBER**; 717 mg **SODIUM**; 145 mg **CHOL**

White Bean Chicken Chili

MAKES 6 servings **PREP** 15 minutes
COOK 10 minutes **SLOW COOK** on HIGH for
3 hours or LOW for 5 hours

- 2 **tbsp canola oil**
- 2 **lb boneless, skinless chicken thighs, cut into 1½-inch pieces**
- 1 **large onion, chopped**
- 4 **cloves garlic, chopped**
- 2 **cups chicken broth**
- 2 **Cubanelle peppers, seeded and sliced**
- 1 **jalapeño, seeded and chopped**
- 2 **tsp ancho chile powder**
- 1 **tsp dried oregano**
- 1 **tsp ground cumin**
- ½ **tsp salt**
- 2 **cans (15 oz each) pinto beans, drained and rinsed**

WHITE BEAN CHICKEN CHILI

SWEET POTATO AND
TURKEY SHEPHERD'S PIE

1 can (15¼ oz) white shoepeg corn, drained

2 tbsp lime juice

½ cup cilantro leaves

Corn bread (optional)

■ Coat a 5- to 6-qt slow cooker with nonstick cooking spray.

■ Heat oil in a large skillet over medium-high heat. Add chicken, onion and garlic. Cook 10 minutes, stirring occasionally, until lightly browned. Add to slow cooker.

■ Stir in broth, Cubanelle peppers, jalapeño, ancho chile powder, oregano, cumin and salt. Mash 1 can of the beans and stir in with remaining can of beans and the corn.

■ Cover and cook on HIGH for 3 hours or LOW for 5 hours.

■ Stir in lime juice and cilantro. Serve with corn bread, if desired.

PER SERVING 440 CAL; 15 g FAT (3 g SAT); 40 g PRO; 39 g CARB; 11 g FIBER; 1,020 mg SODIUM; 147 mg CHOL

Sweet Potato and Turkey Shepherd's Pie

MAKES 10 servings   PREP 15 minutes
COOK 38 minutes   BAKE at 350° for 1 hour

2½ lb sweet potatoes, peeled and cut into 2-inch pieces

¼ cup light brown sugar

4 tbsp unsalted butter

1½ tsp salt

3 tbsp olive oil

2 cups diced yellow onion

3 cups quartered button mushrooms

2 lb ground turkey

1 tbsp minced garlic

2 tsp smoked paprika

2 tsp turmeric

2 tsp ground cumin

½ tsp ground chipotle pepper

8 oz tomato sauce

10 oz frozen spinach, thawed

⅔ cup grated Parmesan

■ Heat oven to 350°. Place sweet potatoes in a medium pot and cover with water. Bring to a boil, reduce to a simmer and cook until fork-tender, about 10 minutes. Drain and return to pot over low heat. Add sugar, butter

and ½ tsp of the salt. Mash sweet potatoes and mix until ingredients are incorporated.

■ Heat 1 tbsp of the oil in a large skillet over medium heat. Add onion and ½ tsp of the remaining salt; cook 5 minutes. Push onion to edge of pan. Pour in another 1 tbsp of the oil and add mushrooms. Cook 2 minutes without stirring, allowing mushrooms to brown. Mix with onion; cook 2 minutes more. Transfer to a plate.

■ Add remaining 1 tbsp oil to pan. Stir in turkey, breaking up meat with a spatula. Season with remaining ½ tsp salt, the garlic, smoked paprika, turmeric, cumin and chipotle. Cook 4 minutes. Stir in onion and mushrooms, tomato sauce, spinach and 1 cup water. Bring to a simmer and cook 10 to 15 minutes, until mixture thickens.

■ Spread turkey mixture into a 9 x 13-inch baking dish. Spread mashed sweet potatoes over the top in an even layer. Sprinkle with Parmesan. Bake at 350° for 1 hour, uncovered.

PER SERVING 360 CAL; 18 g FAT (6 g SAT); 23 g PRO; 28 g CARB; 4 g FIBER; 670 mg SODIUM; 85 mg CHOL

TURKEY MEDALLIONS IN
CURRIED APPLE-SHALLOT SAUCE

Turkey Medallions in Curried Apple-Shallot Sauce

MAKES 4 servings **PREP** 20 minutes
COOK 18 minutes

- 1¼ lb thin boneless, skinless turkey breasts, cut in half crosswise
- ¼ cup all-purpose flour
- ¼ tsp salt
- ¼ tsp black pepper
- ¾ tsp dried thyme
- ¾ tsp dried marjoram
- 2 tbsp extra-virgin olive oil
- 1 tbsp unsalted butter
- 2 Braeburn apples, peeled, cored and chopped
- 2 large shallots, peeled and chopped
- 3 cloves garlic, chopped
- 1 cup chicken broth
- ½ cup white wine
- ¼ cup heavy cream
- 1 tbsp Dijon mustard
- 1½ tsp curry powder
   Steamed green beans (optional side dish)

■ Dredge turkey in flour; season with salt, pepper and ½ tsp each of the thyme and marjoram.

■ In a large skillet, heat 1 tbsp of the oil and the butter over medium-high heat. Add turkey; cook in batches for 3 minutes, turning once, or until cooked through. Remove to a plate, cover and keep warm.

■ Add remaining 1 tbsp oil to skillet. Stir in apples, shallots and garlic; sauté for 2 minutes, stirring occasionally. Add broth, wine, cream, mustard, curry and remaining ¼ tsp each thyme and marjoram. Simmer over medium-low heat 10 minutes, stirring occasionally. Serve turkey with sauce and, if desired, steamed green beans.

PER SERVING 424 **CAL**; 16 g **FAT** (6 g **SAT**); 39 g **PRO**; 28 g **CARB**; 2 g **FIBER**; 602 mg **SODIUM**; 84 mg **CHOL**

Indian Madras Pie

MAKES 6 servings **PREP** 20 minutes
COOK 13 minutes **BAKE** at 350° for 20 minutes

- 2½ lb baking potatoes, peeled and cut into 2-inch pieces
- 2 tbsp vegetable oil
- 1 pkg (20.8 oz) ground turkey
- 1½ cups baby carrots, sliced
- 3 medium parsnips, peeled and sliced
- 2 tsp ground ginger
- 1½ tsp salt
- 1 tsp ground cumin
- 1 tsp ground coriander
- ½ tsp ground cinnamon
- ½ tsp ground turmeric
- ⅛ tsp cayenne pepper
- 1 cup frozen peas, thawed
- ⅔ cup milk
- 2 tbsp unsalted butter
   Pinch cayenne pepper (optional)

■ Heat oven to 350°. Place potatoes in a large pot and cover with cold water. Bring to a boil over high heat; cook, boiling, for 12 minutes. Drain and return to pot.

■ Meanwhile, heat oil in a large, lidded 3- to 4-qt flameproof dish over medium-high heat. Crumble in turkey and cook, breaking apart with a wooden spoon, for 4 minutes. Stir in carrots, parsnips, ginger, ¾ tsp of the salt, the cumin, coriander, cinnamon, turmeric, cayenne and ½ cup water. Cover and cook over medium heat, stirring once or twice, 7 minutes, adding more water if necessary. Uncover and stir in peas. Cook 2 minutes, then remove from heat.

■ Mash potatoes in pot with milk, butter and remaining ¾ tsp salt. Spread potatoes over turkey mixture in dish and sprinkle with cayenne, if desired. Bake, uncovered, at 350° for 20 minutes.

PER SERVING 435 **CAL**; 18 g **FAT** (5 g **SAT**); 24 g **PRO**; 46 g **CARB**; 6 g **FIBER**; 722 mg **SODIUM**; 90 mg **CHOL**

INDIAN MADRAS PIE

TURKEY LASAGNA

Enchiladas Suizas

MAKES 6 servings **PREP** 25 minutes
COOK 14 minutes **BAKE** at 375° for 25 minutes

- 1 **pkg (20.8 oz) lean ground turkey**
- 1 **zucchini (about 8 oz), grated**
- 1 **small onion, chopped**
- ¾ **tsp salt**
- ½ **tsp dried oregano**
- ½ **tsp black pepper**
- ¼ **tsp ground cumin**
- 1 **jar (16 oz) medium salsa verde**
- ¾ **cup half-and-half**
- 4 **oz Monterey Jack cheese, grated (1 cup)**
- 12 **corn tortillas**
   Chopped fresh cilantro (optional)

■ Heat oven to 375°. Coat a 13 x 9 x 2-inch baking dish with nonstick cooking spray.

■ Coat a 12-inch nonstick skillet with nonstick spray and place over medium heat. Crumble in ground turkey and add zucchini and onion. Cook until turkey is no longer pink and most of the liquid has evaporated, 10 minutes. Season with ½ tsp of the salt, the oregano, ¼ tsp of the pepper and the cumin.

■ Meanwhile, combine salsa, half-and-half and remaining ¼ tsp each of the salt and pepper in a blender and pulse until smooth. Stir ¾ cup of the sauce into skillet and heat through. Remove from heat and stir in ¼ cup of the cheese.

■ Pour ⅔ cup of the sauce into prepared dish. Heat a nonstick skillet over medium-high heat; add 1 tortilla. Heat, flipping, 20 seconds. Transfer to a work surface and spoon ¼ cup of the turkey mixture down center. Roll to enclose filling. Transfer, seam side down, to prepared dish. Repeat with remaining tortillas and filling.

■ Pour remaining sauce over enchiladas and top with remaining cheese. Bake at 375° for 25 minutes. Garnish with cilantro, if desired.

PER SERVING 408 **CAL**; 18 g **FAT** (8 g **SAT**); 26 g **PRO**; 33 g **CARB**; 4 g **FIBER**; 773 mg **SODIUM**; 108 mg **CHOL**

Turkey Lasagna

MAKES 8 servings **PREP** 10 minutes
COOK 10 minutes **SLOW COOK** on HIGH for 4 hours or LOW for 5½ hours

- 1 **tbsp canola oil**
- 1 **medium onion, chopped**
- 2 **cloves garlic, chopped**
- 1¼ **lb ground turkey**
- 1 **tsp dried oregano**
- ½ **tsp salt**
- ¼ **tsp black pepper**
- 1 **container (15 oz) low-fat ricotta**
- 1 **cup Italian shredded cheese blend**
- 12 **lasagna noodles, broken in half**
- 1 **pkg (10 oz) frozen chopped broccoli, thawed and squeezed dry**
- 1 **jar (26 oz) chunky tomato sauce**

■ In a large nonstick skillet, heat oil over medium-high heat. Cook onion and garlic 4 minutes or until softened. Add turkey and cook 6 minutes, breaking up with a wooden spoon; season with oregano, salt and pepper. Set aside.

■ In a small bowl, combine ricotta and ½ cup of the shredded cheese.

■ Line a 5- to 6-qt slow cooker with a slow cooker liner. Layer half the uncooked noodles into slow cooker, overlapping as necessary. Spread half the turkey mixture and broccoli over noodles; top with half the tomato sauce and ¼ cup water. Gently spread ricotta mixture on top. Continue layering with remaining noodles, turkey mixture, broccoli, sauce and an additional ¼ cup water.

■ Cover and cook on HIGH for 4 hours or LOW for 5½ hours. Sprinkle remaining ½ cup shredded cheese on top during last 15 minutes of cooking. Use liner to lift lasagna from slow cooker; slice and serve.

PER SERVING 418 **CAL**; 13 g **FAT** (4 g **SAT**); 32 g **PRO**; 44 g **CARB**; 4 g **FIBER**; 706 mg **SODIUM**; 68 mg **CHOL**

ENCHILADAS
SUIZAS

SLOW-COOKED PEPPERY BEEF AND FUSILLI, RECIPE PAGE 98

Beef, Pork & Lamb

Build nutritious meals around flavorful beef, pork or lamb and you will satisfy big appetites any night of the week.

Standing Rib Roast

MAKES 8 servings **PREP** 20 minutes
ROAST at 450° for 20 minutes and at 375° for
1 hour 10 minutes **REST** 15 minutes

- 1 **standing rib roast (3 ribs, about 6 lb total)**
- 1 **tbsp plus ⅓ cup olive oil**
- 4 **cloves garlic, chopped**
- 1 **tsp plus ⅛ tsp salt**
- ½ **tsp plus ⅛ tsp black pepper**
- 1½ **cups fresh parsley leaves**
- ¼ **cup fresh oregano leaves**
- 3 **tbsp red wine vinegar**
- 2 **cloves garlic, chopped**
- ⅛ **tsp red pepper flakes**

■ Heat oven to 450°. Place a rack in a large roasting pan.

■ Rub roast with 1 tbsp oil, then rub with garlic. Season with 1 tsp of the salt and ½ tsp of the pepper. Place roast on rack in pan, rib side down.

■ Roast at 450° for 20 minutes. Reduce oven temperature to 375° and

continue to roast for 70 minutes or until temperature reaches 120°. Tent with foil and let rest 15 minutes.

■ Meanwhile, make chimichurri. Place parsley, oregano, vinegar, garlic, red pepper flakes and remaining ⅛ tsp each salt and black pepper in a blender; pulse until chopped. Gradually add ⅓ cup oil and process until combined. Cover until serving.

■ Thinly slice and serve with chimichurri.

PER SERVING 547 **CAL**; 21 g **FAT** (7 g **SAT**); 82 g **PRO**; 1 g **CARB**; 0 g **FIBER**; 515 mg **SODIUM**; 230 mg **CHOL**

Spicy-Sweet Pot Roast

MAKES 8 servings **PREP** 15 minutes
SLOW COOK on HIGH for 5 hours or
LOW for 10 hours **COOK** 3 minutes

- 2½ **lb boneless beef chuck roast, trimmed**
- 2 **tsp garlic-pepper seasoning**
- 1 **pkg (7 oz) dried fruit mix**
- 1 **tbsp chopped chipotle pepper in adobo**
- 2 **tsp cornstarch**
  Fresh cilantro sprigs (optional)

■ Season meat with garlic-pepper seasoning and place in a 4- to 5-qt slow cooker. Add dried fruit, ½ cup water and chipotle.

■ Cover and cook on HIGH for 5 hours or LOW for 10 hours. Transfer meat and fruit to a serving platter; thinly slice meat. Keep meat and fruit warm.

■ Pour cooking liquid into a bowl and skim off fat. In a medium saucepan, combine 1 tbsp water and cornstarch. Add cooking liquid and simmer over medium heat until thickened, about 3 minutes.

■ Serve meat and fruit with sauce. Garnish with cilantro, if desired.

PER SERVING 351 **CAL**; 18 g **FAT** (7 g **SAT**); 27 g **PRO**; 18 g **CARB**; 1 g **FIBER**; 302 mg **SODIUM**; 107 mg **CHOL**

BALSAMIC LONDON BROIL

Balsamic London Broil

KOSHER STATUS MEAT
MAKES 8 to 10 servings PREP 10 minutes
MARINATE 3 to 6 hours
ROAST at 400° for 50 minutes
REST 5 minutes

- 2½ lb London broil
- 5 cloves garlic, minced
- ¾ cup balsamic vinegar
- ¼ cup plus 1 tbsp olive oil
- 2 medium red onions
- 2 medium yellow onions
- 8 medium shallots
-   Kosher salt
-   Freshly ground black pepper

■ Combine meat with garlic, vinegar and ¼ cup of the olive oil in a large resealable plastic bag. Marinate in refrigerator for 3 to 6 hours.

■ Heat oven to 400°. Remove meat from refrigerator so it can come to room temperature.

■ Cut onions into quarters and halve shallots. On a large rimmed baking sheet, toss together onions, shallots and remaining 1 tbsp olive oil. Season with salt and pepper and roast at 400° until tender, 40 to 50 minutes.

■ After veggies have been roasting for 20 minutes, pour off and discard marinade from meat. Pat meat dry and season it all over with salt and pepper. Heat a large ovenproof skillet over medium-high heat and sear meat until nicely browned, about 5 minutes per side. Transfer skillet to oven and cook alongside vegetables until an instant-read thermometer inserted into meat reads 130° for medium rare, 12 to 18 minutes. Remove meat and veggies from oven. Let meat rest for 5 minutes before slicing.

BEEF TACOS WITH
CHUNKY GUACAMOLE

Beef Tacos with Chunky Guacamole

MAKES 12 tacos, plus 3 cups beef mixture for another meal
PREP 15 minutes COOK 12 minutes
SLOW COOK on HIGH for 6 hours or LOW for 8 hours

- 1 beef chuck roast (about 3½ lb)
- 1 tsp salt
- ½ tsp black pepper
- 2 tbsp vegetable oil
- 2 tsp chili powder
- 1 tsp ground cumin
- ½ tsp cayenne pepper
- 1 onion, chopped
- 1 red sweet pepper, seeded and chopped
- 4 cloves garlic, sliced
- 1 cup beef broth
- 12 fajita-size flour tortillas, heated gently
-   Chunky Guacamole (recipe follows)

■ Season roast with salt and pepper. Heat oil in a large skillet over medium-high heat; add roast and brown on all sides, about 12 minutes total. Remove and discard strings if roast is tied.

■ Coat a 5- to 6-qt slow cooker bowl with nonstick cooking spray. Place roast in slow cooker and season with chili powder, cumin and cayenne. Top with onion, sweet pepper and garlic. Pour broth over top.

■ Cook on HIGH for 6 hours or LOW for 8 hours.

■ Remove roast to a cutting board and shred with 2 forks. Stir meat back into liquid in slow cooker.

■ Wrap ¼ cup beef mixture in each warmed tortilla and top with Chunky Guacamole.

PER TACO 386 CAL; 24 g FAT (6 g SAT); 19 g PRO; 24 g CARB; 6 g FIBER; 517 mg SODIUM; 57 mg CHOL

Chunky Guacamole

Coarsely mash 4 ripe avocados in a medium bowl. Stir in ½ cup finely chopped red onion, ½ cup quartered grape tomatoes, 1 seeded and chopped jalapeño, 2 tbsp lime juice, 2 tbsp chopped cilantro, 1 tbsp olive oil and ¼ tsp salt.

ATLANTA BRISKET

Atlanta Brisket

MAKES 8 servings **PREP** 10 minutes
SLOW COOK on LOW for 8 hours
COOL 10 minutes

- 2 **sweet onions, sliced**
- 1 **beef brisket (about 3 lb), trimmed**
- 1 **packet (1 oz) dry onion soup mix**
- 1½ **cups ketchup**
- 1 **can (12 oz) cola**
  French fries and coleslaw (optional)

■ Coat a 5- to 6-qt slow cooker with nonstick cooking spray.

■ Place onions in slow cooker. Season brisket with soup mix and place on top of onions. Combine ketchup and cola; pour over brisket.

■ Cover and cook on LOW for 8 hours.

■ Remove brisket to a cutting board and allow to cool 10 minutes. Slice against the grain. Serve with french fries and coleslaw, if desired.

PER SERVING 329 **CAL**; 8 g **FAT** (3 g **SAT**); 38 g **PRO**; 26 g **CARB**; 1 g **FIBER**; 1,238 mg **SODIUM**; 73 mg **CHOL**

Peppercorn-Crusted Beef Tenderloin

MAKES 8 servings **PREP** 10 minutes
ROAST at 400° for 45 minutes
REST 10 minutes

- 1 **beef tenderloin (about 3 lb)**
- 1 **tbsp olive oil**
- 3 **tbsp rainbow peppercorns**
- 4 **tsp kosher salt**
  Roasted Garlic Sauce or Red Wine–Shallot Sauce (recipes follow)

■ Bring tenderloin to room temperature 30 minutes before cooking. Heat oven to 400°. Pat tenderloin dry and rub with oil.

■ Crush peppercorns in a spice grinder (or coffee grinder reserved for spices). Mix in a bowl with salt and press onto entire surface of tenderloin. Roast at 400° for 45 minutes or until internal temperature reaches 137°. Let rest 5 to 10 minutes, until temperature reaches 145°, before slicing. Serve with Roasted Garlic Cream Sauce or Red Wine–Shallot Sauce.

PER SERVING 347 **CAL**; 23 g **FAT** (9 g **SAT**); 33 g **PRO**; 1 g **CARB**; 0 g **FIBER**; 1,027 mg **SODIUM**; 111 mg **CHOL**

Roasted Garlic Sauce

MAKES 8 servings **PREP** 5 minutes
ROAST at 400° for 1 hour **COOK** 11 minutes

- 1 **head garlic**
- 2 **tsp olive oil**
- ½ **tsp salt**
  Freshly cracked black pepper
- 1 **tbsp unsalted butter**
- 1 **tbsp all-purpose flour**
- 1 **cup unsalted chicken stock**
- ½ **cup heavy cream**

■ Heat oven to 400°. Slice off top ¼ of garlic head, exposing clove tops. Place on foil and drizzle with oil, ¼ tsp of the salt and freshly cracked pepper. Wrap in foil and roast at 400° for 1 hour, until softened. In a skillet, melt butter over medium heat. Stir in flour; cook for 1 minute. Whisk in stock and heavy cream; squeeze in garlic cloves (discarding skin). Bring to a boil. Simmer for 8 to 10 minutes, until thickened. Stir in remaining salt and more pepper.

PER SERVING 86 **CAL**; 8 g **FAT** (4 g **SAT**); 1 g **PRO**; 3 g **CARB**; 0 g **FIBER**; 168 mg **SODIUM**; 24 mg **CHOL**

Red Wine-Shallot Sauce

MAKES 8 servings **PREP** 5 minutes
COOK 14 minutes

- 3 **tbsp unsalted butter**
- ¼ **cup finely diced shallots**
- 1 **tbsp all-purpose flour**
- 1 **cup unsalted beef stock**
- ¾ **cup dry red wine**
- 1 **tbsp chopped fresh thyme**
- ¼ **tsp plus ⅛ tsp salt**
  Freshly cracked black pepper

■ In a skillet, melt 2 tbsp of the butter over medium heat. Stir in shallots and cook 2 to 3 minutes, until softened. Stir in flour; cook 1 minute. Whisk in stock, wine and thyme. Bring to a boil. Reduce by half and simmer 10 minutes, until thickened. Remove from heat and stir in remaining butter, the salt and cracked pepper.

PER SERVING 65 **CAL**; 4 g **FAT** (3 g **SAT**); 1 g **PRO**; 2 g **CARB**; 0 g **FIBER**; 126 mg **SODIUM**; 11 mg **CHOL**

ROASTED GARLIC
SAUCE

PEPPERCORN-CRUSTED
BEEF TENDERLOIN

RED WINE-
SHALLOT SAUCE

BEER-BRAISED BEEF WITH
POTATOES AND CABBAGE

Beer-Braised Beef with Potatoes and Cabbage

MAKES 4 servings **PREP** 15 minutes
COOK 1 hour 10 minutes

- 1½   lb beef chuck, cut into 1-inch pieces
- 1   cup thinly sliced onion
- 2   cloves garlic, sliced
- 2   tsp chopped fresh thyme
- 2   tbsp all-purpose flour
- 1   tsp salt
- ½   tsp black pepper
- 1   tbsp tomato paste
- 1   cup unsalted beef broth
- 1   cup Guinness beer
- 1½   lb red-skinned potatoes, cut into 2-inch pieces (do not peel)
- 3   cups chopped green cabbage
- ½   cup plain nonfat yogurt
- ½   cup buttermilk
  Fresh parsley (for garnish)

■ In a Dutch oven or heavy-bottomed pot, toss beef cubes with onion, garlic, thyme, flour, ½ tsp of the salt and ¼ tsp of the pepper. Add tomato paste, broth and beer. Cover and bring to a boil. Reduce to a low simmer and cook 1 hour, until beef is tender. With a slotted spoon, remove beef to a bowl.

Increase heat to high and bring sauce to a boil. Simmer 10 minutes, until thickened. Stir beef back into sauce, cover and remove from heat.

■ Meanwhile, add potatoes to a medium pot and fill with cold water. Bring to a boil and cook 9 minutes. Stir in cabbage; cook 3 minutes more. Drain and return to pot. Add yogurt and buttermilk. Mash and stir in remaining ½ tsp salt and ¼ tsp pepper. Serve beef over potato-cabbage mash. Garnish with parsley.

PER SERVING 432 **CAL**; 8 g **FAT** (3 g **SAT**); 43 g **PRO**; 43 g **CARB**; 5 g **FIBER**; 769 mg **SODIUM**; 73 mg **CHOL**

BBQ Short Ribs

MAKES 6 servings **PREP** 15 minutes
SLOW COOK on LOW for 10 hours

- 5 lb short ribs
- 1 large onion, chopped
- 2 cloves garlic, chopped
- 1 cup ketchup
- 1 cup unsalted beef broth
- 2 tbsp sugar
- 2 tbsp white vinegar
- 2 tbsp Worcestershire sauce
- 1 tsp dry mustard
- ¼ tsp black pepper

  Mashed potatoes and sautéed Swiss chard (optional)

■ Spray a 5- to 6 qt slow cooker with nonstick cooking spray. Place ribs in slow cooker.

■ Scatter onion and garlic over ribs. Combine ketchup, broth, sugar, vinegar, Worcestershire sauce, mustard and pepper. Pour over ribs. Cover and cook on LOW for 10 hours.

■ Remove ribs from slow cooker. Skim fat from sauce (there will be more than 1 cup).

■ Serve ribs with sauce and, if desired, mashed potatoes and sautéed Swiss chard.

PER SERVING 727 **CAL**; 39 g **FAT** (16 g **SAT**); 73 g **PRO**; 17 g **CARB**; 1 g **FIBER**; 772 mg **SODIUM**; 223 mg **CHOL**

Balsamic Pot Roast

MAKES 6 servings **PREP** 15 minutes
SLOW COOK on LOW for 10 hours
REST 15 minutes

- 1 beef chuck or bottom round roast, about 3¼ lb
- ½ tsp salt
- ½ tsp dried thyme
- ⅛ tsp black pepper
- 1 onion, chopped
- 3 carrots, chopped
- 3 ribs celery, chopped
- 3 cloves garlic, chopped
- 2 cups unsalted beef stock
- ⅔ cup balsamic vinegar

  Prepared polenta and sautéed sweet peppers (optional)

■ Spray a 5- to 6-qt slow cooker with nonstick cooking spray. Season roast with salt, thyme and black pepper. Place in slow cooker.

■ Scatter onion, carrots, celery and garlic over roast. Pour stock and balsamic vinegar over top. Cover and cook on LOW for 10 hours.

■ Remove roast and allow to rest 15 minutes before slicing. Skim fat from cooking liquid. Mash vegetables in cooking liquid to slightly thicken sauce.

■ Serve sliced roast with sauce and, if desired, polenta and sautéed peppers.

PER SERVING 371 **CAL**; 11 g **FAT** (4 g **SAT**); 53 g **PRO**; 11 g **CARB**; 2 g **FIBER**; 256 mg **SODIUM**; 103 mg **CHOL**

BALSAMIC POT ROAST

BBQ SHORT RIBS

BBQ Beef Brisket

MAKES 8 servings **PREP** 10 minutes
SLOW COOK on HIGH for 6 hours or
LOW for 8 hours
COOK 3 minutes **STAND** 15 minutes

- 2 **tbsp packed dark brown sugar**
- 1 **tbsp Italian seasoning**
- 1 **tsp onion powder**
- ¼ **tsp salt**
- ¼ **tsp black pepper**
- 3 **lb natural beef brisket**
- 2½ **cups beef broth**
- 3 **tbsp molasses**
- 2 **tbsp Worcestershire sauce**
- 3 **dashes liquid smoke (optional)**
- 3 **tbsp cornstarch**
- 1 **tbsp white vinegar**
- 8 **onion rolls**
- 2 **cups prepared creamy coleslaw**

■ In small bowl, combine brown sugar, Italian seasoning, onion powder, salt and pepper. Rub onto brisket and place in a 5- to 6-qt slow cooker.

■ In a bowl, whisk broth, molasses, Worcestershire and, if desired, liquid smoke. Add to slow cooker. Cover and cook on HIGH for 6 hours or LOW for 8 hours.

■ Carefully remove brisket from slow cooker and shred with 2 forks. In a small bowl, combine ¼ cup water, cornstarch and vinegar. Strain liquid in slow cooker into a saucepan and add cornstarch mixture. Bring to a boil over medium-high heat and cook 3 minutes, until thickened and clear. Combine 5 cups of the sauce with brisket in a large bowl. Let stand, covered, for 15 minutes.

■ Split onion rolls and fill with brisket and coleslaw. Serve immediately.

PER SERVING 427 **CAL**; 11 g **FAT** (3 g **SAT**); 43 g **PRO**; 37 g **CARB**; 2 g **FIBER**; 711 mg **SODIUM**; 77 mg **CHOL**

ITALIAN-STYLE STEAK, MUSHROOMS AND ONIONS

BEEF BURGUNDY

Italian-Style Steak, Mushrooms and Onions

MAKES 4 servings **PREP** 15 minutes
SLOW COOK on HIGH for 6 hours or LOW
for 8 hours

- 1½ lb boneless chuck steak, cut into 4 equal pieces
- 1 tsp dried Italian seasoning
- ¼ tsp salt
- ¼ tsp black pepper
- 2 Cubanelle peppers, seeds removed, sliced
- 1 red sweet pepper, seeds removed, sliced
- 1 sweet onion, sliced
- 1 pkg (10 oz) white mushrooms, quartered
- ½ cup beef broth
- 2 tbsp red wine vinegar
- 1 tbsp Worcestershire sauce
- 1 tbsp brown sugar

  Fresh basil leaves

  Purchased tube polenta, sliced into rounds and grilled (optional)

■ Coat a 4- to 5-qt slow cooker with nonstick cooking spray.

■ Season both sides of steaks with Italian seasoning, salt and black pepper. Place in slow cooker. Scatter Cubanelle peppers, sweet pepper, onion and mushrooms over top. In a small bowl, combine broth, vinegar, Worcestershire sauce and brown sugar. Pour over peppers, onions and mushrooms.

■ Cover and cook on HIGH for 6 hours or LOW for 8 hours.

■ Serve steaks with peppers, onions, mushrooms and some of the cooking liquid spooned over the top. Garnish with basil and, if desired, serve with grilled polenta rounds.

PER SERVING 280 **CAL**; 7 g **FAT** (2 g **SAT**); 37 g **PRO**; 19 g **CARB**; 4 g **FIBER**; 432 mg **SODIUM**; 97 mg **CHOL**

Variation: Cut the chuck steak into 1½-inch pieces. In place of Cubanelle peppers and sweet pepper, add 1 lb small red-skinned potatoes, halved. Increase broth to 1 cup. During last 15 minutes of cooking time, add 1 pkg (10 oz) frozen peas, thawed.

Beef Burgundy

MAKES 6 servings **PREP** 15 minutes
COOK 7 minutes **SLOW COOK** on HIGH for
5 hours or LOW for 6½ hours

- 2 lb beef chuck for stew, cut into 1½- to 2-inch chunks
- 5 tbsp all-purpose flour
- ½ tsp salt
- ½ tsp black pepper
- 1 tbsp unsalted butter
- 1 tbsp canola oil
- 1 can (14.5 oz) low-sodium beef broth
- 4 large carrots, peeled and cut on the diagonal into 1½-inch pieces
- 1 pkg (10 oz) brown mushrooms, cleaned (halved or quartered, if large)
- 2 cloves garlic, sliced
- 1 cup red wine
- 1 bag (14.4 oz) frozen pearl onions, thawed

  Mashed potatoes or hot buttered noodles (optional)

■ Combine beef in a large resealable plastic bag with 2 tbsp of the flour, ¼ tsp of the salt and the pepper. Shake to coat. Melt butter and oil in a large stainless-steel skillet over medium-high heat. Add beef and brown for 5 minutes, stirring to sear all sides (cook in 2 batches, if needed). Spoon into a 5- to 6-qt slow cooker. Reduce heat under pan to medium and add 1 cup of the broth. Cook for 2 minutes, stirring up any browned bits on bottom of pan. Pour into slow cooker along with carrots, mushrooms, garlic, red wine and remaining beef broth. Scatter onions over top of vegetables.

■ Cover and cook on HIGH for 5 hours or LOW for 6½ hours. With a slotted spoon, remove beef and vegetables to a large serving bowl.

■ Whisk together remaining 3 tbsp flour with 3 tbsp water in a small bowl. Strain hot liquid from slow cooker into a medium saucepan. Whisk in flour mixture and bring to a boil over medium-high heat. Boil 3 minutes, until thickened, then stir into stew with remaining ¼ tsp salt. Serve stew over mashed potatoes or noodles, if desired.

PER SERVING 500 **CAL**; 12 g **FAT** (4 g **SAT**); 39 g **PRO**; 51 g **CARB**; 6 g **FIBER**; 797 mg **SODIUM**; 69 mg **CHOL**

SLOW-COOKED PEPPERY BEEF AND FUSILLI

- Spoon pasta into a serving bowl and stir in olive oil, vinegar and remaining ¼ tsp salt. Sprinkle remaining ½ tsp coarsely ground pepper over the top. Serve immediately.

PER SERVING 550 CAL; 20 g FAT (6 g SAT); 29 g PRO; 61 g CARB; 4 g FIBER; 341 mg SODIUM; 81 mg CHOL

Lasagna Roll-Up Casserole

MAKES 6 servings PREP 20 minutes
BAKE at 375° for 45 minutes

- 2½ cups beef mixture, from Slow-Cooked Peppery Beef and Fusilli, (left) gently heated
- 2 cups shredded mozzarella
- 1 cup ricotta
- 2 cups jarred marinara sauce, heated
- 12 lasagna noodles (from a 16-oz pkg), cooked per pkg directions
- 2 tbsp grated Parmesan

- Heat oven to 375°. Coat a 13 x 9 x 2-inch baking dish with nonstick cooking spray.

- In a large bowl, gently fold together beef mixture, ½ cup of the mozzarella and the ricotta. Spread 1 cup of the marinara in bottom of prepared dish.

- Place a cooked noodle on a flat work surface and spread about ¼ cup of the beef and cheese mixture over the top. Roll up from a short end and place, seam side down, in baking dish. Repeat with remaining noodles and beef mixture.

- Spoon remaining marinara over roll-ups. Scatter remaining 1½ cups mozzarella over sauce and sprinkle with Parmesan.

- Cover dish with foil and bake at 375° for 30 minutes. Remove foil and bake 15 minutes more. Cool slightly and serve.

PER SERVING 653 CAL; 28 g FAT (12 g SAT); 44 g PRO; 54 g CARB; 5 g FIBER; 985 mg SODIUM; 117 mg CHOL

Slow-Cooked Peppery Beef and Fusilli

MAKES 6 servings, plus 2½ cups beef mixture for Lasagna Roll-Up Casserole (far right)
PREP 10 minutes COOK 10 minutes
SLOW COOK on HIGH for 6 hours

- 2¼ lb beef chuck roast
- 1¼ tsp salt
- ½ tsp finely ground black pepper
- 1 tbsp canola oil
- 2 cups grape tomatoes
- 1½ tsp coarsely ground black pepper
- 1 bag (5 oz) baby spinach
- 1 lb fusilli pasta
- 2 tbsp olive oil
- 2 tbsp balsamic vinegar

- Season beef with 1 tsp of the salt and the finely ground black pepper. In a large skillet, heat canola oil over medium-high heat. Add beef; sear on all sides, about 10 minutes.

- Coat a 4- to 5-qt slow cooker with nonstick cooking spray. Add beef and distribute tomatoes around the sides. Sprinkle ½ tsp of the coarsely ground pepper over beef. Cover and cook on HIGH for 6 hours.

- Remove beef to a cutting board and shred with 2 forks. Return to slow cooker and stir in spinach until wilted. Add ½ tsp of the coarsely ground black pepper. Reserve 2½ cups of the mixture for Lasagna Roll-Up Casserole (recipe, right).

- Meanwhile, cook pasta following package directions, about 11 minutes. Drain and reserve ½ cup pasta cooking water. Toss pasta with remaining 2½ cups beef mixture and pasta water.

SESAME SOBA AND STEAK

Sesame Soba and Steak

MAKES 6 servings **PREP** 10 minutes
COOK 13 minutes **REST** 5 minutes

- 1 pkg (12.8 oz) soba noodles
- 1 tbsp olive oil
- 1 lb flank steak
- ¾ tsp salt
- ⅛ tsp black pepper
- 3 tbsp tahini paste
- 3 tbsp fresh lemon juice
- 2 tbsp harissa
- 2 tbsp honey
- 2 tsp sesame oil
- 1 pint grape tomatoes, halved
- ½ **English cucumber, halved and sliced**
- ½ **cup fresh mint, roughly chopped**
- 2 **tbsp sesame seeds**
   Crumbled feta (optional)

■ Bring a large pot of lightly salted water to a boil. Add soba; cook 3 minutes. Drain and rinse in cold water.

■ Add olive oil to a large skillet over medium-high heat. Pat steak dry and season with ¼ tsp of the salt and the pepper. Cook 5 minutes per side, until medium rare (145°). Let rest 5 minutes, then thinly slice against the grain.

■ In a large bowl, whisk ½ cup water, tahini, lemon juice, harissa, honey, sesame oil and remaining ½ tsp salt. Toss with cooked soba, sliced steak, tomatoes, cucumber, mint and sesame seeds. Garnish with crumbled feta, if desired.

PER SERVING 457 CAL; 15 g **FAT** (3 g **SAT**); 27 g **PRO**; 55 g **CARB**; 3 g **FIBER**; 537 mg **SODIUM**; 25 mg **CHOL**

LENTIL SOUP WITH BEEF

Lentil Soup with Beef

MAKES 6 servings **PREP** 25 minutes
SLOW COOK on HIGH for 3½ hours or
LOW for 7 hours

1	lb boneless beef sirloin steak
4	cups reduced-sodium beef broth
1	cup lentils, rinsed and drained
¾	cup coarsely chopped red sweet pepper
½	cup chopped onion
½	cup sliced carrot
½	cup sliced celery
2	cloves garlic, minced
1	tsp ground cumin
¼	tsp cayenne pepper
⅓	cup snipped fresh parsley

■ Trim fat from meat. Cut into ¾-inch pieces. For a richer soup, cook beef in a nonstick skillet over medium-high heat until browned; otherwise, use uncooked meat. Place in a 3½- or 4-qt slow cooker. Stir in broth, lentils, 1 cup water, the sweet pepper, onion, carrot, celery, garlic, cumin and cayenne.

■ Cover and cook on HIGH for 3½ to 4 hours or LOW for 7 to 8 hours. Stir in parsley. Ladle soup into bowls.

PER SERVING 265 **CAL**; 7 g **FAT** (2 g **SAT**); 26 g **PRO**; 24 g **CARB**; 11 g **FIBER**; 353 mg **SODIUM**; 50 mg **CHOL**

Asian Beef Noodle Soup

MAKES 6 servings **PREP** 15 minutes
SLOW COOK on HIGH for 6 hours or LOW for 8 hours

1½	lb beef chuck or brisket, cut into 1-inch cubes
½	medium yellow onion, thinly sliced
1	piece ginger (2 inches), peeled and sliced
4	cloves garlic, sliced
1	bird's-eye or serrano chile, stemmed and sliced lengthwise
2	tbsp rice vinegar
2	tbsp molasses
¼	cup low-sodium soy sauce
7	cups unsalted beef stock
1	pkg (9.5 oz) udon noodles
6	cups chopped bok choy
1	cup sliced scallions, plus more for garnish
1	cup fresh cilantro, chopped, plus more for garnish

■ Stir beef, onion, ginger, garlic, chile, vinegar, molasses and 2 tbsp of the soy sauce into a 4-qt slow cooker. Pour in beef stock. Cover and cook on HIGH for 6 hours or LOW for 8 hours.

■ During the last 15 minutes of cooking, bring a large pot of lightly salted water to a boil. Add udon; cook 2 minutes. Add bok choy and cook 2 minutes more. Strain. Add noodles, bok choy, scallions, cilantro and remaining 2 tbsp soy sauce to soup. Stir and serve. Garnish with additional scallions and cilantro.

PER SERVING 368 **CAL**; 6 g **FAT** (2 g **SAT**); 34 g **PRO**; 41 g **CARB**; 4 g **FIBER**; 698 mg **SODIUM**; 48 mg **CHOL**

RECIPE NAME

ANCHO MOLE
BEEF STEW

Sesame Steak Salad

MAKES 4 servings PREP 15 minutes
MARINATE 15 minutes
BROIL OR GRILL 6 minutes REST 5 minutes

- 3 tbsp rice vinegar
- 2 tbsp low-sodium soy sauce
- 2 tbsp packed brown sugar
- 1 tbsp minced fresh ginger
- 1 tsp yellow mustard
- 1 tbsp dark sesame oil
- 1¼ lb skirt steak
- 8 cups watercress (2 bunches), tough stems removed
- 1 red sweet pepper, cored, seeded and thinly sliced
- 1 cup shredded carrots
- 3 scallions, trimmed and sliced
- 2 ribs celery, sliced on the diagonal
- 1 tbsp toasted sesame seeds
- ¼ tsp salt

■ In a small bowl, combine vinegar, soy sauce, brown sugar, ginger and mustard. While whisking, add oil.

■ Place steak in a resealable plastic bag and add 3 tbsp of the dressing. Marinate at room temperature for 15 minutes. Heat broiler or gas grill to medium-high heat.

■ Remove steak from bag; discard bag with remaining marinade. Broil or grill steak for 2 to 3 minutes per side, turning once, or until desired doneness. Let rest 5 minutes.

■ Combine watercress, sweet pepper, carrots, scallions and celery in a large bowl. Thinly slice steak across the grain and add to salad. Toss with remaining dressing. Sprinkle with sesame seeds and salt and gently toss again.

PER SERVING 350 CAL; 18 g FAT (11 g SAT); 32 g PRO; 16 g CARB; 3 g FIBER; 535 mg SODIUM; 69 mg CHOL

Ancho Mole Beef Stew

MAKES 6 servings PREP 25 minutes
COOK 1 hour 58 minutes

- ¼ cup all-purpose flour
- 1 tsp plus 2 tsp ancho chile powder
- ½ tsp salt
- 1½ lb beef chuck, cut into 1-inch pieces
- 2 tbsp canola oil
- 1 onion, chopped
- 3 cloves garlic, chopped
- 2 tbsp mole paste (such as La Costeña)
- 3 cups reduced-sodium beef broth
- 1 can (14½ oz) no-salt-added stewed tomatoes
- 1 tsp dried oregano
- 1½ lb small (1 inch round) red potatoes, halved
- ½ lb baby carrots
- 1 can (15 oz) hominy, drained and rinsed
- Fresh cilantro, for garnish

■ Combine flour, 1 tsp ancho chile powder and ⅛ tsp of the salt. Dredge beef in mixture and reserve leftover mixture.

■ In a large pot, heat 1 tbsp of the oil over medium-high heat. Add beef and sauté 5 minutes, turning once. Remove to a plate. Add remaining 1 tbsp oil, the onion and garlic; cook 3 minutes. Stir in reserved flour mixture, mole paste, broth, 1 cup water, tomatoes, oregano and remaining 2 tsp chile powder.

■ Return beef to pot. Cover and simmer over medium-low heat 90 minutes, stirring occasionally. Add potatoes, carrots and remaining ⅜ tsp salt. Simmer an additional 20 minutes, until vegetables are tender.

■ Add hominy and garnish with cilantro.

PER SERVING 406 CAL; 13 g FAT (3 g SAT); 31 g PRO; 44 g CARB; 8 g FIBER; 807 mg SODIUM; 55 mg CHOL

SESAME STEAK SALAD

BACON-WRAPPED
MEATLOAF AND
SMASHED POTATOES

Bacon-Wrapped Meatloaf and Smashed Potatoes

MAKES 6 servings **PREP** 20 minutes
BAKE at 375° for 60 minutes **COOK** 15 minutes

- **2 lb extra-lean ground beef**
- **½ lb white mushrooms, grated**
- **½ cup old-fashioned oats (not quick-cooking)**
- **3 egg whites, lightly beaten**
- **¾ tsp onion salt**
- **½ tsp dried oregano**
- **½ tsp black pepper**
- **¼ cup ketchup**
- **1 tbsp brown sugar**
- **6 slices turkey bacon**
- **2 lb unpeeled Yukon gold potatoes, scrubbed and cut into 1-inch chunks**
- **¾ cup reduced-sodium chicken broth**
- **2 tbsp olive oil**
- **¼ tsp salt**
- **⅛ tsp nutmeg**
- **¼ cup fresh parsley, chopped**

■ Heat oven to 375°. Fit a baking sheet with a rack and coat lightly with nonstick cooking spray.

■ In a large bowl, combine ground beef, mushrooms, oats, egg whites, onion salt, oregano and ¼ tsp of the pepper. Form into a loaf and place on prepared pan. Combine ketchup and brown sugar and spread half on top of meatloaf. Arrange bacon over meatloaf in a crisscross pattern. Bake at 375° for 45 minutes; spread on remaining ketchup mixture and bake for an additional 15 minutes or until internal temperature registers 160°.

■ Meanwhile, place potatoes in a pot and cover with lightly salted water. Bring to a boil; lower heat and simmer, partially covered, for 15 minutes or until fork-tender. Drain and add broth, olive oil, salt, remaining ¼ tsp pepper and the nutmeg. Mash to desired consistency; stir in parsley. Serve with meatloaf.

PER SERVING 414 **CAL**; 14 g **FAT** (4 g **SAT**); 38 g **PRO**; 36 g **CARB**; 3 g **FIBER**; 794 mg **SODIUM**; 95 mg **CHOL**

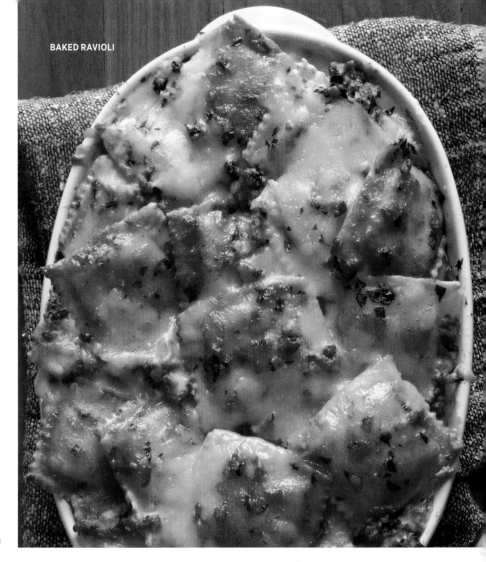

BAKED RAVIOLI

Baked Ravioli

MAKES 8 servings **PREP** 5 minutes
COOK 5 minutes **BAKE** at 350° for 20 minutes
BROIL 2 minutes

- **1 lb lean ground beef**
- **1 jar (24 oz) marinara sauce**
- **¼ cup fresh basil leaves, chopped, plus more for garnish (optional)**
- **¼ cup fresh parsley, chopped**
- **1 pkg (20 oz) refrigerated cheese ravioli**
- **1 pkg (9 oz) refrigerated cheese ravioli**
- **1 bag (8 oz) shredded mozzarella cheese**
- **2 tbsp grated Parmesan cheese**

■ Heat oven to 350°. Coat a 2-qt oval baking dish with nonstick cooking spray. Bring a large pot of lightly salted water to a boil.

■ Crumble ground beef into a large nonstick skillet. Cook for 5 minutes over medium-high heat, until browned. Remove from heat and stir in 1 cup of the marinara sauce, half the basil and half the parsley.

■ Meanwhile, cook ravioli for 5 minutes in boiling water. Drain and return to pot. Stir in remaining sauce, basil and parsley.

■ Pour half the ravioli into prepared dish, spreading level. Top with meat sauce and ¾ cup of the shredded mozzarella. Add remaining ravioli to dish and top with remaining 1¼ cups shredded mozzarella and the Parmesan.

■ Bake at 350° for 20 minutes. Increase oven temperature to broil; broil ravioli for 2 minutes. Garnish with additional chopped basil, if desired.

PER SERVING 542 **CAL**; 22 g **FAT** (12 g **SAT**); 34 g **PRO**; 50 g **CARB**; 5 g **FIBER**; 1,135 mg **SODIUM**; 115 mg **CHOL**

MEXICAN MEATBALLS
IN CHIPOTLE SAUCE

Mexican Meatballs in Chipotle Sauce

MAKES 24 meatballs **PREP** 20 minutes
SLOW COOK on HIGH for 3 hours

- 1½ **lb ground beef, pork and veal mixture or ground chuck**
- 1 **cup bread crumbs**
- ¼ **cup milk**
- 2 **eggs, lightly beaten**
- 2 **tsp chili powder**
- 1 **tsp garlic powder**
- 1 **tsp salt**
- 1 **tsp ground cumin**
- 1 **can (28 oz) fire-roasted crushed tomatoes**
- ½ **cup chicken broth**
- 3 **cloves garlic, chopped**
- 1 **tsp dried oregano**
- 3 **chipotles in adobo, chopped**
- 2 **tbsp chopped cilantro**

■ In a large bowl, combine ground meat, bread crumbs, milk, eggs, chili powder, garlic powder and ½ tsp each of the salt and cumin. Form mixture into 24 meatballs, using about 1 tablespoonful for each.

■ Coat a 3½- or 4-qt slow cooker with nonstick cooking spray. Stir in tomatoes, broth, garlic, oregano, remaining ½ tsp each salt and cumin, and the chipotles. Add meatballs.

■ Cover and cook on HIGH for 3 hours. Stir in cilantro before serving.

PER MEATBALL 88 **CAL**; 4 g **FAT** (1 g **SAT**); 7 g **PRO**; 6 g **CARB**; 1 g **FIBER**; 265 mg **SODIUM**; 34 mg **CHOL**

Bacon Cheeseburger Quiche

MAKES 6 servings **PREP** 20 minutes
MICROWAVE 5 minutes **REST** overnight
COOK 8 minutes **BAKE** at 350° for 25 minutes plus 1 hour 10 minutes **COOL** 10 minutes

- 5 **slices Applegate Farms Good Morning bacon**
- 1 **refrigerated piecrust (rolled out to 12 inches)**
- ½ **lb ground sirloin (90% lean)**
- ½ **cup diced red onion**
- 2 **tsp Worcestershire sauce**

BACON CHEESEBURGER QUICHE

- 3 **cups baby spinach, chopped**
- 1 **medium tomato, seeded and diced**
- ¼ **tsp salt**
- ¼ **tsp black pepper**
- 2 **large eggs**
- 4 **large egg whites**
- ¾ **cup skim milk**
- 3 **tbsp ketchup**
- 2 **tbsp yellow mustard**
- ¾ **cup shredded 2% cheddar cheese**
  Salad (optional)

■ The night before, layer bacon between paper towels on a plate and microwave for 3 to 5 minutes, until crisp. Set aside. Heat oven to 350°. Fit crust into a 9-inch deep-dish pie plate and line crust with foil, pressing down. Bake at 350° for 10 minutes. Remove foil and bake 15 minutes more, until crust holds its shape but small bubbles form. Cool on a wire rack, then cover and store at room temperature overnight.

■ Meanwhile, heat a large nonstick skillet over medium-high heat. Crumble in ground sirloin and add onion and Worcestershire sauce. Cook for 5 minutes. Stir in spinach, crumbled bacon and tomato. Cook for 3 minutes and add salt and pepper. Spoon into a lidded container, cover and refrigerate.

■ The next day, heat oven to 350°. Break filling apart and spoon into piecrust. In a bowl, whisk together eggs, egg whites, milk, ketchup and mustard. Sprinkle cheese over filling in piecrust. Pour in egg mixture and transfer to oven. Bake at 350° for 1 hour 10 minutes, until a toothpick inserted in center comes out clean. Cover edge with foil if it's browning too quickly. Cool 10 minutes before slicing. Serve with salad alongside, if desired.

PER SERVING 348 **CAL**; 18 g **FAT** (8 g **SAT**); 21 g **PRO**; 26 g **CARB**; 1 g **FIBER**; 741 mg **SODIUM**; 119 mg **CHOL**

BEEF GYROS

Asian Lettuce Wraps

MAKES 4 servings **PREP** 7 minutes
COOK 12 minutes

- 2 medium carrots, thinly sliced, or ¾ cup shredded
- 2 heads Boston lettuce
- 1 tbsp canola oil
- 1 pkg (8 oz) sliced mushrooms
- 1 sweet yellow pepper, cored, seeded and cut into ½-inch pieces
- 2 cloves garlic, sliced
- 1¼ lb lean ground beef
- 1 pkg (8.8 oz) fully cooked brown rice
- 1 large egg
- 3 scallions, sliced
- 3 tbsp low-sodium soy sauce
- 3 tbsp rice vinegar
- 2 tsp sugar
- 1 tsp toasted sesame oil
- 1 tsp ground ginger
- Mint leaves, for serving
- Steamed broccoli (optional)

■ Combine carrots and ¼ cup water in a large lidded skillet over medium-high heat. Cover and cook 4 minutes.

■ Meanwhile, remove 16 leaves from lettuce; rinse and pat dry. Set aside.

■ Stir canola oil into skillet with carrots. Add mushrooms, sweet pepper and garlic. Cook 2 minutes. Crumble in ground beef and cook 3 minutes. Add brown rice and cook 2 minutes. Lightly beat egg; push skillet contents to 1 side of pan. Add egg to skillet and scramble, 1 minute. Stir in scallions, soy sauce, vinegar, sugar, sesame oil and ginger. Remove from heat.

■ Serve meat mixture with lettuce leaves (spoon a scant ⅓ cup into each leaf). Sprinkle with mint leaves and, if desired, serve with steamed broccoli on the side.

PER SERVING 503 CAL; 22 g FAT (7 g SAT); 38 g PRO; 35 g CARB; 6 g FIBER; 624 mg SODIUM; 145 mg CHOL

Beef Gyros

MAKES 6 servings **PREP** 25 minutes
SLOW COOK on HIGH for 2 hours or LOW for 4 hours **STAND** 10 minutes

- 1 large sweet onion, cut into thin wedges
- 2 lb extra-lean ground beef
- 2 tsp dried oregano, crushed
- 3 cloves garlic, minced
- ½ tsp salt
- ½ tsp black pepper
- ½ tsp paprika
- 6 oval whole wheat wraps
- 3 roma tomatoes, sliced
- ⅓ cup crumbled reduced-fat feta cheese
- 1 recipe Tzatziki Sauce (recipe follows)

■ Place onion in a 3½- or 4-qt slow cooker. In a large bowl, combine beef, oregano, garlic, salt, pepper and paprika.

■ On wax paper, shape meat mixture into a 5-inch round loaf. Crisscross three 18 x 2-inch foil strips. Place meat loaf in center of strips. Bringing up foil strips, lift and transfer meat and foil to the slow cooker over the onion. Press the meat away from the side of slow cooker to avoid burning.

■ Cover and cook on HIGH for 2 to 2½ hours or on LOW for 4 to 5 hours.

■ Using foil strips, carefully lift meat loaf from the slow cooker and transfer to a cutting board. Let stand for 10 minutes before thinly slicing.*

■ Divide sliced meat and onion among whole wheat wraps. Top with tomatoes, feta cheese and Tzatziki Sauce.

PER SERVING 386 CAL; 11 g FAT (4 g SAT); 45 g PRO; 32 g CARB; 8 g FIBER; 820 mg SODIUM; 97 mg CHOL

Tzatziki Sauce In a medium bowl, stir together 1 carton (6-oz) plain Greek yogurt; 1 cup shredded, seeded cucumber; 1 tbsp lemon juice; 1 tbsp snipped fresh dill weed; 1 tsp honey; 1 clove minced garlic; and ¼ tsp salt. Serve immediately or cover and chill for up to 4 hours.

ASIAN LETTUCE WRAPS

DOUBLE-DECKER
TERIYAKI BURGERS

Double-Decker Teriyaki Burgers

MAKES 4 servings **PREP** 20 minutes
GRILL 9 minutes **REFRIGERATE** 1 hour

- 1 **cup shredded broccoli slaw**
- 2 **tbsp reduced-fat mayonnaise**
- 1 **tbsp rice vinegar**
- ¼ **tsp sugar**
- 1 **lb 95% lean ground beef**
- 4 **oz shiitake mushrooms, stems removed, finely chopped**
- 2 **scallions, trimmed and chopped**
- 2 **tbsp reduced-sodium teriyaki sauce**
- 1 **tbsp finely chopped fresh ginger**
- 4 **canned pineapple slices in juice, drained and patted dry**
- 4 **slices (1 oz each) reduced-fat Muenster or mozzarella cheese**
- 4 **sesame-seed hamburger buns**

■ In a small bowl, combine broccoli slaw, mayonnaise, vinegar and sugar. Refrigerate until serving.

■ In a medium bowl, combine ground beef, mushrooms, scallions, teriyaki sauce and ginger. Form into 8 patties, about 3 inches in diameter; refrigerate for 1 hour.

■ Generously coat stovetop grill pan with nonstick cooking spray. Heat pan over medium-high heat. Grill pineapple slices for 2 minutes per side. Remove to a plate and keep warm. Coat pan again with nonstick cooking spray and add burgers; grill for 3 minutes. Turn and place a slice of cheese on 4 of the burgers; grill 2 more minutes. Top cheese-covered burgers with remaining burgers.

■ To serve, place ¼ cup broccoli slaw mixture on each bun bottom and top with double burger, a pineapple slice and top half of bun.

PER SERVING 412 **CAL**; 12 g **FAT** (5 g **SAT**); 35 g **PRO**; 41 g **CARB**; 3 g **FIBER**; 748 mg **SODIUM**; 73 mg **CHOL**

SPICY CHIPOTLE BURGERS

GAME DAY
DOUBLE-BEEF CHILI

Spicy Chipotle Burgers

MAKES 8 servings PREP 15 minutes
GRILL 10 minutes

- 2 **lb ground beef**
- 3 **chipotles in adobo, seeded and chopped, plus 2 tsp adobo**
- ½ **cup fresh cilantro, chopped, plus more for garnish**
- ⅓ **cup finely grated onion**
- 2 **cloves garlic, finely grated**
- 1 **tsp salt**
- 8 **oz smoked mozzarella, thinly sliced**
- 8 **potato hamburger buns**
- 1 **large tomato, cut into 8 slices**
  Chipotle Sour Cream (optional; recipe follows)

■ Heat a grill or grill pan to medium-high heat. In a large bowl, combine beef, chipotles, adobo, cilantro, onion, garlic and salt. Form into 8 patties. Grill 4 minutes; flip and distribute cheese among burgers. Grill another 3 to 4 minutes for medium, or to desired doneness. Remove to a plate. Grill buns on cut sides 1 to 2 minutes until lightly charred.

■ Place burgers on buns and garnish with tomato slices, cilantro and, if desired, Chipotle Sour Cream.

PER SERVING 400 CAL; 19 g FAT (9 g SAT); 32 g PRO; 25 g CARB; 2 g FIBER; 1,059 mg SODIUM; 89 mg CHOL

Chipotle Sour Cream In a small bowl, combine 1 cup sour cream, 1 seeded and diced chipotle in adobo, 1 tsp adobo and ¼ tsp salt.

Game Day Double-Beef Chili

MAKES 12 servings PREP 20 minutes
COOK 18 minutes SLOW COOK on HIGH for 5 hours or LOW for 8 hours

- 2 **tbsp canola oil**
- 2 **lb ground beef**
- 2 **large onions, chopped**
- 8 **cloves garlic, roughly chopped**
- 2 **lb beef brisket, cut into 1-inch pieces**
- 2 **large green sweet peppers, seeded and diced**
- 1 **can (28 oz) fire-roasted diced tomatoes**
- 2 **cans (8 oz each) tomato sauce**
- ¼ **cup chili powder**
- 1 **tbsp sweet paprika**
- 2 **tsp ground cumin**
- 1½ **tsp salt**
- ¼ **tsp cayenne pepper**
- 6 **cups cooked Texmati rice**
- 1½ **cups shredded Cotija cheese**
  Chopped scallion and red onion for garnish (optional)

■ Coat a 4- to 5-qt slow cooker with nonstick cooking spray.

■ Heat 1 tbsp of the oil in a large nonstick skillet over medium-high heat. Add ground beef, onions and garlic; cook 8 minutes, stirring occasionally. Place in slow cooker. Add remaining 1 tbsp oil and the brisket to skillet; cook 4 to 5 minutes per side, until browned. Place in slow cooker.

■ Stir in sweet peppers, tomatoes, tomato sauce, chili powder, paprika, cumin, salt and cayenne.

■ Cover and cook on HIGH for 5 hours or LOW for 8 hours.

■ Serve with rice and Cotija. Garnish with scallion and red onion, if desired.

PER SERVING 451 CAL; 14 g FAT (6 g SAT); 41 g PRO; 38 g CARB; 4 g FIBER; 865 mg SODIUM; 92 mg CHOL

SEVEN-LAYER
THAI SALAD

Seven-Layer Thai Salad

MAKES 8 servings **PREP** 25 minutes
COOK 7 minutes

- 1 **tbsp canola oil**
- 1½ **lb lean ground beef**
- 2 **tbsp chopped ginger**
- 4 **tbsp reduced-sodium or gluten-free soy sauce**
- 6 **cups shredded iceberg lettuce**
- 2 **sweet red peppers, seeded and thinly sliced**
- 1 **cup packed cilantro leaves, plus more for garnish**
- 2 **cups shelled edamame**
- 1 **large seedless cucumber, peeled and thinly sliced**
- 1 **large bunch scallions, trimmed and sliced**
- ½ **cup smooth peanut butter**
- 1 **tsp chopped garlic**
- ⅔ **cup light mayonnaise**
  Chopped peanuts, for garnish

■ In a large nonstick skillet, heat oil over medium-high heat. Crumble in beef and add ginger; cook 7 minutes, stirring occasionally. Stir in 2 tbsp of the soy sauce and allow to cool.

■ In the bottom of a 14-cup trifle dish, place lettuce and pack down slightly.

Top with a layer of red peppers followed by layers of cilantro (packing down each), cooled beef mixture, edamame, cucumber and scallions.

■ In a small bowl, whisk peanut butter with 2 tbsp warm water and remaining 2 tbsp soy sauce until smooth. Stir in garlic and mayonnaise.

■ Spread peanut butter dressing over top of salad. Garnish with chopped peanuts and, if desired, cilantro. If desired, toss salad before serving.

PER SERVING 341 **CAL**; 22 g **FAT** (4 g **SAT**); 25 g **PRO**; 14 g **CARB**; 4 g **FIBER**; 619 mg **SODIUM**; 52 mg **CHOL**

Lamb Meatballs, Greek Potatoes and Broccoli Rabe

MAKES 4 servings **PREP** 25 minutes
ROAST at 450° for 30 minutes **BROIL** 1 minute

- 1¼ **lb ground lamb**
- ⅓ **cup plain bread crumbs**
- 1 **lightly beaten egg**
- 2 **tbsp chopped fresh mint**
- 1 **tsp garlic salt**
- 1 **tsp onion powder**
- 1 **tsp dried oregano**
- ¼ **tsp cinnamon**
- ¼ **tsp black pepper**
- 1½ **lb potato wedges**
- 2 **tsp olive oil**
- ½ **tsp plus ⅛ tsp salt**
- ½ **tsp plus ⅛ tsp black pepper**
- ½ **lb trimmed broccoli rabe**
- 2 **containers (5.3 oz each) plain Greek yogurt**
- ½ **peeled and diced cucumber**
- ½ **tsp lemon juice**

■ Line a 13 x 9-inch rimmed sheet pan with nonstick foil. Combine lamb, bread crumbs, egg, mint, garlic salt, onion powder, dried oregano, cinnamon, and pepper. Form into 28 meatballs.

■ In prepared sheet pan, toss potato wedges (½ inch thick) with olive oil and ½ tsp each salt and pepper. Scatter broccoli rabe over potatoes. Arrange meatballs on top.

■ Roast at 450° for 30 minutes. Broil 1 minute. For yogurt sauce, combine Greek yogurt, cucumber, ⅛ tsp each salt and pepper, and lemon juice. Serve with sauce.

Lamb Curry

MAKES 6 servings **PREP** 20 minutes
SLOW COOK on LOW for 10 hours and HIGH for 15 minutes

- 2 **lb boneless lamb shoulder, cut into 2-inch pieces**
- 1 **tsp garam masala**
- 1 **tsp ground coriander**
- 1 **tsp salt**
- 1 **tsp black pepper**

LAMB CURRY

- ½ **tsp turmeric**
- 1 **large onion, chopped**
- 2 **tbsp chopped ginger**
- 2 **cloves garlic, chopped**
- 1 **can (15 oz) diced tomatoes**
- 1 **cup vegetable broth**
- 1 **green sweet pepper, cored, seeded and cut into 1-inch pieces**
- 1 **red sweet pepper, cored, seeded and cut into 1-inch pieces**
- ½ **cup fresh cilantro leaves**
- ½ **cup plain yogurt**
  Basmati rice and naan (optional)

■ Coat a 4½- to 5-qt slow cooker bowl with nonstick cooking spray. Place lamb in slow cooker.

■ In a small bowl, combine garam masala, coriander, ½ tsp of the salt, ½ tsp of the black pepper and the turmeric. Season meat with spice mixture. Scatter onion, ginger and garlic over lamb.

■ Pour tomatoes and broth over top. Cover and cook on LOW for 10 hours.

■ Stir in sweet peppers and remaining ½ tsp each salt and black pepper. Cook on HIGH for 15 minutes.

■ Stir in cilantro. Serve with yogurt and, if desired, basmati rice and naan.

PER SERVING 363 **CAL**; 21 g **FAT** (9 g **SAT**); 31 g **PRO**; 11 g **CARB**; 2 g **FIBER**; 817 mg **SODIUM**; 110 mg **CHOL**

SMOKY PORK TENDERLOIN WITH
PINEAPPLE-MANGO SALSA

Smoky Pork Tenderloin with Pineapple-Mango Salsa

MAKES 4 servings **PREP** 15 minutes
ROAST at 450° for 20 minutes
REST 10 minutes

SALSA

- 2 **cups cubed pineapple**
- 2 **cups cubed mango (about 1 large)**
- ½ **cup chopped red onion**
- 2 **scallions, thinly sliced**
- ¼ **cup cilantro leaves, chopped**
- 1 **jalapeño pepper, seeded and chopped**
- 2 **tbsp canola oil**
- ¼ **tsp salt**

PORK

- 1 **pork tenderloin (about 1¼ lb)**
- 1 **tbsp canola oil**
- 1 **tsp smoked paprika**
- ½ **tsp salt**
- ⅛ **tsp black pepper**
  Citrus-Chili Sweet Potatoes (optional; recipe follows)

■ **Salsa.** In a large bowl, combine pineapple, mango, red onion, scallions, cilantro, jalapeño, canola oil and salt. Cover and refrigerate until serving.

■ **Pork.** Heat oven to 450°. Rub tenderloin with canola oil and season all sides with smoked paprika, salt and black pepper. Place in a roasting pan on a rack and roast at 450° for 20 minutes or until internal temperature reaches 145°. Tent with foil and allow to rest 10 minutes before slicing thinly.

■ Serve pork with salsa and, if desired, Citrus-Chili Sweet Potatoes.

PER SERVING 378 **CAL**; 16 g **FAT** (3 g **SAT**); 31 g **PRO**; 30 g **CARB**; 4 g **FIBER**; 512 mg **SODIUM**; 92 mg **CHOL**

Citrus-Chili Sweet Potatoes Bake 2 lb sweet potatoes at 450° for 45 minutes, until fork-tender. Spoon flesh into a large bowl; add ¼ cup orange juice, 1 tbsp brown sugar, ¼ tsp each cinnamon and chili powder and ⅛ tsp salt. Mash to desired consistency.

Pork Loin Roast with Two Sauces

MAKES 8 servings **PREP** 15 minutes
ROAST at 450° for 20 minutes and at 325° for 80 minutes
REST 10 minutes **COOK** 3 minutes

- 4 **cloves garlic, chopped**
- 1 **tbsp lemon juice**
- 1 **tbsp coarsely chopped sage**
- 1 **tsp coarsely chopped fresh savory or fresh oregano**
- 1 **tsp chopped thyme**
- ½ **tsp salt**
- ¼ **tsp black pepper**
- 1 **center-cut pork loin roast with 6 ribs (about 4½ lb)**
- 1 **tbsp olive oil**
- 3 **tbsp flour**
- 2 **cups vegetable broth**
  Fig and Port Sauce (recipe follows)

■ Heat oven to 450°. Fit a large roasting pan with a rack.

■ In a small bowl, combine garlic, lemon juice, sage, savory, thyme, salt and pepper. Brush pork roast with olive oil and rub with garlic-and-herb mixture.

■ Place pork in prepared pan and roast at 450° for 20 minutes. Lower oven heat to 325° and roast an additional 80 to 90 minutes or until internal temperature reaches 145°. Let rest 10 minutes.

■ While pork is resting, prepare gravy. Pour off all but 2 tbsp of the fat from roasting pan. Place pan over medium heat and sprinkle with flour. Cook 1 minute, scraping up any browned bits from bottom of pan. Gradually whisk in vegetable broth and 1 cup water. Bring to a boil and cook 2 minutes, whisking constantly. Strain into a small saucepan and keep warm. Slice pork and serve with gravy and Fig and Port Sauce.

PER SERVING 398 **CAL**; 24 g **FAT** (8 g **SAT**); 40 g **PRO**; 4 g **CARB**; 0 g **FIBER**; 515 mg **SODIUM**; 115 mg **CHOL**

Fig and Port Sauce

MAKES 1¼ cups **PREP** 5 minutes
COOK 9 minutes

- 2 **sliced shallots**
- 1 **tbsp plus 2 tbsp butter**
- 1 **tbsp flour**
- 1 **cup ruby port**
- 6 **quartered dried figs**
- ⅛ **tsp salt**
- ⅛ **tsp pepper**

■ Cook shallots in 1 tbsp butter 3 minutes. Add flour and cook 1 minute. Whisk in port; simmer 3 minutes. Add figs and cook 2 minutes. Stir in 2 tbsp water and 2 tbsp butter. Season with salt and pepper.

PORK LOIN ROAST WITH TWO SAUCES

Salsa Verde Pork Ribs

MAKES 8 servings **PREP** 10 minutes
SLOW COOK on HIGH for 6 hours or
LOW for 8 hours **BROIL** 4 minutes

- 1 **jar (16 oz) tomatillo salsa**
- ½ **red onion, diced**
- 2 **jalapeños, seeded and diced**
- ½ **cup cilantro leaves**
- 3 **cloves garlic, chopped**
- 1 **tsp salt**
- ¾ **tsp black pepper**
- 4 **lb pork ribs, cut into 2 sections**
- ¾ **tsp ground coriander**
- ½ **tsp ground cumin**
-    **Pepitas and chopped scallion, for garnish (optional)**

■ Coat a 6-qt slow cooker with nonstick cooking spray. In a large bowl, combine tomatillo salsa, onion, jalapeños, cilantro, garlic and ½ tsp each of the salt and black pepper.

■ Season ribs with remaining ½ tsp salt and ¼ tsp black pepper, the coriander and cumin. Place in slow cooker; pour tomatillo mixture over top.

■ Cover and cook on HIGH for 6 hours or LOW for 8 hours.

■ Heat broiler to high. Cut ribs apart; place on a broiler pan and spoon some sauce over top. Broil 3 to 4 minutes, until browned and slightly crispy.

■ Serve ribs garnished with pepitas and scallion, if desired.

PER SERVING 336 **CAL**; 24 g **FAT** (8 g **SAT**); 27 g **PRO**; 3 g **CARB**; 0 g **FIBER**; 666 mg **SODIUM**; 99 mg **CHOL**

Double Smoky Country Ribs

MAKES 8 servings **PREP** 10 minutes
BAKE at 450° for 30 minutes and at 300° for 60 minutes **BROIL** 10 minutes

- 2 **tbsp smoked paprika**
- 1 **tsp salt**
- ½ **tsp dried thyme**
- ½ **tsp garlic powder**
- ½ **tsp onion powder**

DOUBLE SMOKY COUNTRY RIBS

- ¼ **tsp cayenne pepper**
- 8 **bone-in country-style pork ribs, 4 to 5 lb**
- 1 **tbsp canola oil**
- 1 **recipe Texas Rib Sauce (recipe follows)**

■ Heat oven to 450°.

■ In a small bowl, combine smoked paprika, salt, thyme, garlic powder, onion powder and cayenne. Brush ribs with oil and season with smoked paprika mixture.

■ Place ribs in a large roasting dish and add ½ cup water. Cover very tightly with aluminum foil. Bake at 450° for 30 minutes. Reduce oven temperature to 300° and bake an additional 60 minutes.

■ Heat broiler. Set rack 6 inches from heat source. Brush ribs generously with some of the Texas Rib Sauce. Broil 4 to 5 minutes per side, turning once.

■ Serve with remaining Rib Sauce on the side.

PER SERVING 374 **CAL**; 17 g **FAT** (5 g **SAT**); 35 g **PRO**; 18 g **CARB**; 1 g **FIBER**; 958 mg **SODIUM**; 115 mg **CHOL**

Texas Rib Sauce

MAKES Eight 1½ cup servings **PREP** 10 minutes
COOK 16 minutes

- 1 **tbsp canola oil**
- 2 **cloves garlic, chopped**
- 6 **tbsp tomato paste**
- ½ **cup beef broth**
- ½ **cup packed light brown sugar**
- ¼ **cup Worcestershire sauce**
- ¼ **cup lemon juice**
- 1 **chipotle chile pepper in adobo, seeded and chopped**
- 1 **tbsp adobo sauce**

■ In a medium saucepan, heat oil over medium heat. Add garlic and cook 1 minute. Add tomato paste, broth, brown sugar, Worcestershire sauce, lemon juice, chipotle and adobo sauce. Whisk until smooth.

■ Bring to a boil. Reduce heat to medium-low and simmer 15 minutes, stirring occasionally. Sauce will reduce to about 1½ cups.

PER SERVING 89 **CAL**; 2 g **FAT** (0 g **SAT**); 1 g **PRO**; 17 g **CARB**; 1 g **FIBER**; 555 mg **SODIUM**; 0 mg **CHOL**

HARVEST PORK ROAST

Harvest Pork Roast

MAKES 10 servings **PREP** 20 minutes
MARINATE at least 3 hours or overnight
BAKE at 400° for 15 minutes and at 350° for
45 minutes **BROIL** 8 minutes

PORK

- 1 **can (6 oz) apple juice concentrate, thawed**
- 3 **tbsp maple syrup**
- 2 **tbsp cider vinegar**
- 2 **tbsp olive oil**
- 2 **tsp Worcestershire sauce**
- 1 **tsp salt**
- ½ **tsp cinnamon**
- ¼ **tsp black pepper**
- 1 **boneless pork roast (about 3 lb)**
- 1 **tbsp cornstarch**

APPLES

- 4 **tbsp butter, melted**
- 4 **tbsp maple syrup**
- ¼ **tsp cinnamon**
- 4 **Granny Smith apples, peeled, cored and cut into ½-inch-thick slices**

■ **Pork.** In a large resealable plastic bag, combine apple juice concentrate, maple syrup, cider vinegar, olive oil, Worcestershire sauce, salt, cinnamon and pepper. Add pork roast and marinate at least 3 hours or overnight, turning occasionally.

■ Heat oven to 400°. Remove pork from plastic bag and reserve marinade. Roast at 400° for 15 minutes. Reduce oven temperature to 350° and roast 40 to 45 minutes more, until internal temperature reaches 140°. Place on a serving platter and tent with foil. Allow to rest for 10 minutes.

■ **Apples.** Meanwhile, heat broiler to high. In a bowl, combine butter, maple syrup and cinnamon. Place apple slices on a large broiler pan and brush with butter mixture. Broil about 4 minutes per side, turning once, until tender, brushing occasionally with butter mixture.

■ Place marinade in a small saucepan and bring to a simmer. Combine cornstarch with 1 tbsp water; stir into saucepan and simmer for 1 minute.

■ To serve, slice pork and serve with apples and sauce.

PER SERVING 363 **CAL**; 17 g **FAT** (7 g **SAT**); 27 g **PRO**; 26 g **CARB**; 1 g **FIBER**; 312 mg **SODIUM**; 87 mg **CHOL**

Pulled-Pork Cemita

MAKES 8 servings **PREP** 10 minutes
COOK 6 minutes **SLOW COOK** on HIGH for
6 hours or LOW for 8 hours

- 1 **bone-in pork loin roast (about 3 lb)**
- ¼ **tsp salt**
- ¼ **tsp black pepper**
- 2 **tbsp oil**
- 1 **medium onion, sliced**
- 1 **can (10 oz) enchilada sauce**
- 3 **tbsp lime juice**
- 2 **tsp chili powder**
- 8 **sesame seed rolls, split**
- ¾ **cup jarred black bean spread**
- ¾ **cup prepared guacamole or smashed ripe avocado**
- 1 **large tomato, sliced**
- 4 **oz goat cheese, crumbled**
   Fresh cilantro leaves

■ Place pork on a cutting board; season with salt and pepper. Heat oil in a large stainless skillet over high heat. Brown pork on all sides, about 6 minutes total. Remove from heat.

■ Place onion in a 4- to 5-qt slow cooker. Whisk in enchilada sauce, ½ cup water, lime juice and chili powder. Add pork to slow cooker; cover and cook on HIGH for 6 hours or LOW for 8 hours.

■ Remove pork to a clean cutting board. Cool slightly. When cool enough to handle, separate and discard bones, fat and connective tissue from meat, leaving pork in pieces as large as possible. Place pork on a platter and drizzle with about 1 cup of the liquid from slow cooker.

■ Assemble sandwiches: Spread bottom cut sides of rolls with an equal amount of bean spread (about 2 tbsp each); spread remaining halves with guacamole. Top bean spread with pork, tomato slices, goat cheese and cilantro.

PER SERVING 418 **CAL**; 20 g **FAT** (8 g **SAT**); 33 g **PRO**; 29 g **CARB**; 2 g **FIBER**; 883 mg **SODIUM**; 76 mg **CHOL**

KOREAN PORK CHOPS

Korean Pork Chops

MAKES 4 servings **PREP** 15 minutes
MARINATE 60 minutes
GRILL OR BROIL 4 minutes **COOK** 5 minutes

- ⅓ **cup orange juice**
- ½ **cup orange marmalade**
- 4 **cloves garlic, chopped**
- 3 **tbsp reduced-sodium soy sauce**
- 2 **tbsp brown sugar**
- 2 **tbsp rice vinegar**
- 1 **tbsp toasted sesame oil**
- 2 **tsp Asian chili paste**
- 4 **bone-in rib pork chops (about 7 oz each)**
- 8 **oz sugar snap peas**
- 4 **oz angel hair pasta**
- 1 **tsp toasted sesame seeds**

■ In a resealable bag, combine orange juice, marmalade, garlic, soy sauce, brown sugar, vinegar, sesame oil and chili paste. Add pork chops, seal bag and marinate in refrigerator 60 minutes.

■ Heat a grill pan to medium-high or broiler to high. Remove chops from plastic bag, reserving marinade. Grill or broil chops 2 minutes per side or until internal temperature reaches 145°. Place marinade in a small saucepan and boil 5 minutes.

■ Meanwhile, bring a large pot of lightly salted water to a boil. Add snap peas and cook 1 minute. Stir in angel hair and cook 2 minutes. Drain. Place in a bowl, toss with ⅔ cup of the reserved marinade and sprinkle with sesame seeds.

■ Serve pork chops with pasta, snap peas and remaining marinade.

PER SERVING 492 **CAL**; 15 g **FAT** (4 g **SAT**); 36 g **PRO**; 47 g **CARB**; 2 g **FIBER**; 628 mg **SODIUM**; 85 mg **CHOL**

Add remaining 1 tbsp oil to skillet and repeat with remaining 4 chops.

■ Pour chicken broth into empty skillet. Whisk in mustard and release browned bits on bottom of pan. Bring to a simmer. Reduce heat to medium and simmer 3 to 4 minutes, until slightly thickened. Stir in mushroom mixture.

■ Meanwhile, reheat squash in a lidded medium pot with milk, remaining ½ tsp salt and remaining ¼ tsp pepper. Serve pork over squash. Ladle mushroom sauce on top.

PER SERVING 429 CAL; 19 g FAT (3 g SAT); 36 g PRO; 30 g CARB; 6 g FIBER; 543 mg SODIUM; 91 mg CHOL

Delicata Squash Heat oven to 400°. Cut 2 delicata squash in half lengthwise and scoop out seeds. Coat halves with 1 tbsp olive oil and sprinkle cavities with ⅛ tsp salt. Place, cut sides down, on 2 baking sheets. Roast at 400° for 30 minutes. Let cool slightly and scoop out flesh.

Ancho Pork and Black Bean Tostadas

MAKES 10 tostadas plus 5 cups pork mixture for another meal PREP 30 minutes
SLOW COOK on HIGH for 6 hours or LOW for 8 hours COOK 10 minutes

3½	lb boneless pork shoulder or butt
1	tsp salt
½	tsp black pepper
2	tsp ancho chile powder
1	tsp ground cumin
1	tsp dried oregano
¼	tsp cinnamon
1	onion, chopped
4	cloves garlic, chopped
8	plum tomatoes, seeded and chopped
1	cup chicken broth
1	can (15 oz) black beans, drained and rinsed
2	cups vegetable oil
10	corn tortillas
3	cups shredded iceberg lettuce
	Pineapple-Habanero Salsa (recipe follows)

Pork Scaloppine with Winter Squash

MAKES 4 servings PREP 20 minutes
COOK 22 minutes

3	tbsp canola oil
½	lb sliced cremini mushrooms
¼	cup sliced shallots
1	tbsp chopped fresh sage
4	thick boneless center-cut pork chops (about 1¼ lb)
½	cup all-purpose flour
1	tsp salt
½	tsp black pepper
1	cup low-sodium chicken broth
1	tsp Dijon mustard
	Cooked delicata squash (recipe follows)
½	cup milk

■ Heat oven to 200°. In a large skillet, heat 1 tbsp of the oil over medium-high heat. Add mushrooms and cook 8 minutes, stirring a couple of times, until lightly browned. Add sliced shallots; cook 2 minutes. Mix in sage; remove to a bowl. Turn off heat and reserve pan.

■ Carefully split pork chops in half lengthwise (knife parallel to cutting board), making 8 thin chops. Pound each to ⅛-inch thickness in between 2 pieces of plastic wrap on a cutting board. On a plate, combine flour, ½ tsp of the salt and ¼ tsp of the pepper. Dredge chops in flour mixture, gently shaking to remove any excess; place on another plate.

■ In same skillet, over medium-high heat, add 1 tbsp of the oil. Sauté 4 of the chops for 2 minutes; flip and cook another 2 minutes. Remove to a baking sheet and place in warm oven.

ANCHO PORK AND BLACK BEAN TOSTADAS

■ Coat a 3½- to 4-qt slow cooker with nonstick cooking spray. Season pork with salt and pepper. Place in slow cooker. Sprinkle with ancho chile powder, cumin, oregano and cinnamon.

■ Place onion, garlic and tomatoes around pork. Pour broth down sides of bowl.

■ Cover and cook on HIGH for 6 hours or LOW for 8 hours.

■ Remove pork to a cutting board and shred with 2 forks. Return to slow cooker; stir in beans and heat through.

■ Heat oil in a skillet to 375°. Cook tortillas in batches 1 minute per side or until crisp. Place on a paper towel-lined baking sheet.

■ Top each tortilla with ½ cup of the pork, some shredded lettuce and Pineapple-Habanero Salsa.

PER TOSTADA 255 **CAL**; 16 g **FAT** (2 g **SAT**); 11 g **PRO**; 20 g **CARB**; 4 g **FIBER**; 312 mg **SODIUM**; 24 mg **CHOL**

Pineapple-Habanero Salsa Combine 2½ cups diced fresh pineapple; ¼ cup finely chopped sweet pepper; 1 habanero pepper, seeded and chopped; 2 tbsp chopped cilantro; and 1 tbsp each lime and olive oil. Season with ⅛ tsp salt.

MALAYSIAN PORK CURRY
NOODLE SOUP

BRAZILIAN BLACK
BEAN STEW

Winter Vegetable and Spelt Soup

MAKES 6 servings **SOAK** overnight
PREP 20 minutes **COOK** 45 minutes

- 1 cup spelt
- 1 tbsp olive oil
- 3 links (3 oz each) sweet Italian sausage, casings removed
- 2 cups peeled and cubed butternut squash (cut into 1-inch pieces)
- 1½ cups peeled and sliced carrots (cut into 1-inch pieces)
- 1½ cups peeled and sliced parsnips (cut into 1-inch pieces)
- 1 large onion, diced
- 3 cloves garlic, chopped
- 1 tbsp chopped fresh thyme
- 4 cups low-sodium chicken broth
- ¾ tsp salt
- ¼ tsp black pepper

■ Soak spelt in cold water overnight. Drain and set aside.

■ In a large lidded pot, heat olive oil over medium heat. Add sausage, breaking up with a wooden spoon. Cook 8 to 10 minutes, until browned. Stir in butternut squash, carrots, parsnips, onion, garlic and thyme. Cook 5 minutes, stirring occasionally. Add chicken broth, 1 cup water and the spelt. Bring to a boil. Reduce heat to a simmer and cook, covered, for 30 minutes or until spelt is tender. Stir in salt and pepper.

PER SERVING 277 **CAL**; 9 g **FAT** (2 g **SAT**); 11 g **PRO**; 41 g **CARB**; 7 g **FIBER**; 623 mg **SODIUM**; 12 mg **CHOL**

Malaysian Pork Curry Noodle Soup

MAKES 8 servings **PREP** 15 minutes
SLOW COOK on HIGH for 6 hours or LOW for 8 hours

- 3 lb boneless pork shoulder
- 1 large yellow onion, diced
- 1 3-inch piece ginger, peeled and chopped
- 3 cloves garlic, chopped
- 2 cups unsalted chicken stock
- 1 can (13.5 oz) coconut milk
- 2 tbsp lime juice
- 1 tbsp curry powder
- 2 tsp sugar
- 1 tsp salt
- ½ tsp red pepper flakes
- 1 box (8 oz) pad thai rice noodles
  Scallions and chow mein noodles (optional)

■ Place pork shoulder, onion, ginger and garlic in a 4-qt slow cooker. In a bowl, whisk stock, coconut milk, lime juice, curry powder, sugar, ½ tsp of the salt and the red pepper flakes. Pour over pork. Cover and cook on HIGH for 6 hours or LOW for 8 hours.

■ Remove pork to a cutting board and shred. Stir remaining ½ tsp salt into liquid and return shredded pork to slow cooker. Meanwhile, prepare rice noodles per package directions.

■ Divide rice noodles among 8 bowls, then ladle pork and broth on top. Garnish with scallions and chow mein noodles, if desired.

PER SERVING 350 **CAL**; 16 g **FAT** (11 g **SAT**); 21 g **PRO**; 30 g **CARB**; 1 g **FIBER**; 400 mg **SODIUM**; 65 mg **CHOL**

Brazilian Black Bean Stew

MAKES 10 servings **PREP** 15 minutes
SLOW COOK on HIGH for 5 hours or LOW for 7 hours

- 2½ lb pork spare ribs
- 3 oz diced cured chorizo, casing removed
- 1 large yellow onion, diced
- 4 cloves garlic, sliced
- 1 lb collard greens, large stems discarded, roughly chopped
- 2 cups unsalted chicken stock
- ½ tsp salt
- ¼ tsp black pepper
- 2 cans (15.5 oz each) black beans, rinsed and drained
- 1 tbsp white vinegar
- 6 cups cooked white or brown rice
- 1 large orange, peeled and cut into segments

■ Place ribs, chorizo, onion and garlic in a 3½- or 4-qt slow cooker. Place collard greens on top, pressing down firmly. Whisk stock, salt and pepper, then pour on top. Cover and cook on HIGH for 5 hours or LOW for 7 hours.

■ Carefully remove ribs to a cutting board and shred; discard bones. Stir beans and vinegar into liquid. Stir meat back into slow cooker.

■ To serve, scatter about ½ cup rice into each bowl. Ladle stew on top and garnish with orange segments.

PER SERVING 500 **CAL**; 24 g **FAT** (8 g **SAT**); 25 g **PRO**; 46 g **CARB**; 10 g **FIBER**; 525 mg **SODIUM**; 75 mg **CHOL**

Schnitzel and Salad

MAKES 4 servings **PREP** 14 minutes
COOK 6 minutes

- **8** small thinly sliced boneless pork chops (about 1½ lb)
- **¾** cup plain bread crumbs
- **½** tsp plus ¼ tsp salt
- **1** large egg
- **½** cup all-purpose flour
- **1** pkg (11 oz) mixed salad greens
- **2** medium oranges
- **2** lemons
- **2** tsp honey
- **1** tsp Dijon mustard
- **⅛** tsp black pepper
- **2** tbsp olive oil
- **3** tbsp vegetable oil

■ If needed, pound pork chops to ¼-inch thickness. Place bread crumbs and ½ tsp of the salt in a shallow bowl. Whisk egg plus 2 tbsp water in a second bowl. Place flour in a third bowl.

■ Coat 1 pork chop in flour. Dip into egg mixture, allowing excess to drip back into bowl. Coat with bread crumbs and transfer to a large platter. Repeat with remaining pork chops.

■ Place salad greens in a large bowl. Peel oranges and slice into half-moons. Add to greens. Juice 1 lemon to yield ¼ cup juice; cut second lemon into wedges. Whisk lemon juice with honey, mustard, remaining ¼ tsp salt and the pepper. Whisk in olive oil and toss with salad greens.

■ Heat 1½ tbsp of the vegetable oil in a large skillet over medium-high heat. Add 4 pork chops; cook 3 minutes, turning once. Repeat with remaining 1½ tbsp vegetable oil and 4 pork chops.

■ Divide salad among 4 plates. Top each with 2 pieces pork schnitzel. Serve with lemon wedges on the side.

PER SERVING 402 **CAL**; 18 g **FAT** (3 g **SAT**); 31 g **PRO**; 28 g **CARB**; 3 g **FIBER**; 804 mg **SODIUM**; 115 mg **CHOL**

Pork Tenderloin Salad

MAKES 4 servings **PREP** 20 minutes
ROAST at 425° for 35 minutes
REFRIGERATE overnight

- **1** bag (24 oz) baby red potatoes, quartered
- **2** tbsp olive oil
- **½** tsp salt
- **¼** tsp black pepper
- **1** canned chipotle in adobo, chopped, plus 2 tsp adobo
- **1** tbsp light mayonnaise
- **2½** tsp Dijon mustard
- **2** tsp fresh oregano, chopped
- **1** pork tenderloin (1¼ lb)
- **3** tbsp red wine vinegar
- **1** tsp honey
- **1** pkg (5 oz) salad greens
- **1** pear, cored and diced

■ The night before, heat oven to 425°. Toss potatoes with 1 tbsp of the oil, ¼ tsp of the salt and ⅛ tsp of the pepper. Spread onto a rimmed baking sheet. In a small bowl, blend chipotle,

1 tsp of the adobo, the mayonnaise, 2 tsp of the mustard, 1 tsp of the oregano, ⅛ tsp of the salt and remaining ⅛ tsp pepper. Brush onto pork tenderloin on a rimmed baking sheet.

■ Roast potatoes at 425° for 35 minutes, stirring occasionally. Roast pork at 425° for 30 minutes, or until it registers 140° on an instant-read thermometer. Remove from oven and cover pork with foil. Cool both pork and potatoes; refrigerate overnight.

■ Meanwhile, whisk together vinegar, remaining 1 tbsp oil, ⅛ tsp salt, 1 tsp adobo, 1 tsp oregano and the honey. Wrap and store at room temperature overnight.

■ To serve, in a large bowl, toss together roasted potatoes, salad greens, diced pear and dressing. Divide among 4 bowls. Thinly slice pork and fan on top.

PER SERVING 427 **CAL**; 13 g **FAT** (3 g **SAT**); 34 g **PRO**; 43 g **CARB**; 5 g **FIBER**; 802 mg **SODIUM**; 93 mg **CHOL**

SCHNITZEL AND SALAD

SLOW COOKER MAC AND CHEESE WITH BACON

SPRING CARBONARA

Slow Cooker Mac and Cheese with Bacon

MAKES 6 servings **PREP** 15 minutes
SLOW COOK on LOW for 3 hours

- 12 oz (about 4 cups) uncooked radiatore pasta (or your favorite shape)
- 8 slices bacon, cooked
- 2 cups milk
- 1 can (12 oz) evaporated milk
- 2 tsp Dijon mustard
- 1 tsp onion powder
- ¼ tsp salt
- ¼ tsp black pepper
- 6 oz thinly sliced deli American cheese, cut into thin strips
- 1 cup (4 oz) grated Gouda cheese

■ Coat a 4- to 5-qt slow cooker with nonstick cooking spray.

■ Bring a pot of lightly salted water to a boil and cook pasta 2 minutes less than package directions. Drain. Crumble 6 slices of the bacon and add to slow cooker with milk, evaporated milk, mustard, onion powder, salt and pepper. Whisk until blended, then stir in pasta. Cover and cook on LOW for 2½ hours.

■ Stir in cheeses and cook an additional 30 minutes. Crumble remaining 2 slices bacon and sprinkle on top of servings.

PER SERVING 516 **CAL**; 22 g **FAT** (14 g **SAT**); 26 g **PRO**; 52 g **CARB**; 3 g **FIBER**; 813 mg **SODIUM**; 66 mg **CHOL**

Spring Carbonara

MAKES 6 servings **PREP** 15 minutes
COOK 17 minutes

- 4 oz pancetta, diced
- 1 cup sliced leeks
- 3 cloves garlic, sliced
- 6 eggs
- 1 cup grated Pecorino cheese, plus more for garnish (optional)
- 1 tsp freshly cracked black pepper, plus more for garnish (optional)
- ½ tsp salt
- 1 lb linguine
- 2 cups shelled fresh peas
- 1 lb asparagus, trimmed and sliced into ½-inch pieces
- ⅓ cup roughly chopped fresh parsley

■ Bring a large pot of lightly salted water to a boil. In a large skillet over medium heat, cook pancetta 4 minutes. Remove to a plate with a slotted spoon.

Add leeks and garlic; cook 3 minutes. Turn off heat and set aside.

■ In a bowl, whisk eggs, Pecorino, pepper and salt. Set aside.

■ Cook linguine in boiling salted water 9 minutes. (Add peas and asparagus to water after 7 minutes.) Drain, reserving ½ cup of the pasta water.

■ Return pan to medium heat. Add linguine, peas, asparagus and pancetta to leeks and garlic. Cook 1 minute, stirring well. Vigorously mix in egg mixture, making sure not to scramble. Stir in reserved pasta water, if needed, and parsley. Serve immediately, garnishing with more Pecorino and pepper, if desired. (If pan isn't large enough, pasta can be tossed in the pot once linguine is drained.)

PER SERVING 525 **CAL**; 16 g **FAT** (7 g **SAT**); 27 g **PRO**; 68 g **CARB**; 6 g **FIBER**; 785 mg **SODIUM**; 237 mg **CHOL**

Spanish Tortilla

MAKES 4 servings **PREP** 10 minutes
ROAST at 400° for 25 minutes
COOK 47 minutes

- 1 **bag (28 oz) small red-skin potatoes, cut into 1-inch pieces**
- 2 **tbsp extra-virgin olive oil**
- ¾ **tsp salt**
- ¼ **tsp plus ⅛ tsp black pepper**
- 2 **oz (½ cup) cured Spanish chorizo, casing removed, diced**
- 1 **yellow onion, thinly sliced**
- 7 **eggs**
  Fresh parsley, for garnish

■ Heat oven to 400°. On a rimmed baking sheet, toss potatoes with 1 tbsp of the oil, ¼ tsp of the salt and ⅛ tsp of the pepper. Roast at 400° for 15 minutes, flip and roast another 10 minutes.

■ In a 10-inch nonstick skillet, cook chorizo 5 minutes over medium heat. Remove to a plate with a slotted spoon. Pour in remaining 1 tbsp oil. Add onion; cook 5 to 7 minutes, until softened. Stir in potatoes and chorizo. Reduce heat to medium-low.

■ In a bowl, beat eggs with remaining ½ tsp salt and ¼ tsp pepper. Pour over mixture in skillet. Cook 10 minutes, then cover with foil. Cook 20 minutes, then loosen with a silicone spatula, place a plate on top of skillet and carefully flip tortilla onto plate. Slide tortilla back into skillet, uncooked side down. Cook another 5 minutes.

■ Flip onto a new plate, garnish with parsley and slice into 4 pieces.

PER SERVING 425 **CAL**; 22 g **FAT** (6 g **SAT**); 19 g **PRO**; 39 g **CARB**; 4 g **FIBER**; 823 mg **SODIUM**; 383 mg **CHOL**

Meatball and Barley Soup

MAKES 6 servings **PREP** 25 minutes
COOK 40 minutes

- 1 **tbsp olive oil**
- 2 **medium carrots, peeled and diced**
- 2 **ribs celery, diced**
- 1 **cup diced onion**
- 3 **cloves garlic, finely diced**

MEATBALL AND BARLEY SOUP

- 6 **cups low-sodium chicken broth**
- 1¼ **cups barley**
- 1 **lb ground pork**
- ¾ **cup shredded Parmesan cheese, plus more for garnish (optional)**
- 2 **tbsp chopped fresh parsley**
- 1½ **tsp salt**
- ½ **tsp pepper**
- 1 **can (15.5 oz) cannellini beans, drained and rinsed**
- 8 **cups roughly chopped escarole**

■ In a large pot, heat oil over medium heat. Add carrots, celery and onion; cook 8 minutes. Stir in garlic and cook 2 minutes. Add broth, 2 cups water and barley. Bring to a boil. Reduce heat to medium-low, cover and cook 25 minutes.

■ Meanwhile, mix together ground pork, ¼ cup of the Parmesan, the parsley, ¼ tsp of the salt and ¼ tsp of the pepper. Roll into 30 meatballs, about 1 tbsp each.

■ Drop meatballs into soup. Stir in beans. Return to a simmer and cook 5 minutes. Stir in escarole and remaining ½ cup Parmesan, 1¼ tsp salt and ¼ tsp pepper. Ladle into bowls and, if desired, garnish with grated Parmesan.

PER SERVING 450 **CAL**; 17 g **FAT** (6 g **SAT**); 23 g **PRO**; 51 g **CARB**; 13 g **FIBER**; 772 mg **SODIUM**; 46 mg **CHOL**

CHICKPEA, WHITE BEAN
AND ESCAROLE STEW

Chickpea, White Bean and Escarole Stew

MAKES 12 cups **PREP** 15 minutes
SOAK overnight **COOK** 1 hour 40 minutes

- 1½ **cups dried white beans**
- 1½ **cups dried chickpeas**
- 2 **tbsp olive oil**
- 2 **onions, chopped**
- 3 **carrots, diced**
- 2 **ribs celery, diced**
- 6 **cloves garlic, sliced**
- 6 **plum tomatoes, seeds removed, chopped**
- 1 **sprig rosemary**
- 4 **sprigs thyme**
- 2 **bay leaves**
- 1 **pkg (10 oz) frozen lima beans, thawed**
- 4 **oz sliced prosciutto, cut into ribbons**
- 1 **tsp salt**
- ¼ **tsp black pepper**
- 1 **large bunch escarole (about 1 lb), sliced**

  Shaved Parmesan (optional)

  Extra-virgin olive oil, for drizzling (optional)

■ Place beans and chickpeas in a large pot and cover with cold water. Soak overnight.

■ Heat olive oil in a large pot over medium-high heat. Add onions, carrots, celery and garlic; cook 8 minutes, stirring occasionally. Add tomatoes, rosemary, thyme and bay leaves. Stir in drained beans and 6 cups water. Bring to a boil. Lower heat and simmer, covered, 90 minutes.

■ Add lima beans, prosciutto, salt and pepper. Return to a simmer and gradually add escarole. Cook 2 minutes, until escarole is tender. Remove and discard bay leaves.

■ Ladle into bowls. Top with shaved Parmesan and drizzle with olive oil, if desired.

PER SERVING 257 **CAL**; 4 g **FAT** (1 g **SAT**); 15 g **PRO**; 42 g **CARB**; 12 g **FIBER**; 415 mg **SODIUM**; 0 mg **CHOL**

Mushroom, Sausage and Whole Grain Soup

MAKES 6 servings **PREP** 15 minutes
COOK 7 minutes
SLOW COOK on HIGH for 5 hours

- 1 **lb sweet Italian sausage, casings removed**
- 2 **tbsp white wine vinegar**
- 1¼ **cups Bob's Red Mill whole grain medley**
- 2 **cups diced sweet onion**
- 1 **lb sliced wild mushrooms**
- 2 **ribs celery, sliced**
- 3 **cloves garlic, chopped**
- 1 **tbsp chopped fresh thyme**
- 6 **cups unsalted chicken stock**
- ¾ **tsp salt**
- ¼ **tsp black pepper**

  Fresh parsley, for garnish

■ Heat a large sauté pan over medium-high heat. Add sausage, breaking apart with a spoon. Cook for 7 minutes, stirring occasionally, until browned. Add vinegar, scraping up browned bits from bottom of pan.

■ Transfer sausage to a 4-qt slow cooker. Stir in grains, onion, mushrooms, celery, garlic and thyme. Pour chicken stock on top, making sure all grains are submerged. Cover and cook on HIGH for 5 hours. Stir in salt and pepper. Garnish with parsley.

PER SERVING 370 **CAL**; 12 g **FAT** (4 g **SAT**); 21 g **PRO**; 43 g **CARB**; 7 g **FIBER**; 904 mg **SODIUM**; 22 mg **CHOL**

MUSHROOM, SAUSAGE AND WHOLE GRAIN SOUP

BAJA FISH TACOS WITH GRILLED AVOCADO, RECIPE PAGE 137

Fish & Shellfish

Versatile fish and shellfish are quick-cooking and convenient, and most store well in the freezer for flavorful meals any time.

SEARED WILD SALMON
WITH PISTACHIO
GREMOLATA

Wild Salmon Caesar

MAKES 4 servings PREP 25 minutes
ROAST 14 minutes at 450°

- 1 wild-caught salmon fillet
     (1 lb), cut into 4 pieces
- 1 bunch thin asparagus, trimmed
- 2 tbsp olive oil
- ¾ tsp salt
- ½ tsp black pepper
- ½ cup reduced-fat sour cream
- 2 tbsp lemon juice
- 2 cloves garlic, finely chopped
- 1 tsp spicy brown mustard
- 1 tsp Worcestershire sauce
- 1 tsp anchovy paste (optional)
- 5 tbsp grated Parmesan
- 8 cups sliced romaine
- ½ small red onion, sliced
- 1 cup grape tomatoes

■ Heat oven to 450°. Place salmon and asparagus on separate baking pans. Drizzle 1 tbsp of the olive oil over asparagus; season salmon and asparagus with ½ tsp of the salt and ¼ tsp of the pepper. Roast at 450° for 12 to 14 minutes, until salmon flakes and asparagus is tender. Cut asparagus into 1-inch pieces.

■ Meanwhile, whisk sour cream, remaining 1 tbsp olive oil, the lemon juice, garlic, mustard, Worcestershire, anchovy paste (if using), remaining ¼ tsp each salt and pepper and 3 tbsp of the Parmesan. Set aside.

■ In a large bowl, toss romaine, onion, tomatoes and asparagus. Add half the dressing and remaining 2 tbsp Parmesan; toss to coat.

■ Serve salad with salmon and remaining dressing on the side.

PER SERVING 387 CAL; 21 g FAT (6 g SAT); 34 g PRO; 17 g CARB; 7 g FIBER; 661 mg SODIUM; 87 mg CHOL

Seared Wild Salmon with Pistachio Gremolata

MAKES 4 servings PREP 25 minutes
COOK 49 minutes

FARRO PILAF

- 3 tbsp olive oil
- 8 oz sliced wild mushrooms
- 1 large shallot, sliced
- ¾ cup farro
- ¼ cup dry white wine
- 2 cups chicken broth
- ¼ tsp salt
- ⅛ tsp black pepper

GREMOLATA

- ⅓ cup shelled pistachios, finely chopped
- ¼ cup fresh parsley, chopped
- ¼ cup fresh mint, chopped
- 1 tbsp lemon zest
- 1 tbsp olive oil
- 1 garlic clove, finely chopped
   Pinch of salt

SALMON

- 2 tbsp olive oil
- 1 lb salmon fillet, cut into 4 squares
   Pinch of salt and pepper

■ **Farro Pilaf.** In a large skillet, heat 2 tbsp of the olive oil over medium-high heat. Add mushrooms and sauté 5 minutes, until lightly browned. Transfer to a bowl. Heat remaining 1 tbsp of the oil in a medium saucepan over medium heat. Add shallot and cook 3 minutes. Stir in farro and wine; cook 1 minute. Add broth, salt and pepper; bring to a simmer. Cover and simmer 35 to 40 minutes, until tender. Stir in sautéed mushrooms.

■ **Gremolata.** In a small bowl, combine pistachios, parsley, mint, lemon zest, oil, garlic and salt. Set aside.

■ **Salmon.** Meanwhile, heat oil in same skillet over medium-high heat. Season salmon with salt and pepper and place in skillet, skin sides down. Cook 3 minutes, turn and cook an additional 3 minutes.

■ Spoon gremolata over salmon and serve with farro.

PER SERVING 587 CAL; 35 g FAT (5 g SAT); 34 g PRO; 33 g CARB; 4 g FIBER; 755 mg SODIUM; 72 mg CHOL

WILD SALMON CAESAR

PANKO FRIED FISH
AND SMOKY CHIPS

Panko Fried Fish and Smoky Chips

MAKES 4 servings **PREP** 10 minutes
BAKE at 450° for 20 minutes **COOK** 6 minutes

- 1 **lb (from a 2-lb bag) frozen straight-cut fries**
- 1 **tsp smoked paprika**
- 4 **tilapia fillets (about 4 oz each)**
- ½ **tsp salt**
- ¼ **tsp black pepper**
- 2 **egg whites, lightly beaten**
- 1 **cup whole wheat panko**
- 3 **tbsp canola oil**
   Lemon wedges for squeezing
   Ketchup and tartar sauce (optional)

■ Heat oven to 450°. Place fries on an ungreased baking sheet in single layer. Bake at 450° for 10 minutes. Sprinkle with smoked paprika and bake for an additional 8 to 10 minutes, until crispy, turning once.

■ Meanwhile, season tilapia with ¼ tsp of the salt and the pepper. Dip in egg whites and coat with panko.

■ Heat oil in a large nonstick skillet over medium-high heat. Add tilapia and cook for 2 to 3 minutes per side, until golden.

■ Sprinkle tilapia with remaining ¼ tsp salt. Serve with fries and lemon wedges. Accompany with ketchup and tartar sauce, if desired.

PER SERVING 399 **CAL**; 15 g **FAT** (1 g **SAT**); 30 g **PRO**; 39 g **CARB**; 3 g **FIBER**; 763 mg **SODIUM**; 57 mg **CHOL**

Baja Fish Tacos with Grilled Avocado

MAKES 4 servings **PREP** 20 minutes
COOK 4 minutes per batch **GRILL** 4 minutes

- 3 **cups coleslaw mix**
- ⅓ **cup reduced-fat yogurt**
- 1 **scallion, sliced**
- ¾ **tsp salt**
- ¼ **tsp black pepper**
- ½ **cup all-purpose flour**
- 2 **egg whites, lightly beaten**
- 1 **cup chipotle-seasoned panko**

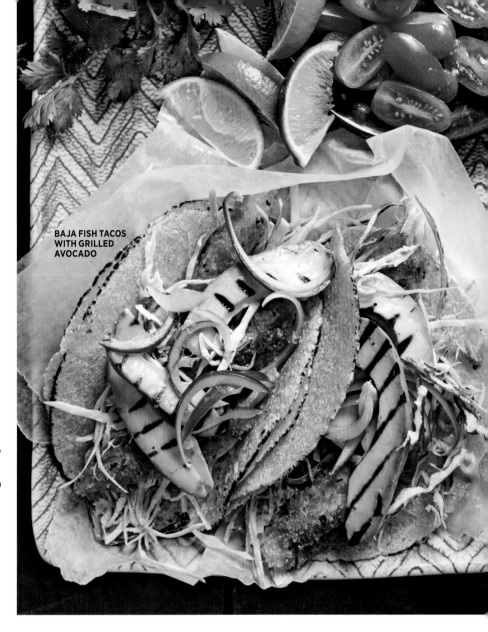

BAJA FISH TACOS WITH GRILLED AVOCADO

- 1 **lb tilapia, cut diagonally into 1-inch strips**
- ¼ **cup canola oil**
- 1 **avocado**
- 16 **corn tortillas**
   Cilantro, halved grape tomatoes and sliced red onion (optional)
   Lime wedges, chipotle hot sauce and sour cream (optional)

■ In a medium bowl, combine coleslaw mix, yogurt, scallion, ¼ tsp of the salt and the pepper. Cover and refrigerate.

■ Place flour, egg whites and panko in separate shallow dishes. Whisk remaining ½ tsp salt into flour. Coat fish with flour, egg whites and panko.

■ In a large nonstick skillet, heat oil over medium-high heat. Cooking in batches, sauté fish 2 minutes per side, until golden. Place on a wire rack and keep warm.

■ Heat a grill pan to medium-high. Slice avocado in half; remove skin and pit. Grill 2 minutes per side. Thinly slice, then place on a plate.

■ Gently heat tortillas in microwave.

■ To assemble tacos, double up tortillas and place a few pieces of fish, some slaw and some avocado on each. Garnish with cilantro, tomatoes and onion, if desired. Serve with lime wedges, hot sauce and sour cream, if desired.

PER SERVING 517 **CAL**; 16 g **FAT** (2 g **SAT**); 33 g **PRO**; 61 g **CARB**; 6 g **FIBER**; 621 mg **SODIUM**; 58 mg **CHOL**

HALIBUT, PEARL COUSCOUS AND HARISSA

GINGER AND SCALLION STEAMED SEA BASS

Halibut, Pearl Couscous and Harissa

MAKES 4 servings PREP 5 minutes
COOK 17 minutes

- 1 tbsp canola oil
- 4 halibut or swordfish steaks (about 5 oz each)
- ¾ tsp salt
- ½ tsp black pepper
- 1 cup sliced onion
- 2 tbsp chopped garlic
- 2½ cups vegetable broth
- 1¼ cups pearl couscous (also called Israeli couscous)
- 1 pkg (5 oz) baby spinach
- 4 plum tomatoes, roughly chopped
- 3 tbsp harissa
- 2 tbsp chopped fresh parsley
- 1 lemon, cut into wedges

■ Heat oil in a large skillet over medium-high heat. Season fish with ¼ tsp each of the salt and pepper. Add to skillet; cook for 3 minutes per side. Remove to a plate.

■ Add onion and garlic; cook for 2 minutes, stirring so that garlic doesn't burn. Add broth and couscous; simmer, covered, for 4 minutes. Stir in spinach, tomatoes, harissa and remaining ½ tsp salt and ¼ tsp pepper; cook for 2 minutes. Return fish to skillet. Cover and simmer for 3 minutes or until couscous is tender.

■ To serve, garnish with parsley and lemon wedges.

PER SERVING 414 CAL; 7 g FAT (1 g SAT); 37 g PRO; 49 g CARB; 6 g FIBER; 724 mg SODIUM; 45 mg CHOL

Ginger and Scallion Steamed Sea Bass

MAKES 4 servings PREP 20 minutes
MARINATE 15 minutes COOK 15 minutes
STEAM 8 minutes

- ¼ cup low-sodium soy sauce
- 3 tbsp rice vinegar
- 2 tbsp light brown sugar
- 1 tsp sesame oil
- ½ tsp five-spice powder
- 1 cup thinly sliced scallions
- 4 tbsp julienned ginger
- 1¼ lb sea bass or cod (4 fillets)
- 1 lb baby bok choy
- 1¼ cups jasmine rice
- ⅓ cup unsalted chicken stock
- 1 tsp cornstarch

■ Mix soy sauce, vinegar, brown sugar, sesame oil and five-spice powder in a bowl. Pour ¼ cup of the soy mixture into a small saucepan and set aside. Stir ½ cup of the scallions and 3 tbsp of the ginger into remaining ¼ cup soy mixture. Pour half over fillets in a resealable plastic bag. Marinate 15 minutes. Toss bok choy with remaining marinade.

■ Meanwhile, bring 2½ cups water to a boil in a small lidded pot. Add rice, cover and return to a boil. Reduce heat and cook 15 minutes, until water is absorbed. Keep covered but remove from heat.

■ Fill a large skillet with ½ inch water. Stack 2 bamboo steamer baskets on top with lid. Bring water to a boil. Place fish fillets in bottom basket and bok choy in top basket. Cover with lid; steam for 6 to 8 minutes, just until fish flakes easily with a fork.

■ While fish and bok choy are cooking, add stock and cornstarch to contents in saucepan; bring to a boil. Cook 2 minutes, until thickened. Fluff rice. Serve fish and bok choy over rice, spoon sauce on top and garnish with remaining ½ cup scallions.

PER SERVING 313 CAL; 4 g FAT (1 g SAT); 33 g PRO; 34 g CARB; 2 g FIBER; 788 mg SODIUM; 62 mg CHOL

Maple-Mustard Glazed Salmon

MAKES 8 servings PREP 10 minutes
ROAST at 400° for 15 minutes

- 1 whole skin-on salmon fillet (about 2½ lb)
- 2 tbsp light brown sugar
- 1 tsp salt
- ⅛ tsp black pepper
- 2 tbsp maple syrup
- 1 tbsp unsalted butter, melted
- 1 tbsp grainy mustard
- Fresh parsley, for garnish (optional)

■ Heat oven to 400°. Dry salmon with paper towels and place in an oven-safe baking dish. In a small bowl, combine brown sugar, salt and pepper; pat onto salmon. In a bowl, stir maple syrup, butter and mustard. Pour evenly over salmon. Roast at 400° for 15 minutes or until desired doneness. Garnish with parsley, if desired.

PER SERVING 270 CAL; 12 g FAT (2 g SAT); 32 g PRO; 7 g CARB; 0 g FIBER; 408 mg SODIUM; 93 mg CHOL

MAPLE-MUSTARD
GLAZED SALMON

GREENS AND
GRAIN SALAD

Greens and Grain Salad

MAKES 4 servings **PREP** 15 minutes
MICROWAVE 3 minutes

- 1   **container (6 oz) plain fat-free yogurt (not Greek)**
- 2   **tbsp white wine vinegar**
- ⅓   **cup chopped fresh dill**
- 1   **tsp sugar**
- ½   **tsp salt**
- ¼   **tsp black pepper**
- 1   **cup frozen fully cooked wheat berries**
- 1   **cup cooked lentils**
- 1   **pkg (8.8 oz) refrigerated cooked beets, diced**
- 8   **cups chopped butter lettuce**
- 8   **cups baby spinach**
- ½   **cup chopped unsalted pistachios**
- 1   **can (6 oz) canned salmon, drained (optional)**

■ In a large bowl, stir together yogurt, vinegar, fresh dill, sugar, salt and pepper. Set aside.

■ Heat wheat berries in a microwave-safe bowl for 2 minutes; stir and heat 1 minute more, until thawed.

■ Toss wheat berries, lentils, beets, lettuce, spinach and pistachios in bowl with dressing. Fold in salmon, if desired, or serve salad with salmon.

PER SERVING 424 **CAL**; 10 g **FAT** (1 g **SAT**); 33 g **PRO**; 64 g **CARB**; 15 g **FIBER**; 765 mg **SODIUM**; 20 mg **CHOL**

Salmon Skewers over Roasted Vegetables

MAKES 4 servings **PREP** 20 minutes
ROAST at 425° for 40 minutes
BROIL 5 minutes

- 2   **tbsp red wine vinegar**
- 1   **tsp Dijon mustard**
- ½   **tsp smoked or traditional paprika, plus more for sprinkling**
- ¾   **tsp salt**
- ½   **tsp black pepper**
- 2   **tbsp plus 2 tsp olive oil**
- 1½ **lb red-skinned potatoes, cut into 1½-inch pieces**
- ½   **red onion**
- 1   **lb asparagus, tough ends discarded, or green beans**
- 1   **lb skinless salmon fillet, cut into 1½-inch cubes**
- 16 **cherry tomatoes**

■ Heat oven to 425°.

■ In a small bowl, whisk together vinegar, mustard, paprika, ¼ tsp of the salt and ⅛ tsp of the pepper. While whisking, add the oil in a stream.

■ Toss potatoes with 2 tbsp of the dressing and spread onto a rimmed baking sheet. Sprinkle paprika on cut side of onion and add to pan, cut side up. Roast at 425° for 20 minutes.

■ Stir potatoes and push to one side of the pan. Remove onion to a cutting board. Toss asparagus with 1 tbsp of the remaining dressing and add to pan. Continue to roast at 425° for 20 minutes.

■ Meanwhile, toss salmon with remaining 2 tbsp dressing. Cut onion into 4 wedges, then cut wedges in half. Thread eight 6- to 8-inch skewers with salmon, onion and cherry tomatoes. Season with ¼ tsp salt and ⅛ tsp pepper.

■ Remove potatoes and asparagus from oven. Season with remaining ¼ tsp salt and ¼ tsp pepper. Turn oven temperature up to broil.

■ Broil skewers, 4 inches from heat, for 5 minutes, turning once. Serve skewers over roasted vegetables.

PER SERVING 433 **CAL**; 18 g **FAT** (3 g **SAT**); 32 g **PRO**; 38 g **CARB**; 7 g **FIBER**; 538 mg **SODIUM**; 72 mg **CHOL**

SALMON SKEWERS OVER ROASTED VEGETABLE

SEAFOOD AND SPRING VEGGIE CHOWDER

Poached Salmon Salad

MAKES 6 servings **PREP** 20 minutes
COOK 10 minutes **REFRIGERATE** at least 1 hour

SALMON

- 3 cups low-sodium vegetable broth
- 1 small onion, halved
- 3 cloves garlic, sliced
- 10 whole peppercorns
- ½ tsp red pepper flakes
- 1¼ lb salmon fillets, thawed, if frozen
- ⅛ tsp salt

DRESSING AND SALAD

- ¼ cup orange juice
- 2 tbsp red wine vinegar
- 2 tsp spicy brown mustard
- ¾ tsp salt
- ½ tsp hot sauce
- 2 tbsp olive oil
- 12 oz fresh kale leaves (8 packed cups), tough stems removed, chopped
- 1½ cups seedless red grapes, halved, if large
- ¼ cup roasted, salted sunflower seeds

■ **Salmon.** Combine broth, onion, garlic, peppercorns and red pepper flakes in a straight-sided sauté pan. Cover and bring to a boil, then reduce heat to medium. Simmer 5 minutes. Season salmon with salt and add to pan. Cover and cook at very low simmer for 5 minutes. Remove fish to a plate with a large spatula and refrigerate at least 1 hour.

■ **Dressing and Salad.** In a small bowl, whisk together orange juice, vinegar, mustard, ½ tsp of the salt and the hot sauce. While whisking, add olive oil in a thin stream.

■ Combine the kale, grapes and sunflower seeds in a large bowl. Remove salmon skin. Flake salmon into bite-size pieces and add to bowl. Pour dressing over salad and season with remaining ¼ tsp salt. Gently salad toss to combine.

PER SERVING 339 CAL; 18 g **FAT** (3 g **SAT**); 23 g **PRO**; 22 g **CARB**; 3 g **FIBER**; 751 mg **SODIUM**; 56 mg **CHOL**

Seafood and Spring Veggie Chowder

MAKES 5 servings **PREP** 24 minutes
SLOW COOK on HIGH for 4 hours 30 minutes plus 15 minutes or LOW for 6 hours 45 minutes plus 15 minutes

- 2 leeks, white and light-green parts only, sliced and cleaned well
- 2 medium carrots, peeled and sliced in half-moons
- 1 large rib celery, diced
- 1 lb russet potatoes, peeled and diced
- 2 cups milk
- 2 cups reduced-sodium vegetable broth
- 1 tsp Old Bay seasoning
- ½ tsp garlic powder
  Pinch ground nutmeg
- 1 bunch pencil-thin asparagus, trimmed and cut into ¼- to ½-inch pieces
- ½ lb peeled, deveined shrimp, cut in half
- ½ lb small bay scallops (thawed, if frozen)
- ½ lb lump crabmeat or imitation crab (surimi), torn into small pieces
- 3 tbsp instant potato flakes
  Salt and pepper to taste (optional)

■ Coat a 3½- or 4-qt slow cooker with nonstick cooking spray. Add leeks, carrots, celery and potatoes. Stir in milk, vegetable broth, Old Bay seasoning, garlic powder and nutmeg. Cover and cook on HIGH for 4½ hours or LOW for 6 hours 45 minutes.

■ Uncover and stir in asparagus, shrimp, scallops, crab and potato flakes. Recover and cook for an additional 15 minutes (on either HIGH or LOW; see Note). Season to taste with salt and pepper, if desired.

Tip: Seafood cooks very quickly and can easily get tough. Make sure that shrimp and scallops are opaque yet tender and crab is heated through.

PER SERVING 330 CAL; 5 g **FAT** (2 g **SAT**); 29 g **PRO**; 44 g **CARB**; 5 g **FIBER**; 957 mg **SODIUM**; 103 mg **CHOL**

POACHED
SALMON SALAD

SCALLOP
FRISÉE SALAD

- In the same skillet, add corn and cook until charred, about 3 minutes. Stir occasionally.

- In a large bowl, toss greens, frisée and fennel with half the dressing. Add scallops and corn. Serve with remaining dressing and, if desired, lemon wedges.

PER SERVING 496 CAL; 22 g FAT (3 g SAT); 44 g PRO; 36 g CARB; 4 g FIBER; 800 mg SODIUM; 103 mg CHOL

Straw-and-Hay Linguine with Arrabbiata Sauce and Bay Scallops

MAKES 6 servings PREP 15 minutes
COOK 16 minutes

- 2 tbsp olive oil
- 4 cloves garlic, sliced
- 1 can (28 oz) San Marzano tomatoes, drained and broken up
- 1 tsp red pepper flakes
- 1 tsp sugar
- ½ tsp salt
- 1½ lb frozen bay scallops, thawed
- ½ lb spinach linguine
- ½ lb traditional linguine
- ⅓ cup shredded ricotta salata
- ½ cup sliced fresh basil

- In a medium saucepan, heat oil over medium-high heat; add garlic and cook 2 minutes. Add tomatoes, red pepper flakes, sugar and salt. Simmer, covered, 10 minutes, stirring occasionally.

- Stir in scallops and simmer an additional 3 to 4 minutes or until cooked through.

- Meanwhile, cook pasta following package directions, about 8 minutes. Drain, reserving ¼ cup pasta cooking water.

- In a large serving bowl, toss pasta with tomato sauce and scallops. Add pasta water as needed to loosen sauce.

- Top with ricotta salata and basil. Serve immediately.

PER SERVING 470 CAL; 9 g FAT (2 g SAT); 25 g PRO; 72 g CARB; 5 g FIBER; 855 mg SODIUM; 30 mg CHOL

Scallop Frisée Salad

MAKES 4 servings PREP 20 minutes
COOK 7 minutes

DRESSING

- ½ cup buttermilk
- ¼ cup reduced-fat sour cream
- ¼ cup reduced-fat mayonnaise
- ¼ cup snipped chives
- 1 tsp lemon juice
- ¼ tsp salt
- ¼ tsp black pepper
- ½ cup finely chopped, peeled seedless cucumber

SCALLOPS AND SALAD

- 3 tbsp canola oil
- 1¼ lb large sea scallops, halved horizontally
- ⅓ cup all-purpose flour
- ¼ tsp salt
- ¼ tsp black pepper
  Kernels from 3 ears of corn
- 8 cups spring salad greens
- ½ large bunch frisée
- ½ fennel bulb, trimmed and thinly sliced
  Lemon wedges (optional)

- Dressing. In a medium bowl, whisk buttermilk, sour cream, mayonnaise, chives, lemon juice, salt and pepper. Stir in cucumber. Refrigerate.

- Scallops and Salad. Heat 2 tbsp of the oil in a large nonstick skillet over medium-high heat. Coat scallops in flour and add half to skillet; cook 2 minutes per side. Season with ⅛ tsp each of the salt and pepper. Remove to a plate. Add remaining 1 tbsp oil to skillet and cook remaining scallops. Season with remaining ⅛ tsp each salt and pepper. Remove to plate.

**STRAW-AND-HAY LINGUINE WITH
ARRABBIATA SAUCE AND BAY SCALLOPS**

SHRIMP FETTUCCINE WITH
CREAMY CAPER SAUCE

Shrimp Fettuccine with Creamy Caper Sauce

MAKES 4 servings **PREP** 15 minutes
COOK 12 minutes

- 1 **box (12 oz) spinach fettuccine**
- 1 **tbsp olive oil**
- 1 **small red onion, halved and sliced**
- 2 **cloves garlic, sliced**
- 1 **lb cleaned raw shrimp, thawed, if frozen**
- ⅔ **cup garden vegetable cream cheese**
- ⅓ **cup heavy cream**
- 2 **tbsp fresh dill, chopped**
- 2 **tbsp capers**
- 2 **tbsp lemon juice**
- ½ **tsp black pepper**
- ¼ **tsp salt**

■ Bring a large pot of lightly salted water to a boil. Add fettuccine and stir so strands do not stick together. Cook 12 minutes or per package directions. Drain, reserving ½ cup of the pasta water.

■ Meanwhile, heat oil in a large nonstick skillet over medium heat. Add onion and garlic and cook 5 minutes. Stir in shrimp, cream cheese, cream, dill, capers, lemon juice, pepper and salt. Cook 3 to 5 minutes, until shrimp are cooked through.

■ Stir cooked pasta into sauce, along with some of the reserved pasta water. Serve immediately.

PER SERVING 597 **CAL**; 23 g **FAT** (12 g **SAT**); 33 g **PRO**; 66 g **CARB**; 4 g **FIBER**; 745 mg **SODIUM**; 221 mg **CHOL**

Linguine with Scallops, Red Pepper and Broccolini

MAKES 4 servings **PREP** 10 minutes
COOK 10 minutes

- 8 **oz linguine**
- 1 **bunch Broccolini, cut into 1-inch pieces**
- 1 **red sweet pepper, seeded and thinly sliced**
- 2 **tbsp olive oil**
- 2 **tbsp unsalted butter**

LINGUINE WITH SCALLOPS, RED PEPPER AND BROCCOLINI

- 1 **lb scallops, tough muscle removed, rinsed**
- 3 **tbsp Wondra flour**
- ¾ **tsp salt**
- ½ **tsp black pepper**
- 6 **cloves garlic, finely chopped**
- 2 **tsp cornstarch**
- ½ **cup vegetable broth**
- 3 **tbsp chopped fresh parsley**
- 2 **tbsp lemon juice**
- 2 **tbsp grated Parmesan cheese**

■ Cook pasta according to package directions, about 9 minutes; add Broccolini and red pepper during last 2 minutes of cooking. Reserve ½ cup cooking water. Drain.

■ Meanwhile, heat 1 tbsp each of the oil and butter in a large stainless skillet over medium-high heat. Coat scallops with flour and season with ¼ tsp each of the salt and black pepper. Sauté 2 minutes per side; reserve. Add remaining 1 tbsp oil and butter to skillet and cook garlic for 30 seconds. Combine cornstarch and broth; add to skillet and simmer for 1 minute.

■ Add pasta, parsley, lemon juice, remaining ½ tsp salt, remaining ¼ tsp pepper and scallops. Toss gently to combine and simmer for 1 minute. Add some of the reserved cooking water, if needed.

■ Spoon into a large serving bowl. Sprinkle with Parmesan.

PER SERVING 500 **CAL**; 15 g **FAT** (5 g **SAT**); 30 g **PRO**; 59 g **CARB**; 4 g **FIBER**; 702 mg **SODIUM**; 55 mg **CHOL**

Lemony Shrimp Linguine

MAKES 6 servings **PREP** 15 minutes
COOK 13 minutes

1	box (12 oz) whole wheat linguine
¼	cup olive oil
⅓	cup fresh lemon juice, plus 1 tbsp lemon zest
½	tsp salt
¼	tsp black pepper
1½	lb peeled and deveined shrimp
1	bulb fennel, cored, thinly sliced
½	sweet onion, thinly sliced
3	cloves garlic, sliced
½	cup chopped pitted Kalamata olives
½	cup fresh parsley, chopped

■ Bring a pot of lightly salted water to a boil. Add linguine and cook 9 minutes or until al dente.

■ Meanwhile, in a small bowl, whisk 2 tbsp of the olive oil with the lemon juice, lemon zest, salt and pepper. Set aside.

■ Heat 1 tbsp of the olive oil in a large skillet over medium heat. Add shrimp. Sauté 1 minute; flip and sauté 1 to 2 minutes more, until just cooked. Remove to a plate. Add remaining 1 tbsp olive oil to skillet; stir in fennel and onion. Cook 7 minutes, until softened. Stir in garlic; cook 1 minute. Stir in reserved olive oil-lemon mixture. Bring to a simmer and cook 1 minute.

■ Remove cooked pasta from pot with tongs and add to skillet, along with 1 cup of the pasta water, the cooked shrimp and olives. Bring to a simmer and cook 1 minute. Stir in parsley. Serve immediately.

PER SERVING 402 **CAL**; 14 g **FAT** (2 g **SAT**); 27 g **PRO**; 49 g **CARB**; 9 g **FIBER**; 582 mg **SODIUM**; 168 mg **CHOL**

Singapore Shrimp Noodles

MAKES 4 servings **PREP** 15 minutes
SOAK 10 minutes **MICROWAVE** 2 minutes

1	pkg (7 oz) vermicelli rice noodles
3	tbsp vegetable oil
3	tbsp low-sodium soy sauce
2	tbsp rice vinegar

- 2 tbsp curry powder
- 2 tsp sesame oil
- 1 1-inch piece ginger, peeled and grated
- 1 clove garlic, grated
- 1 lb frozen cooked, peeled and deveined shrimp, thawed
- 1 red sweet pepper, thinly sliced
- 1 bunch scallions, sliced
- 1 cup bean sprouts
- 1 jalapeño, thinly sliced
- ¼ cup fresh cilantro, chopped

■ In a large bowl, cover rice noodles with 2 inches of very hot water. Soak for 10 minutes. Microwave for 2 minutes. Let cool slightly, then carefully remove noodles to a cutting board, reserving ¼ cup of the soaking liquid. Cut noodles into thirds.

■ In the same bowl, whisk together reserved liquid, vegetable oil, soy sauce, vinegar, curry powder, sesame oil, ginger and garlic. Return noodles to bowl; toss with shrimp, red pepper, scallions, bean sprouts, jalapeño and cilantro.

PER SERVING 427 CAL; 15 g FAT (2 g SAT); 29 g PRO; 44 g CARB; 4 g FIBER; 717 mg SODIUM; 221 mg CHOL

Moroccan Shrimp and Couscous

MAKES 4 servings PREP 20 minutes
COOK 12 minutes BAKE at 400° for 12 minutes

- 1 tsp ground cumin
- ½ tsp salt
- ½ tsp ground cinnamon
- ½ tsp ground turmeric
- ¼ tsp ground ginger
- ⅛ tsp ground cayenne
- 1 tbsp olive oil
- ¼ cup minced shallots
- 2 cloves garlic, minced
- 1 cup whole wheat Israeli couscous
- 1¼ lb peeled and deveined shrimp (tails left on)
- 1 cup dried apricots
- 1 cup pitted dates
- 8 large Italian- or Spanish-style green olives with pits

MOROCCAN SHRIMP AND COUSCOUS

- 2 tbsp lemon juice, plus 1 tsp zest
- 2 tbsp white wine, chicken broth or water
- ½ cup fresh parsley, chopped
- ½ cup fresh cilantro, chopped
- ¼ cup chopped almonds

■ Heat oven to 400°. In a small bowl, combine cumin, salt, cinnamon, turmeric, ginger and cayenne.

■ Heat olive oil in a medium pot over medium heat. Add half each of the shallots, garlic and spice mixture. Cook 2 minutes, until soft. Stir in couscous and 1¼ cups water; cover and bring to a boil. Reduce to a simmer and cook for 8 to 10 minutes. Set aside, covered.

■ In a large bowl, toss shrimp with apricots, dates, olives, lemon juice and zest, wine and remaining shallots, garlic and spice mixture. Transfer to 2 large parchment cooking bags (such as PaperChef brand) and seal per package directions. Place bags on a rimmed baking sheet. Bake at 400° for 10 to 12 minutes. Carefully open to release steam; toss in a bowl with parsley, cilantro and almonds. Serve shrimp over couscous.

PER SERVING 550 CAL; 10 g FAT (1 g SAT); 30 g PRO; 88 g CARB; 10 g FIBER; 882 mg SODIUM; 211 mg CHOL

SHRIMP
MARINARA

Shrimp Marinara

MAKES 6 servings **PREP** 20 minutes
COOK 34 minutes

- 2 **tbsp olive oil**
- 6 **cloves garlic, sliced**
- 2 **cans (28 oz each) crushed tomatoes**
- 1 **can (14.5 oz) no-salt-added diced tomatoes**
- 2 **tsp sugar**
- 2 **tsp dried oregano**
- 1 **tsp salt**
- ½ **tsp red pepper flakes**
- 1 **lb medium shrimp, peeled and deveined**
- 1 **cup frozen green peas, thawed**
- 1 **pkg (13.25 oz each) whole wheat penne**
- ½ **cup fresh basil leaves, torn (optional)**
- **Sautéed broccoli rabe (optional)**

■ Heat oil in a large pot over medium-high heat; add garlic and cook for 1 to 2 minutes, until golden. Stir in crushed tomatoes, diced tomatoes, sugar, oregano, salt and red pepper flakes. Bring to a boil; reduce heat to medium and simmer, with lid ajar, for 30 minutes. Stir occasionally.

■ Spoon half the sauce, about 3½ cups, into a container and cool. Cover and refrigerate or freeze for another use.

■ Stir shrimp and peas into remaining sauce. Cook for 2 minutes or until shrimp are cooked through.

■ Meanwhile, cook penne following package directions.

■ To serve, toss remaining penne with shrimp sauce and, if desired, basil. Serve with sautéed broccoli rabe, if desired.

PER SERVING 410 **CAL**; 5 g **FAT** (1 g **SAT**); 27 g **PRO**; 62 g **CARB**; 10 g **FIBER**; 552 mg **SODIUM**; 115 mg **CHOL**

Shrimp Pad Thai

MAKES 4 servings **PREP** 15 minutes
SOAK 30 minutes **COOK** 9 minutes 30 seconds

- ½ **pkg (16 oz) rice noodles (8 oz total)**
- 3 **tbsp packed light brown sugar**
- 2 **tbsp plus 1 tsp fish sauce**
- 1 **tbsp balsamic vinegar**
- ¼ **tsp cayenne pepper**
- 2 **tbsp canola oil**
- 3 **cloves garlic, chopped**
- ¾ **lb raw peeled and deveined shrimp**
- 3 **eggs**
- 1 **cup bean sprouts**
- 1 **cup sliced scallions**
- ⅓ **cup chopped roasted unsalted peanuts, plus more for garnish**
- 1 **lime, cut into wedges (optional)**
- **Fresh cilantro (optional)**

■ Soak noodles in water for 30 minutes or according to package directions. Drain; set aside.

■ In a small bowl, stir together brown sugar, fish sauce, vinegar and cayenne; set aside. Heat oil in a large nonstick skillet over medium-high heat. Add garlic; sauté 30 seconds. Stir in shrimp; sauté 2 minutes, flipping once. Move garlic and shrimp to side of pan closest to handle. Tilt skillet so that empty side is closest to burner; add noodles and ½ cup water. Stir noodles for 3 to 4 minutes, until almost all the water is absorbed, keeping skillet tilted and shrimp untouched. Return entire pan to burner. Pour in fish sauce-brown sugar mixture and stir, combining shrimp and noodles. Make a well in the center. Add 1 egg; when white starts to set (it takes about 1 minute), break yolk with a rubber spatula, scramble and mix into shrimp-noodle mixture. Repeat with remaining 2 eggs, making a well each time. Stir in bean sprouts, ¾ cup of the scallions and the peanuts.

■ Serve immediately. Garnish with remaining ¼ cup scallions and, if desired, chopped peanuts, a squeeze of lime and fresh cilantro.

PER SERVING 498 **CAL**; 18 g **FAT** (3 g **SAT**); 26 g **PRO**; 59 g **CARB**; 3 g **FIBER**; 1,020 mg **SODIUM**; 285 mg **CHOL**

SHRIMP PAD THAI

SHRIMP TOSTADAS

lettuce, tomatoes, onion, cucumber and cilantro. Squeeze a wedge of lime over each. Serve with salsa and, if desired, sour cream on the side.

PER SERVING 329 **CAL**; 13 g **FAT** (2 g **SAT**); 22 g **PRO**; 31 g **CARB**; 4 g **FIBER**; 741 mg **SODIUM**; 179 mg **CHOL**

Hoisin Shrimp with Bok Choy, Shiitakes and Peppers

MAKES 4 servings **PREP** 20 minutes
ROAST 20 minutes at 450°

- ¼ cup hoisin sauce
- 2 tbsp reduced-sodium soy sauce, plus more for serving (optional)
- 1 tbsp rice wine vinegar
- 2 tsp sesame oil
- 1 tsp sriracha
- 1 large bok choy, cut into 3-inch pieces
- 2 red sweet peppers, seeded and cut into ½-inch strips
- 1 lb small shiitake mushrooms, stems removed
- 2 tbsp canola oil
- 1½ lb jumbo shrimp, peeled and deveined
- 2 tsp toasted sesame seeds
  Chopped scallions (optional)

■ Heat oven to 450°. Line a 13 x 9-inch rimmed sheet pan with nonstick foil.

■ In a small bowl, combine hoisin, soy sauce, vinegar, sesame oil and sriracha. Set aside.

■ Place bok choy, peppers and shiitakes on prepared sheet pan. Combine 3 tbsp of the hoisin mixture with canola oil. Pour over vegetables and toss to coat.

■ Toss shrimp with remaining hoisin mixture. Place shrimp over vegetables.

■ Roast at 450° for 20 minutes. Garnish with sesame seeds and, if desired, scallions. Serve with additional soy sauce, if desired.

Shrimp Tostadas

MAKES 4 servings **PREP** 20 minutes
BAKE at 450° for 7 minutes **BROIL** 4 minutes

- ½ cup reduced-fat mayonnaise
- 1 tbsp lime juice
- 1 tsp brown sugar
- ¼ tsp chipotle chile powder
- 8 white corn tortillas
- 1 lb large shrimp, shells removed, deveined
- ¼ tsp salt
- ⅛ tsp black pepper
- 4 cups shredded iceberg lettuce
- 2 plum tomatoes, cored and diced
- 1 small red onion, chopped
- ½ cucumber, peeled and cut into thin matchsticks
- ½ cup cilantro leaves
- 1 lime, cut into wedges
- ½ cup prepared tomato salsa
  Sour cream (optional)

■ In a small bowl, whisk together mayonnaise, lime juice, brown sugar and chile powder. Refrigerate.

■ Heat oven to 450°. Place 2 racks on each of 2 baking sheets. Place tortillas on racks and lightly spritz both sides with nonstick cooking spray. Bake at 450° for 5 to 7 minutes or until crisp. Remove tortillas from oven and reserve.

■ Heat broiler. Coat broiler pan with nonstick cooking spray. Season shrimp with salt and pepper and place on broiler pan. Broil for 2 minutes per side or until cooked through. Remove shrimp to a plate.

■ Spread top of each tortilla with about 1 tbsp of mayonnaise mixture. Top with equal amounts shrimp,

HOISIN SHRIMP WITH
BOK CHOY, SHIITAKES
AND PEPPERS

WHITE PIZZA WITH
ARUGULA, LEMON,
PARMESAN AND RICOTTA,
RECIPE PAGE 163

Vegetarian

Let meat take a backseat once in a while with vegetarian recipes that can satisfy even the heartiest appetite.

about 3 minutes. Transfer to a bowl. Sprinkle tops of macaroni and cheese with crumbs. Bake on a cookie sheet at 350° on the middle rack until hot and crumbs are golden brown, about 20 minutes.

PER SERVING 390 **CAL**; 18 g **FAT** (11 g **SAT**); 15 g **PRO**; 42 g **CARB**; 2 g **FIBER**; 432 mg **SODIUM**; 53 mg **CHOL**

Fettuccine Alfredo

MAKES 6 servings **PREP** 10 minutes
COOK 10 minutes

- 1 **lb fettuccine**
- 1 **cup frozen peas, thawed**
- 1 **small red sweet pepper, cored, seeded and thinly sliced**
- ½ **cup fat-free half-and-half**
- ⅓ **cup heavy cream**
- 2 **tbsp unsalted butter**
- 1 **tsp garlic powder**
- ¾ **tsp salt**
- ¼ **tsp black pepper**
- 4 **tbsp reduced-fat cream cheese**
- ¾ **cup grated Parmesan cheese**
- ¼ **cup fresh parsley, chopped**

■ Cook fettuccine following package directions, about 10 minutes. Add peas and red pepper during last minute of cooking. Drain.

■ Meanwhile, in a medium saucepan, combine half-and-half, cream, butter, garlic powder, salt and black pepper. Bring to a simmer; gradually whisk in cream cheese and take off heat. Stir in ½ cup of the Parmesan.

■ Place drained pasta mixture in a large bowl and toss with sauce. Sprinkle with remaining ¼ cup Parmesan and the chopped parsley. Serve immediately.

PER SERVING 412 **CAL**; 18 g **FAT** (11 g **SAT**); 18 g **PRO**; 47 g **CARB**; 3 g **FIBER**; 655 mg **SODIUM**; 96 mg **CHOL**

INDIVIDUAL MAC AND CHEESE

Individual Mac and Cheese

MAKES 8 servings **PREP** 45 minutes
COOK 15 minutes **BAKE** at 350° for 20 minutes

- 4 **tbsp unsalted butter**
- 1 **small onion, chopped**
- 1 **rib celery, chopped**
- 1½ **tsp chopped fresh thyme**
- 2 **tbsp all-purpose flour**
- 1½ **cups hot whole milk**
- ¼ **lb cheddar cheese, coarsely grated**
- ¼ **lb Fontina cheese, coarsely grated**
- ½ **tsp finely grated fresh nutmeg**
- ¾ **lb tubular pasta, such as tubetti or tubettini**
- **Salt and black pepper to taste**
- 1½ **cups fresh bread crumbs (from about 3 slices firm white sandwich bread)**

■ Melt 2 tbsp of the butter in a large skillet over medium heat. Add onion, celery and thyme; cook, stirring, until vegetables are softened, about 4 minutes. Add flour and cook, stirring constantly, until flour is golden, about 4 minutes. Add milk in a slow stream, whisking constantly. Cook until thickened and reduced to 1½ cups, about 4 minutes. Remove pan from heat; whisk in cheeses and nutmeg.

■ Meanwhile, bring a large pot of salted water to a boil. Stir in pasta; cook until al dente, about 7 minutes. Drain pasta; return to pot. Gently stir together pasta, cheese mixture and salt and pepper to taste. Spoon into eight 5- to 8-oz ovenproof dishes.

■ Heat oven to 350°. Melt remaining 2 tbsp butter in a nonstick skillet over medium heat. Add bread crumbs and cook, stirring, until golden,

FETTUCCINE ALFREDO

Summertime Linguine

MAKES 6 servings **PREP** 15 minutes
COOK 14 minutes

- 4 ears yellow corn, shucked
- ½ lb haricots verts, halved
- 1 lb linguine or fettuccine
- ¼ cup extra-virgin olive oil
- 6 plum tomatoes (about 14 oz), cored and cut into 1-inch pieces
- 1 orange sweet pepper, sliced
- 2 cloves garlic, sliced
- 3 scallions, sliced
- 2 tbsp fresh lemon juice
- 2 tbsp chopped fresh parsley
- ¾ tsp salt
- ¼ tsp cracked black pepper
- Grated Parmesan cheese (optional)

■ Bring a large pot of lightly salted water to a boil. Add corn and haricots verts; cook for 2 minutes. Remove with a slotted spoon to a large bowl.

■ Return water to a boil and add linguine. Cook for 12 minutes or per package directions. Drain, reserving ½ cup of the pasta water.

■ Meanwhile, heat 3 tbsp of the olive oil in a large skillet over medium heat. Cut corn kernels from cobs and set aside. Add tomatoes, sweet pepper, garlic and scallions to skillet. Cook, stirring, for 3 minutes.

■ In a large bowl, toss pasta with remaining 1 tbsp olive oil. Add tomato mixture, corn, haricots verts, lemon juice, parsley, salt and black pepper. Gently toss and add some reserved pasta water if mixture is too dry. If desired, stir in Parmesan to taste.

PER SERVING 466 **CAL**; 13 g **FAT** (2 g **SAT**); 16 g **PRO**; 77 g **CARB**; 6 g **FIBER**; 354 mg **SODIUM**; 3 mg **CHOL**

Swiss Chard and Mushroom Lasagna

MAKES 8 servings **PREP** 30 minutes
COOK 17 minutes **BAKE** at 400° for 50 minutes
COOL 20 minutes

- 2 tbsp olive oil
- 3 cloves garlic, chopped
- 1 lb Swiss chard, stems removed, cut crosswise into 1-inch slices
- 1 lb baby bella mushrooms, sliced
- ½ tsp salt
- ¼ tsp black pepper
- 2 tbsp unsalted butter
- ¼ cup all-purpose flour
- 2½ cups fat-free milk
- ¼ tsp ground nutmeg
- ⅛ tsp cayenne pepper
- 12 uncooked lasagna noodles
- 1 container (15 oz) part-skim ricotta cheese
- 1 cup shredded Fontina cheese

1 egg, lightly beaten

2 cups shredded part-skim mozzarella

½ cup grated Grana Padano or Parmigiano-Reggiano cheese

■ Heat oven to 400°. Coat a 13 x 9 x 2-inch baking dish with nonstick cooking spray.

■ In a large nonstick skillet, heat olive oil over medium-high heat. Add garlic, Swiss chard, mushrooms, ¼ tsp of the salt and the black pepper. Cook 7 minutes, stirring occasionally. Spoon off any excess liquid.

■ Meanwhile, in a medium saucepan, melt butter over medium heat; stir in flour and cook 1 minute. Gradually whisk in milk. Bring to a simmer; cook, stirring frequently, 3 minutes or until thickened. Add remaining ¼ tsp salt, the nutmeg and cayenne.

■ Cook lasagna noodles following package directions, about 10 minutes. Drain. Combine ricotta, Fontina and egg.

■ Spread ¼ cup of white sauce in baking dish. Layer as follows: 3 noodles, ricotta mixture, 3 noodles, 1 cup of the sauce, chard mixture, ½ cup of the mozzarella, 3 noodles, remaining 1½ cups mozzarella and 3 noodles. Spread remaining ¾ cup sauce over noodles and sprinkle Grana Padano over top.

■ Cover and bake at 400° for 30 minutes. Uncover and bake an additional 20 minutes. Cool 20 minutes before serving.

PER SERVING 458 CAL; 20 g FAT (10 g SAT); 29 g PRO; 43 g CARB; 3 g FIBER; 790 mg SODIUM; 87 mg CHOL

Easy Veggie Lasagna

MAKES 10 servings PREP 30 minutes
BROIL 10 minutes BAKE at 375° for 1 hour 5 minutes STAND 20 minutes

12 traditional lasagna noodles

4 zucchini (about 1¾ lb), trimmed and sliced lengthwise (24 slices total)

1 tbsp olive oil

¼ tsp salt

¼ tsp black pepper

EASY VEGGIE LASAGNA

2 containers (16 oz each) 2% cottage cheese

2 egg yolks

¼ cup fresh basil, chopped

1 jar (24 oz) marinara sauce

1 can (14.5 oz) diced tomatoes, drained

1 box (9 oz) frozen artichoke hearts, thawed and chopped

3 cups shredded part-skim mozzarella

Chopped fresh parsley (optional)

■ Place dry noodles in a large bowl and add the hottest tap water you can. Soak 20 minutes.

■ Meanwhile, heat broiler. Toss zucchini with oil and ⅛ tsp each of the salt and pepper. Spread onto 1 large or 2 small baking sheets. Broil 5 minutes; flip slices over and broil an additional 5 minutes. Set aside. Lower oven temp to 375°.

■ In a medium bowl, beat cottage cheese, egg yolks, basil and remaining ⅛ tsp each salt and pepper.

■ Coat a 13 x 9 x 2-inch baking dish with nonstick cooking spray. Spread ½ cup of the marinara on bottom

of dish. Top with 3 of the soaked noodles. Top noodles with 2 cups of the cottage cheese mixture. Add 3 more noodles to dish. Top noodles with half the zucchini slices. Combine remaining marinara sauce, the diced tomatoes and chopped artichoke hearts. Spread half over zucchini. Top with 3 noodles. Layer with remaining 2 cups cottage cheese mixture, remaining zucchini slices and 1 cup of the mozzarella. Add remaining 3 noodles and remaining marinara mixture. Top with remaining 2 cups mozzarella.

■ Cover with nonstick foil and bake at 375° for 35 minutes. Uncover dish and bake an additional 30 minutes, until cheese is melted, edges are bubbly and noodles are tender when pierced with a knife. Sprinkle lasagna with chopped parsley, if desired, and let stand 20 minutes before slicing.

PER SERVING 390 CAL; 13 g FAT (6 g SAT); 26 g PRO; 42 g CARB; 5 g FIBER; 965 mg SODIUM; 74 mg CHOL

HEARTY TUSCAN LINGUINE

Cheesy Noodle Casserole

MAKES 6 servings **PREP** 25 minutes
SLOW COOK on HIGH for 3½ hours or LOW for 7 hours, plus 20 minutes on HIGH

2½	cups water
1	can (10.75 oz) reduced-fat and reduced-sodium condensed cream of mushroom soup
1	can (14.5 oz) no-salt-added diced tomatoes, undrained
1	cup sliced celery (2 stalks)
1	cup sliced carrots (2 medium)
1	cup chopped onion (1 large)
1½	tsp dried Italian seasoning, crushed
2	cloves garlic, minced
¼	tsp salt
¼	tsp black pepper
8	oz dried extra-wide noodles
1	pkg (16-oz) extra-firm tofu (fresh bean curd), drained, if necessary, and cubed*
½	cup shredded reduced-fat cheddar cheese (2 oz)

■ In a 3½- or 4-qt slow cooker whisk together the water and cream of mushroom soup. Stir in tomatoes, celery, carrots, onion, Italian seasoning, garlic, salt and pepper.

■ Cover and cook on HIGH for 3½ to 4 hours or LOW for 7 to 8 hours

■ Stir in uncooked noodles; cover and cook on HIGH for 20 to 30 minutes more or until tender, stirring once halfway through cooking. Gently stir in tofu cubes. Sprinkle with cheese; cover and let stand until cheese is melted.

*Tip: To drain tofu, place it on a paper towel-lined plate for 15 minutes.

PER SERVING 316 CAL; 8 g FAT (2 g SAT); 17 g PRO; 42 g CARB; 4 g FIBER; 447 mg SODIUM; 44 mg CHOL

Hearty Tuscan Linguine

MAKES 6 servings **PREP** 15 minutes
SLOW COOK on HIGH for 4 hours or LOW for 6 hours

1	large onion, sliced
½	cup packed in oil sun-dried tomatoes, drained and sliced
4	cloves garlic, sliced
1½	cups reduced-sodium vegetable broth
¼	cup tomato paste
1	tsp fresh rosemary, chopped
½	tsp dried oregano
½	tsp salt
¼	tsp black pepper
2	cans (15 oz each) cannellini beans, drained and rinsed
1	small bunch kale, rinsed and torn into bite-size pieces (about 6 cups)
1	lb linguine, cooked per pkg directions
2	tbsp olive oil
½	cup grated Parmesan cheese
½	cup toasted pine nuts

■ Coat a 3½- or 4-qt slow cooker with nonstick cooking spray.

■ Place onion, sun-dried tomatoes, garlic, broth, tomato paste, rosemary, oregano, ¼ tsp of the salt and the pepper in slow cooker. Stir to blend. Stir in beans; place kale on top.

■ Cover and cook on HIGH for 4 hours or LOW for 6 hours.

■ Add remaining ¼ tsp salt. In a large bowl, toss sauce with cooked linguine and olive oil. Stir in Parmesan and sprinkle with pine nuts.

PER SERVING 487 CAL; 17 g FAT (3 g SAT); 23 g PRO; 72 g CARB; 12 g FIBER; 762 mg SODIUM; 45 mg CHOL

Spaghetti with Brussels Sprouts and Hazelnuts

MAKES 8 servings **PREP** 15 minutes
COOK 8 minutes

1½	lb Brussels sprouts (about 7 cups), trimmed
1	lb spaghetti
6	tbsp extra-virgin olive oil
¼	cup sliced shallots
4	cloves garlic, sliced
½	cup hazelnuts, chopped
½	tsp salt
	Freshly cracked black pepper
1	cup grated Pecorino Romano cheese

■ Shred Brussels sprouts in a food processor fitted with a slicing blade. Set aside.

■ Bring a pot of salted water to a boil. Add spaghetti; cook 8 minutes. Drain, reserving ½ cup of the pasta water.

■ Meanwhile, in a large skillet, heat oil over medium heat. Stir in shallots and garlic; cook 2 minutes. Mix in shredded Brussels sprouts; cook 4 minutes. Using tongs, add spaghetti to skillet. Stir in pasta water, hazelnuts, salt, freshly cracked pepper to taste and ¾ cup of the Pecorino Romano. Toss well. Place in a serving bowl and sprinkle with remaining ¼ cup cheese.

PER SERVING 460 CAL; 21 g FAT (5 g SAT); 18 g PRO; 52 g CARB; 6 g FIBER; 422 mg SODIUM; 15 mg CHOL

SPAGHETTI WITH BRUSSELS
SPROUTS AND HAZELNUTS

GUACAMOLE WITH
GRILLED
QUESADILLAS

Guacamole with Grilled Quesadillas

MAKES 6 servings   **PREP** 20 minutes
COOK 10 minutes   **GRILL** 2 minutes per batch

GUACAMOLE

- **3** ripe avocados, peeled and pitted
- **2** tbsp fresh lime juice
- **¼** tsp salt
- **⅛** tsp black pepper
- **1** plum tomato, seeded and finely diced
- **¼** cup fresh cilantro leaves, chopped
- **1** jalapeño, seeded and finely chopped
- **2** large cloves garlic, chopped

GRILLED QUESADILLAS

- **1** tbsp unsalted butter
- **1** sweet onion, thinly sliced
- **¼** tsp salt
- **6** large tortillas (wraps)
- **3** cups grated Manchego cheese (12 oz.)

■ **Guacamole.** Cut avocados into large chunks and place in a medium bowl. Add lime juice, salt and black pepper and mash to desired consistency. Stir in tomato, cilantro, jalapeño and garlic. Set aside.

■ **Quesadillas.** Heat grill to medium-high heat. Melt butter in a cast-iron skillet set on grill rack. Add onion and salt and cook 10 minutes, stirring frequently. Carefully remove pan from grill.

■ Place 2 tortillas on grill and spread half of each with some of the onion. Grill 30 seconds. Sprinkle ½ cup of the cheese over each tortilla and fold to enclose filling. Grill 1 minute, then flip over and grill 30 more seconds. Repeat with remaining tortillas, onion and cheese. Cut each quesadilla into wedges and serve with guacamole.

PER ⅓ CUP GUACAMOLE 166 **CAL**; 15 g **FAT** (2 g **SAT**); 2 g **PRO**; 10 g **CARB**; 7 g **FIBER**; 105 mg **SODIUM**; 0 mg **CHOL**

PER QUESADILLA 465 **CAL**; 25 g **FAT** (13 g **SAT**); 23 g **PRO**; 36 g **CARB**; 8 g **FIBER**; 940 mg **SODIUM**; 64 mg **CHOL**

White Pizza with Arugula, Lemon, Parmesan and Ricotta

MAKES 6 servings   **PREP** 15 minutes
BAKE at 500° for 15 minutes

- **3** tbsp olive oil, plus more to grease pan and brush crust
- **1** lb pizza dough (homemade or purchased; thawed, if frozen)
- **1** ball (8 oz) fresh mozzarella, thinly sliced
- **5** cups packed arugula
- **½** cup freshly grated Parmesan cheese
- **2** tbsp fresh lemon juice (about half a lemon)
- **¼** tsp salt
- **⅛** tsp black pepper
- **¾** cup ricotta cheese

■ Heat oven to 500°. Grease a 17 x 12-inch rimmed baking sheet with olive oil. Drop pizza dough into center of greased sheet and use fingers to press out and flatten dough so it spreads as close as possible to corners of pan.

■ Scatter mozzarella slices over dough and brush exposed edge with olive oil. Bake for 15 minutes, until crust is crispy and cheese is bubbly. (If cheese browns too quickly, cover center of pizza with foil.)

■ While pizza bakes, toss together arugula, Parmesan, the 3 tbsp oil, the lemon juice, salt and pepper. When pizza is ready, let cool for about 2 minutes and top with salad. Top with 12 spoonfuls of ricotta (1 tbsp each). Cut into squares and serve.

WHITE PIZZA WITH ARUGULA, LEMON, PARMESAN AND RICOTTA

EGGPLANT PARMESAN

Eggplant Parmesan

MAKES 8 servings **PREP** 30 minutes
SLOW COOK on LOW for 6 hours
COOK 10 minutes

- **3 large eggs**
- **⅓ cup prepared pesto**
- **¼ cup milk**
- **1½ cups plain bread crumbs**
- **¼ cup plus 2 tbsp grated Parmesan**
- **4 cups spicy pasta sauce**
- **2 medium eggplants (about 2½ lb total), peeled and cut into ½-inch rounds**
- **1 pkg (8 oz) Italian cheese blend**
- **1 lb spaghetti**
- **2 tbsp olive oil**
- **Fresh basil (optional)**

■ In a medium bowl, whisk eggs, pesto and milk. In a second bowl, toss bread crumbs and ¼ cup Parmesan.

■ Set aside ½ cup of the sauce. Coat a 4- to 5-qt slow cooker with nonstick cooking spray. Spoon ½ cup of the sauce on bottom of slow cooker.

■ Dip each eggplant slice in egg mixture, then bread crumb mixture, and place on a cutting board. Layer one-third of the eggplant slices into slow cooker (about 8 pieces). Top with 1 cup sauce and ⅔ cup Italian cheese blend. Repeat twice. Cover and cook on LOW for 5½ to 6 hours.

■ During last 30 minutes of cooking time, bring a large pot of lightly salted water to a boil. Add spaghetti and cook 10 minutes. Drain and toss with remaining 2 tbsp Parmesan and the olive oil. Heat reserved sauce gently in microwave or saucepan. Serve alongside eggplant and spaghetti. Garnish with basil, if desired.

PER SERVING 606 **CAL**; 25 g **FAT** (8 g **SAT**); 25 g **PRO**; 73 g **CARB**; 10 g **FIBER**; 982 mg **SODIUM**; 108 mg **CHOL**

PUMPKIN FARROTTO

Pumpkin Farrotto

MAKES 6 servings **PREP** 15 minutes
COOK 6 minutes
SLOW COOK on HIGH for 4 hours

- 4 tbsp unsalted butter
- 1 medium onion, diced
- 2 cloves garlic, minced
- ¼ cup white wine (optional)
- 1½ cups whole farro (not pearled)
- 4 cups unsalted vegetable stock
- 1 can (15 oz) pumpkin puree
- 6 tbsp grated Parmesan
- 1 tbsp fresh sage, chopped
- 1 box (10 oz) frozen peas, thawed
- 1 tsp salt
- ¼ tsp black pepper
- ½ cup toasted walnuts, chopped

■ Melt 3 tbsp of the butter in a large skillet over medium heat. Add onion and cook, stirring, 3 minutes. Stir in garlic; cook 2 minutes. Add wine and farro; cook 1 minute or until most of the wine evaporates. Transfer to a 4-qt slow cooker.

■ Stir in vegetable stock, pumpkin, 4 tbsp of the Parmesan and the sage. Cover and cook on HIGH for 4 hours. Uncover and gently stir in peas, remaining 1 tbsp butter, the salt and pepper. Spoon into bowls and top with walnuts and remaining 2 tbsp Parmesan.

PER SERVING 436 **CAL**; 17 g **FAT** (6 g **SAT**); 16 g **PRO**; 55 g **CARB**; 14 g **FIBER**; 663 mg **SODIUM**; 24 mg **CHOL**

BUTTERNUT SQUASH–SWISS CHARD FRITTATA

Butternut Squash–Swiss Chard Frittata

MAKES 4 servings **PREP** 15 minutes
MICROWAVE 5 minutes **COOK** 11 minutes
BAKE at 400° for 10 minutes
REST 5 minutes

- 12 oz butternut squash, peeled and cut into ½-inch cubes
- 6 large eggs
- 4 egg whites
- ¾ tsp salt
- ⅛ tsp black pepper
- 2 tbsp olive oil
- ¼ cup diced shallots
- 2 cloves garlic, sliced
- 8 oz Swiss chard, chopped
- 2 oz plain goat cheese

■ Heat oven to 400°. Microwave squash and ¼ cup water in a dish, covered and vented, for 5 minutes. In a large bowl, whisk eggs, egg whites, salt and pepper. Heat oil in a 10-inch cast-iron skillet over medium heat. Sauté shallots and garlic 2 minutes. Add Swiss chard. Increase heat to high; cook 5 minutes, until water is mostly absorbed. Carefully stir in cubed squash; cook 2 minutes. Pour in eggs. Reduce heat to medium. Dot cheese on top. Cook 2 minutes.

■ Place skillet in oven and bake at 400° for 10 minutes, until set. Let rest 5 minutes, then loosen edges with a nonstick spatula. Slice into 4 pieces.

PER SERVING 271 **CAL**; 17 g **FAT** (5 g **SAT**); 18 g **PRO**; 13 g **CARB**; 3 g **FIBER**; 764 mg **SODIUM**; 324 mg **CHOL**

MEDITERRANEAN
GRATIN

Mediterranean Gratin

MAKES 4 servings **PREP** 20 minutes
BAKE at 400° for 1 hour 15 minutes
COOL 10 minutes

- 1½ **lb plum tomatoes, cut into ¼-inch slices**
- 1 **lb zucchini, cut into ¼-inch slices**
- 1 **lb small eggplant, cut into ¼-inch slices**
- ½ **medium red onion, cut into ¼-inch half-moons**
- 4 **cloves garlic, coarsely chopped**
- 6 **tbsp extra-virgin olive oil**
- ¾ **tsp coarse sea salt**
- ¼ **tsp black pepper**
- 1 **tbsp fresh marjoram leaves**
- ¾ **cup ricotta**
- 3 **tbsp grated Asiago cheese**
- 3 **tbsp whole-grain panko**

■ Heat oven to 400°. Grease a 2-qt oval baking dish.

■ Around edge of dish, alternately fan tomato and zucchini slices. They will be standing up on edge once finished. In middle of dish, fan eggplant slices so that they overlap. Randomly tuck in onion slices and sprinkle garlic over top. Drizzle 4 tbsp of the olive oil over gratin and season with salt and pepper. Sprinkle marjoram leaves over top.

■ Cover with foil and bake at 400° for 60 minutes. Dollop ricotta over top and sprinkle with Asiago and panko. Bake, uncovered, for an additional 15 minutes or until vegetables are tender.

■ Cool 10 minutes. Drizzle with remaining 2 tbsp olive oil and serve.

PER SERVING 375 **CAL**; 29 g **FAT** (8 g **SAT**); 11 g **PRO**; 23 g **CARB**; 8 g **FIBER**; 555 mg **SODIUM**; 28 mg **CHOL**

Israeli Poached Eggs (Shakshuka)

MAKES 4 servings **PREP** 10 minutes
COOK 25 minutes **STAND** 5 minutes

- 1 **tbsp olive oil**
- 1 **cup diced yellow onion**
- 3 **cloves garlic, sliced**
- 1 **tsp harissa paste**

ISRAELI POACHED EGGS
(SHAKSHUKA)

- 1 **tsp ground cumin**
- 1 **tsp ground turmeric**
- 1 **can (28 oz) Cento crushed tomatoes**
- 1 **jar (12 oz) roasted red peppers, drained and diced**
- ¼ **tsp salt**
- ½ **cup fresh cilantro, chopped, plus more for garnish**
- ½ **cup crumbled feta**
- 8 **eggs**
- 4 **whole wheat pitas, warmed (optional)**

■ Heat olive oil in a deep-sided skillet over medium heat. Add onion; cook

3 minutes. Stir in garlic, harissa, cumin and turmeric. Cook 2 more minutes. Mix in tomatoes, roasted peppers and salt. Simmer 10 minutes.

■ Stir in cilantro and two-thirds of the feta. Crack eggs, one by one, into a small dish and carefully pour them into sauce. Simmer 10 minutes. Cover and remove from heat. Let stand about 5 minutes, depending on desired doneness. Sprinkle with remaining feta. Garnish with additional cilantro. If desired, serve in bowls with pitas.

PER SERVING 395 **CAL**; 18 g **FAT** (6 g **SAT**); 23 g **PRO**; 35 g **CARB**; 9 g **FIBER**; 807 mg **SODIUM**; 440 mg **CHOL**

SPAGHETTI SQUASH
AND BLACK BEAN TACOS
WITH QUESO FRESCO

Spaghetti Squash and Black Bean Tacos with Queso Fresco

MAKES 4 servings PREP 15 minutes
MICROWAVE 17 minutes COOK 16 minutes

- **3** lb spaghetti squash (1 large)
- **2** tbsp lime juice
- **1** tbsp chili powder
- **½** tsp ground cumin
- **½** tsp ground coriander
- **½** tsp coarse salt
- **16** 6-inch corn tortillas
- **1** can (15 oz) black beans, drained and rinsed
- **4** oz queso fresco, feta or Cotija cheese, crumbled
- **¼** cup finely diced red or white onion
- **¼** cup chopped fresh cilantro
  Hot sauce and lime wedges (optional)

■ Pierce squash (about 1 inch deep) all over with a knife. Place in a microwave-safe dish and microwave for 7 minutes. Turn squash over and microwave another 8 to 10 minutes, until slightly soft. Cool 5 minutes. (Alternatively, you can roast squash. Cut in half lengthwise, scoop out seeds and roast, cut sides down, in an oiled baking pan at 375° for 40 minutes.)

■ Scoop squash flesh into a bowl, discarding seeds and skin. In a small bowl, whisk lime juice, chili powder, cumin, coriander and salt. Pour over squash and gently toss.

■ Heat a skillet over medium-high heat. Warm and slightly blister tortillas, about 30 seconds per side. Transfer to a platter and top each tortilla with 2 tbsp each beans and squash and 2 tsp cheese. Garnish with onion and cilantro and, if desired, hot sauce and lime wedges.

PER SERVING 430 CAL; 10 g FAT (4 g SAT); 17 g PRO; 69 g CARB; 15 g FIBER; 814 mg SODIUM; 20 mg CHOL

Pear-and-Pecan-Stuffed Squash

MAKES 4 servings PREP 20 minutes
ROAST at 400° for 30 minutes
MICROWAVE 1 minute
BROIL 3 minutes COOK 5 minutes

- **2** delicata or acorn squash, halved lengthwise and seeded
- **1** tbsp plus 1 tsp olive oil
- **½** tsp salt
- **1** cup cooked wheat berries
- **1** pear, peeled, cored and diced into small cubes
- **½** cup shredded Parmesan cheese
- **⅓** cup roughly chopped pecans
- **2** tsp chopped fresh sage
- **¼** tsp black pepper
- **4** cloves garlic, chopped
- **1** bag (10 oz) frozen kale
- **1** can (15.5 oz) butter beans, drained and rinsed
- **1** tsp lemon juice

■ Heat oven to 400°. Coat squash halves with 1 tbsp of the olive oil. Sprinkle cavities with ⅛ tsp of the salt. Place, cut sides down, on 2 baking sheets. Roast at 400° for 30 minutes.

■ Turn on broiler. In a microwave-safe bowl, combine cooked wheat berries, pear, ¼ cup of the Parmesan, the pecans, sage, ¼ tsp of the salt and ⅛ tsp of the pepper. Microwave for 1 minute. Carefully fill squash halves with mixture. Sprinkle with remaining ¼ cup Parmesan and broil for 2 to 3 minutes, until cheese is melted and lightly browned.

■ Meanwhile, in a medium pot, heat remaining 1 tsp olive oil over medium heat. Stir in garlic; cook 1 minute. Mix in frozen kale and ½ cup water. Bring to a boil. Cover and cook 3 minutes. Stir in butter beans, lemon juice, remaining ¼ tsp salt and remaining ⅛ tsp pepper. Cook 2 minutes, until beans are heated. Serve with squash.

PER SERVING 516 CAL; 16 g FAT (3 g SAT); 21 g PRO; 83 g CARB; 16 g FIBER; 787 mg SODIUM; 9 mg CHOL

RUSTIC GRILLED
VEGETABLE TART

Rustic Grilled Vegetable Tart

MAKES 8 servings **PREP** 30 minutes
GRILL 10 minutes **BAKE** at 450° for 10 minutes
and at 350° for 65 minutes **COOL** 15 minutes

- 1 **large ear of corn, shucked**
- 2 **plum tomatoes, halved lengthwise and seeded**
- 2 **scallions, trimmed**
- 1 **tbsp vegetable oil**
- 1 **refrigerated ready-to-roll piecrust (from a 14.1-oz pkg)**
- ¾ **cup shredded dill Havarti cheese**
- ⅛ **tsp salt**
- 3 **eggs**
- 1 **egg yolk**
- ½ **cup heavy cream**
- 1 **tbsp grainy mustard**
- **Dill for garnish (optional)**

■ Heat grill to medium-high. Brush corn, tomatoes and scallions with oil and place on grill. Grill corn 8 to 10 minutes, until lightly charred, turning often. Grill tomatoes and scallions 3 minutes, turning once until lightly charred. Chop tomatoes and scallions; cut kernels from cob.

■ Heat oven to 450°. On a well-floured surface, roll crust into a 17 x 7-inch rectangle and fit into a 13½ x 4½-inch rectangular tart pan with removable bottom. Prick bottom and sides of crust with fork. Line with foil; fill with pie weights or dry beans.

■ Bake at 450° for 10 minutes. Remove from oven, remove foil and weights. Reduce heat to 350°.

■ Toss together Havarti, corn, tomatoes and scallions; season with salt. Scatter over tart. Whisk together eggs, egg yolk, cream and mustard. Pour over corn and tomato mixture.

■ Place tart pan on a baking sheet. Bake at 350° for 55 to 65 minutes or until a knife inserted near center comes out clean. Remove to a wire rack and cool 15 minutes before removing side of pan. Garnish with dill, if desired.

PER SERVING 286 **CAL**; 20 g **FAT** (10 g **SAT**); 7 g **PRO**; 19 g **CARB**; 1 g **FIBER**; 280 mg **SODIUM**; 140 mg **CHOL**

HEIRLOOM
TOMATO PIE

Heirloom Tomato Pie

MAKES 6 servings **PREP** 15 minutes
LET STAND 10 minutes **BAKE** at 375° for
45 minutes **COOL** 15 minutes

- 2½ **lb heirloom tomatoes, sliced ¼ inch thick**
- ½ **tsp salt**
- 1 **refrigerated piecrust**
- ¼ **cup plain bread crumbs**
- 8 **oz fresh mozzarella, sliced ⅛ inch thick**
- ½ **cup fresh basil leaves**
- ¼ **cup shredded Parmesan**
- **Freshly cracked pepper**
- 1 **egg, beaten (optional)**

■ Heat oven to 375°. Place sliced tomatoes in a single layer on paper towels. Sprinkle 1 side of tomatoes with ¼ tsp of the salt; let stand for 10 minutes. Gently pat salted side of tomatoes with paper towels to absorb some of the moisture. Flip tomatoes and sprinkle with remaining ¼ tsp of the salt.

■ Meanwhile, fit piecrust into a 9-inch pie plate. Sprinkle bread crumbs evenly on the bottom. Place half the mozzarella over the bread crumbs, along with a third of the tomatoes and a third of the basil. Sprinkle with 2 tbsp of the Parmesan. Layer with a third of the tomatoes, a third of the basil and remaining mozzarella. Layer with remaining tomatoes, basil and Parmesan. Season with pepper and, if desired, brush edges of crust with beaten egg.

■ Bake at 375° for 40 to 45 minutes, until crust is browned. Cool 10 to 15 minutes before slicing.

PER SERVING 347 **CAL**; 20 g **FAT** (11 g **SAT**); 13 g **PRO**; 30 g **CARB**; 3 g **FIBER**; 687 mg **SODIUM**; 36 mg **CHOL**

Tip: For a less juicy pie seed the tomatoes.

PORTOBELLO PIZZA
CHEESEBURGERS

Portobello Pizza Cheeseburgers

MAKES 6 servings **PREP** 5 minutes
BROIL 15 minutes

- **1 lb small sweet peppers (such as Pero Family Farms)**
- **2 tbsp olive oil**
- **¼ tsp salt**
- **¼ tsp black pepper**
- **6 medium portobello mushrooms**
- **1 can (14.5 oz) Italian-seasoned diced tomatoes**
- **1 cup reduced-fat shredded Italian 4-cheese blend**
- **1 loaf (about 12 oz) crusty Italian bread, sliced in half horizontally and cut into 6 equal pieces**

■ Heat broiler to high. Set one rack 6 inches from heat source. Place second rack as far from heat source as possible.

■ Place peppers on a rimmed baking sheet. Toss with 1 tbsp of the olive oil and ⅛ tsp each of the salt and black pepper. Place on lower rack of oven and cook for 15 minutes, turning once halfway through, until peppers are tender and slightly browned.

■ Meanwhile, clean mushrooms and remove gills. Brush with remaining 1 tbsp oil and place on a separate baking sheet, cap sides up. Place on top rack and broil for 4 minutes. Turn and season with remaining ⅛ tsp each salt and pepper. Broil

for an additional 3 minutes. Fill with tomatoes and top each mushroom with 3 tbsp cheese. Broil for 3 to 4 minutes.

■ Place mushrooms between bread slices. Serve peppers on the side.

PER SERVING 307 **CAL**; 11 g **FAT** (3 g **SAT**); 13 g **PRO**; 40 g **CARB**; 5 g **FIBER**; 689 mg **SODIUM**; 10 mg **CHOL**

Hearty Veggie Chowder

MAKES 6 servings **PREP** 25 minutes
SLOW COOK on HIGH for 6 hours or LOW for 8 hours

- **2 large leeks (white and light green parts only), cleaned and thinly sliced**

HEARTY VEGGIE CHOWDER

1 lb diced butternut squash

½ lb parsnips, peeled and diced

½ lb carrots, sliced

⅔ cup barley

2 cloves garlic, sliced

1 box (32 oz) vegetable broth

1 can (14.5 oz) petite-cut diced tomatoes

1 tsp fresh thyme, chopped

1 box (10 oz) frozen corn, thawed

½ cup heavy cream

¼ cup chopped fresh parsley

¾ tsp salt

¼ tsp black pepper

⅛ tsp cayenne pepper

■ Combine leeks, squash, parsnips, carrots, barley and garlic in a 5-qt slow cooker. Stir in broth, 4 cups water, tomatoes and thyme. Cover and cook on HIGH for 6 hours or LOW for 8 hours.

■ Stir in corn, heavy cream, parsley, salt, black pepper and cayenne. Let sit until corn is heated through.

PER SERVING 309 CAL; 8 g FAT (5 g SAT); 7 g PRO; 56 g CARB; 10 g FIBER; 1,132 mg SODIUM; 27 mg CHOL

Potato-Broccoli Soup

MAKES 8 servings PREP 20 minutes
SLOW COOK on HIGH for 3 hours or LOW for 7 hours MICROWAVE 4 minutes

3½ lb russet potatoes, peeled and cut into 1½-inch pieces

1 large onion, cut into wedges

2 cloves garlic, coarsely chopped

POTATO-BROCCOLI SOUP

2 cans (14.5 oz each) vegetable broth

1 can (12 oz) evaporated milk

1 tsp salt

⅛ tsp ground nutmeg

1 lb broccoli florets, cut into bite-size pieces

8 oz sharp cheddar, shredded (white or orange)

½ cup sour cream

¼ tsp black pepper

Snipped fresh chives

■ Combine potatoes, onion and garlic in a 5-qt slow cooker. Add 1 can of broth, evaporated milk, ½ tsp of the salt and nutmeg. Cover and cook on HIGH for 3 hours or LOW for 7 hours.

■ Place broccoli in a microwave-safe bowl and add ½ cup water. Cover with plastic and microwave 3 to 4 minutes, until tender. Set aside 1½ cups of the broccoli; add remaining broccoli to slow cooker along with remaining can of vegetable broth and 1 cup of the cheddar. Puree with an immersion blender until completely smooth.

■ Stir in remaining ½ tsp salt and 1 cup cheddar, reserved broccoli, the sour cream and pepper. Ladle into bowls and sprinkle with chives just before serving.

PER SERVING 385 CAL; 15 g FAT (10 g SAT); 16 g PRO; 47 g CARB; 4 g FIBER; 988 mg SODIUM; 54 mg CHOL

WHITE BEAN AND FENNEL SOUP

Tomato Soup and Grilled Cheese Panini

MAKES 5 servings **PREP** 20 minutes
REFRIGERATE overnight **SLOW COOK** on HIGH
for 6 hours or on LOW for 8 hours
COOK 3 minutes per batch

- 3 **lb plum tomatoes**
- 2 **cloves garlic**
- 1 **can (14.5 oz) reduced-sodium vegetable broth**
- ¼ **cup fresh basil leaves, plus 15 large leaves for sandwiches**
- ¼ **tsp salt**
- ¼ **tsp black pepper**
- 10 **slices whole grain bread**
- 1 **tbsp jarred basil pesto**
- 8 **oz fresh mozzarella**
- 1 **large tomato**

■ The night before cooking, core, halve and seed plum tomatoes. Thinly slice garlic and combine in a resealable plastic bag with tomatoes. Refrigerate.

■ In the morning, combine tomatoes and garlic with broth and the ¼ cup basil leaves in a 4½-qt slow cooker. Season with salt and pepper, cover and cook on HIGH for 6 hours or on LOW for 8 hours.

■ Once soup is almost done, heat a panini press. Place 5 slices of the bread on a work surface. Spread ½ tsp pesto on each slice. Cut mozzarella and the large tomato into 10 thin slices each. Place 2 slices of the mozzarella on bread. Add 3 basil leaves to each sandwich and top each with 2 slices tomato. Top with 5 remaining bread slices and coat both sides of sandwiches with nonstick cooking spray. Cook sandwiches in panini press for 3 minutes, until browned and cheese is melted.

■ While sandwiches cook, ladle half the tomato mixture into a blender. Blend until smooth. Add remaining tomato mixture to blender if there is space (or do in batches); blend until smooth (or you can use an immersion blender). Divide among 5 bowls (about 1⅓ cups per serving). Serve each with a sandwich.

PER SERVING 408 **CAL**; 17 g **FAT** (8 g **SAT**); 19 g **PRO**; 42 g **CARB**; 9 g **FIBER**; 795 mg **SODIUM**; 47 mg **CHOL**

White Bean and Fennel Soup

MAKES 6 servings **PREP** 25 minutes
SOAK overnight **SLOW COOK** on HIGH for 6 hours **COOK** 9 minutes

- 1 **bag (16 oz) dried cannellini beans**
- 1 **fennel bulb, trimmed, quartered, cored and sliced**
- 1 **medium onion, chopped**
- 2 **cloves garlic, sliced**
- 1 **tsp Italian seasoning**
- 6 **cups vegetable stock**
- 1 **head escarole, cored, rinsed and chopped**
- 1 **can (14.5 oz) diced tomatoes, drained**
- 1 **cup mini pasta, such as farfellini**
- 1 **tsp salt**
  Grated Parmesan and freshly ground black pepper

■ Place cannellini beans in a bowl with 4 cups cold water. Cover with plastic and soak overnight.

■ Drain beans and transfer to a 6-qt slow cooker. Add fennel, onion, garlic and Italian seasoning. Pour in stock and 2 cups water. Cover and cook on HIGH for 5½ hours.

■ Uncover and stir in escarole and diced tomatoes. Recover and cook 30 minutes more.

■ Meanwhile, bring a medium saucepan of lightly salted water to a boil. Add pasta and cook 9 minutes or as per package directions. Drain. Stir pasta into soup along with salt. Ladle into bowls and top with Parmesan and black pepper.

PER SERVING 429 **CAL**; 3 g **FAT** (1 g **SAT**); 28 g **PRO**; 76 g **CARB**; 18 g **FIBER**; 994 mg **SODIUM**; 6 mg **CHOL**

TOMATO SOUP AND GRILLED CHEESE PANINI

INDIAN TOMATO
AND LENTIL SOUP

Indian Tomato and Lentil Soup

MAKES 6 servings **PREP** 15 minutes
SLOW COOK on HIGH for 5 hours

3	cups low-sodium vegetable broth
4	plum tomatoes, seeded and chopped (about 2 cups)
1	cup brown lentils
1	large onion, chopped
2	ribs celery, diced
1	large carrot, peeled and diced
3	cloves garlic, chopped
4	tsp garam masala
1¼	tsp salt
1	can (15 oz) chickpeas, drained and rinsed
1	bag (5 oz) baby spinach
½	cup plain Greek yogurt
	Lemon wedges, for squeezing

■ Coat a 4- to 6-qt slow cooker bowl with nonstick cooking spray.

■ Add broth, 1 cup water, the tomatoes, lentils, onion, celery, carrot, garlic, garam marsala and 1 tsp of the salt to the slow cooker.

■ Cover and cook on HIGH for 5 hours. During last 30 minutes, stir in remaining ¼ tsp salt, the chickpeas and spinach.

■ Just before serving, stir in yogurt. Serve with yogurt and lemon wedges.

PER SERVING 230 **CAL**; 2 g **FAT** (0 g **SAT**); 15 g **PRO**; 41 g **CARB**; 14 g **FIBER**; 755 mg **SODIUM**; 1 mg **CHOL**

RED LENTIL SOUP

Red Lentil Soup

MAKES 8 servings **PREP** 15 minutes
SLOW COOK on HIGH for 4 hours or LOW for 6 hours

¾	cup blanched almonds, plus more for garnish (optional)
2	large carrots, peeled and sliced into 2-inch pieces
1	medium onion, peeled and quartered
2	ribs celery, finely diced
1	bag (16 oz) red lentils
2	large vegetable bouillon cubes, crumbled
1	tbsp curry powder
½	tsp salt
2	cloves garlic, halved
¾	cup heavy cream
	Chopped fresh cilantro for garnish (optional)

■ Combine blanched almonds, carrots, onion and celery in a 5- to 6-qt slow cooker. Pick through lentils and rinse. Add lentils to slow cooker along with bouillon, curry powder, salt, garlic and 7 cups water.

■ Cover and slow cook on HIGH for 4 hours or LOW for 6 hours. Uncover and puree with an immersion blender until smooth (alternately, transfer soup in batches to a blender and puree until smooth). Stir in heavy cream and heat through. Garnish with cilantro and additional blanched almonds, if desired.

PER SERVING 370 **CAL**; 16 g **FAT** (6 g **SAT**); 18 g **PRO**; 40 g **CARB**; 6 g **FIBER**; 675 mg **SODIUM**; 31 mg **CHOL**

BUTTERNUT SQUASH AND
BLACK BEAN CHILI

Spicy Vegetable and Barley Chili

MAKES 6 servings **PREP** 20 minutes
SLOW COOK on HIGH for 4 hours or LOW
for 6 hours

- 4 **cups low-sodium spicy vegetable juice**
- 2 **tbsp chili powder**
- 1¼ **tsp salt**
- 1 **tsp dried oregano**
- 1 **tsp ground cumin**
- 1 **large onion, chopped**
- 4 **cloves garlic, chopped**
- 4 **cups cauliflower florets (about half a head)**
- 2 **cups frozen corn, thawed**
- 1 **large zucchini, cut into 1-inch dice**
- 1 **large summer squash, cut into 1-inch dice**
- 1 **orange sweet pepper, seeded and cut into 1-inch dice**
- 2 **ribs celery, sliced**
- 1 **cup pearled barley**
- 1 **can (15 oz) kidney beans, drained and rinsed**
- 1 **pkg frozen chopped spinach, thawed**
- ¼ **cup cilantro, chopped**

■ Coat a 5-qt slow cooker bowl with nonstick cooking spray.

■ Stir in 3 cups of the vegetable juice, the chili powder, salt, oregano, cumin, onion and garlic. Stir in cauliflower, corn, zucchini, squash, sweet pepper, celery and barley.

■ Cover and cook on HIGH for 4 hours or LOW for 6 hours. During last 30 minutes of cooking time, stir in remaining 1 cup vegetable juice, the beans and spinach. Garnish with cilantro and serve.

PER SERVING 341 **CAL**; 2 g **FAT** (0 g **SAT**); 15 g **PRO**; 72 g **CARB**; 19 g **FIBER**; 791 mg **SODIUM**; 0 mg **CHOL**

Butternut Squash and Black Bean Chili

MAKES 8 servings **PREP** 20 minutes
SLOW COOK on HIGH for 6 hours or LOW for 8 hours

- 2 **large onions, chopped**
- 4 **cloves garlic, chopped**
- 1 **butternut squash (2 lb) seeded, peeled and cut into 1½-inch pieces (5 cups)**
- 1 **large green sweet pepper, seeded and chopped**
- 1 **large jalapeño pepper, seeded and chopped**
- 2 **cans (14.5 oz each) stewed tomatoes**
- 4 **tsp ancho chili powder**
- 2 **tsp ground cumin**
- 1 **tsp salt**
- 2 **cans (15 oz each) black beans, drained and rinsed**
- ½ **red sweet pepper, seeded and cut into 1-inch dice**
- ½ **yellow sweet pepper, seeded and cut into 1-inch dice**
- ½ **orange sweet pepper, seeded and cut into 1-inch dice**
- ¼ **cup fresh cilantro, chopped**
- 1 **cup shredded taco cheese**
- 2 **scallions, thinly sliced**

■ Coat a 4-qt slow cooker with nonstick cooking spray.

■ Add onions, garlic, squash, green sweet pepper and jalapeño. Combine tomatoes, chili powder, cumin and salt. Pour over squash and peppers.

■ Cover and cook on HIGH for 6 hours or LOW for 8 hours. Add beans and red, yellow and orange peppers during last 30 minutes.

■ To serve, stir in cilantro. Top with cheese and scallions.

PER SERVING 209 **CAL**; 5 g **FAT** (3 g **SAT**); 10 g **PRO**; 38 g **CARB**; 11 g **FIBER**; 977 mg **SODIUM**; 13 mg **CHOL**

SPICY VEGETABLE AND
BARLEY CHILI

CHURRASCO AND TOSTONES,
RECIPE PAGE 192

Grilling

Fire up the grill and cook a mouthwatering meal for family and friends.

PORK AND PLUM SKEWERS

down. Brush with remaining sauce. Grill for 3 minutes, then flip over. Grill for 3 minutes more, until pork is no longer pink. Season with remaining ⅛ tsp salt and serve with couscous salad.

PER SERVING 439 CAL; 16 g FAT (4 g SAT); 38 g PRO; 34 g CARB; 3 g FIBER; 492 mg SODIUM; 89 mg CHOL

Grilled Spareribs with Texas Rib Sauce

MAKES 8 servings PREP 15 minutes
COOK 1 hour 6 minutes GRILL 10 minutes

- 4   lb pork spareribs, cut into individual ribs
- 1   tbsp canola oil
- 2   cloves garlic, chopped
- 6   tbsp tomato paste
- ½   cup beef broth
- ½   cup packed light brown sugar
- ¼   cup Worcestershire sauce
- ¼   cup lemon juice
- 1   chipotle pepper in adobo, seeded and chopped
- 1   tbsp adobo sauce

■ Bring a large pot of lightly salted water to a boil. Add ribs; gently simmer 60 minutes. Drain and remove ribs to a large cutting board.

■ Meanwhile, for the Texas Rib Sauce, in a medium saucepan, heat oil over medium heat. Add garlic and cook 1 minute. Add tomato paste, broth, brown sugar, Worcestershire sauce, lemon juice, chipotle and adobo sauce. Whisk until smooth.

■ Bring to a boil. Reduce heat to medium-low and simmer 15 minutes, stirring occasionally. Sauce will reduce to about 1½ cups.

■ Heat a gas grill to medium-high or the coals in a charcoal grill to medium-hot.

■ Generously brush ribs with Texas Rib Sauce. Grill about 5 minutes per side, brushing with more sauce as needed, until ribs are nicely browned.

■ Serve with remaining sauce.

PER SERVING 618 CAL; 41 g FAT (12 g SAT); 26 g PRO; 34 g CARB; 2 g FIBER; 1,239 mg SODIUM; 127 mg CHOL

Pork and Plum Skewers

MAKES 4 servings PREP 15 minutes
COOK 8 minutes GRILL 6 minutes

- ½   tsp ground cinnamon
- ½   tsp ground cumin
- 1   tsp ground ginger
- ½   tsp black pepper
- ¼   cup plum preserves
- ¼   cup cider vinegar
- ¾   tsp plus ⅛ tsp salt
- 2   tbsp olive oil
- 2   lb boneless pork loin, trimmed and cut into 1½-inch pieces
- ½   red onion, cut into 1½-inch pieces
- 3   red plums, pitted, each cut into 6 wedges
- 1   cup Israeli pearl couscous
- 2   cups packed baby spinach, shredded
- ¼   cup crumbled feta cheese
- ¼   cup toasted sliced almonds

■ In a small bowl, whisk together cinnamon, cumin, ginger, pepper, preserves, vinegar and ½ tsp of the salt. While whisking, add oil in a thin stream. Set aside 3 tbsp of the sauce.

■ Thread 6 metal skewers with pork, onion and plum wedges: Use 5 or 6 pieces of pork per skewer, alternating with 3 plum wedges and as much red onion as desired.

■ Heat grill to medium-high. While grill is heating, cook couscous in lightly salted boiling water for 8 minutes. Drain and rinse with cool water. Toss with spinach, feta, almonds, ¼ tsp of the remaining salt and reserved 3 tbsp sauce. Set aside.

■ Brush skewers with some of the sauce. Place on oiled grill, sauce sides

**GRILLED SPARERIBS
WITH TEXAS RIB SAUCE**

COFFEE-MOLASSES
ST. LOUIS–STYLE RIBS

BROWN SUGAR-
BOURBON-GLAZED
BABY BACK RIBS

Brown Sugar-Bourbon-Glazed Baby Back Ribs

MAKES 8 servings **PREP** 15 minutes
COOK 15 minutes **MARINATE** overnight
GRILL 60 minutes

- 1   cup bourbon
- 2   tbsp canola oil
- 1   cup red onion, chopped
- 4   cloves garlic, chopped
- 1   cup ketchup
- ½   cup dark brown sugar
- ¼   cup cider vinegar
- ½   tsp red pepper flakes
- ½   tsp salt
- ¼   tsp black pepper
- 1   rack baby back ribs, about 3½ lb, cut into 2 equal pieces

■ Place bourbon in a medium saucepan and place over medium heat. Gently simmer until reduced to ⅔ cup, about 5 minutes.

■ In another medium saucepan, heat oil over medium-high heat. Add onion and garlic; cook 5 minutes, stirring occasionally. Carefully stir in ketchup, reduced bourbon, brown sugar, vinegar, red pepper flakes, salt and pepper.

■ Place ribs in a large baking dish and add bourbon-ketchup sauce. Turn to coat evenly. Cover with plastic wrap and refrigerate overnight.

■ Heat a gas grill to medium-high or the coals in a charcoal grill to medium-hot. Lightly grease grates of grill. Add ribs meaty sides ups and grill, covered, 20 minutes, until lightly charred. Baste with sauce, turn and grill 20 minutes more. Baste ribs again and turn. Grill an additional 20 minutes.

■ Place remaining sauce in a small pot. Simmer 5 minutes.

■ Place racks on a cutting board and slice into individual ribs. Serve with remaining sauce on the side.

PER SERVING 484 **CAL**; 24 g **FAT** (8 g **SAT**); 24 g **PRO**; 23 g **CARB**; 0 g **FIBER**; 639 mg **SODIUM**; 86 mg **CHOL**

Coffee-Molasses St. Louis–Style Ribs

MAKES 8 servings **PREP** 10 minutes
MARINATE overnight **GRILL** over indirect heat 2 hours, then over direct heat 6 minutes
COOK 2 minutes

- 1   cup very strong brewed black coffee
- 1   cup sweet onion, chopped
- ⅓   cup molasses
- ¼   cup ketchup
- ¼   cup cider vinegar
- ¼   cup reduced-sodium soy sauce
- 2   tbsp Frank's hot sauce
- 2   racks St. Louis-style ribs (about 5 lb total)

■ In a medium bowl, combine coffee, onion, molasses, ketchup, vinegar, soy sauce and hot sauce.

■ Place ribs in a large baking dish and pour marinade over the top. Evenly coat ribs with marinade. Cover with plastic wrap and refrigerate overnight.

■ Set a gas or charcoal grill for indirect heat. Wrap ribs tightly in a single layer in heavy-duty aluminum foil. Grill ribs in foil over indirect heat for 2 hours, turning after 1 hour.

■ Remove ribs to a cutting board and cut into 3 portions. Set grill to high. Brush ribs with marinade and grill about 3 minutes per side. Place marinade in a saucepan, bring to a rolling boil and cook 3 minutes. Cool.

■ Serve ribs with cooled marinade as a dipping sauce.

PER SERVING 460 **CAL**; 29 g **FAT** (10 g **SAT**); 35 g **PRO**; 14 g **CARB**; 0 g **FIBER**; 670 mg **SODIUM**; 123 mg **CHOL**

PEANUT PORK AND NOODLES

■ Toss noodle mixture with remaining dressing and the salt. Slice pork into thin strips and scatter over salad. Sprinkle with peanuts and serve immediately.

PER SERVING 438 **CAL**; 14 g **FAT** (3 g **SAT**); 26 g **PRO**; 53 g **CARB**; 7 g **FIBER**; 800 mg **SODIUM**; 31 mg **CHOL**

Grilled Pork with Pasta Salad

MAKES 6 servings
PREP 10 minutes   REST 5 minutes
COOK 7 minutes   GRILL 8 minutes

- 2   **pork tenderloins (about 2 lb)**
- ½   **cup light Caesar salad dressing**
- ½   **box (8 oz; about 2¾ cups) radiatore (or your favorite short-shape pasta)**
- 1   **can (15.5 oz) reduced-sodium chickpeas, drained and rinsed**
- 1   **can (14 oz) artichoke hearts, drained and quartered**
- 1   **pint cherry tomatoes, cut in half**
- 1   **cucumber, cut into half-moons**
- ¼   **cup pitted olives (optional)**
- ¼   **cup light mayonnaise**

■ Heat grill to medium-high. Bring a large pot of lightly salted water to boiling. Split tenderloins lengthwise almost all the way through and flatten like a book.

■ Place in a glass dish and add ¼ cup of the Caesar dressing, turning to coat.

■ Cook pasta in boiling water for 7 minutes or per package directions. Drain and rinse. Meanwhile, grill pork, covered, for 4 minutes per side, turning once. Transfer to a cutting board and let rest 5 minutes.

■ Combine pasta, chickpeas, artichoke hearts, tomatoes, cucumber and, if desired, olives. Blend remaining ¼ cup dressing and the mayonnaise. Toss with pasta mixture. Slice pork; serve with pasta salad.

PER SERVING 469 **CAL**; 11 g **FAT** (3 g **SAT**); 44 g **PRO**; 54 g **CARB**; 9 g **FIBER**; 773 mg **SODIUM**; 105 mg **CHOL**

Peanut Pork and Noodles

MAKES 4 servings   PREP 25 minutes
MARINATE 15 minutes   COOK 3 minutes
GRILL 4 minutes

DRESSING

- ¼   **cup rice vinegar**
- ¼   **cup creamy peanut butter**
- 3   **tbsp low-sodium soy sauce**
- 2   **tbsp honey**
- 1   **tbsp minced garlic**
- 1   **tbsp minced ginger**
- 1   **tsp garlic-chili paste**

SALAD

- 8   **oz sliced boneless pork chops**
- 2   **pkg (3 oz each) ramen noodles, flavor packets discarded**
- 8   **oz snow peas, tough strings removed, sliced**
- 8   **oz baby bok choy, trimmed, cleaned and sliced crosswise**
- 1   **red sweet pepper, cored, seeded and thinly sliced**
- ⅛   **tsp salt**
- 3   **tbsp dry-roasted unsalted peanuts**

■ **Dressing.** In a small bowl, combine vinegar, peanut butter, 3 tbsp water, the soy sauce, honey, garlic, ginger and chili paste. Whisk until smooth.

■ **Salad.** Heat grill or grill pan to medium-high heat. Combine pork chops and ⅓ cup of the dressing in a resealable plastic bag. Marinate at least 15 minutes.

■ Meanwhile, bring a large pot of water to a boil. Break up ramen noodles, stir into pot and cook 2 minutes. Add snow peas and bok choy. Return to a boil, cook 1 minute, then drain and rinse in cold water. Drain and place mixture in a large bowl with sliced red pepper.

■ Remove pork from marinade; discard marinade. Grill for 3 to 4 minutes, turning halfway through. Transfer to a cutting board.

GRILLED PORK WITH PASTA SALAD

PORK BURGERS STUFFED
WITH MANCHEGO

ESCAROLE, BEAN
AND PORK SALAD

Pork Burgers Stuffed with Manchego

MAKES 8 servings **PREP** 20 minutes
GRILL 10 minutes

- **2 lb ground pork**
- **¼ cup light mayonnaise, plus more for serving (optional)**
- **1 tsp dried oregano**
- **½ tsp salt**
- **½ tsp coarsely ground pepper**
- **½ tsp dried thyme**
- **½ tsp onion powder**
- **½ tsp hot paprika**
- **4 oz Manchego cheese**
- **8 egg challah rolls, split**
- **8 tbsp dried onion topping**
- **Sliced hot cherry peppers (optional)**

■ In a large bowl, combine pork, mayonnaise, oregano, salt, black pepper, thyme, onion powder and paprika. Form into 8 burgers.

■ Cut Manchego into pieces about 1 inch square and ¼ inch thick. Make an indentation in each burger and insert a piece of cheese. Close meat around cheese and flatten burger.

■ Heat a gas grill to medium-high or the coals in a charcoal grill to medium-hot. Lightly grease grates. Grill burgers about 5 minutes per side, until internal temperature reaches 160°.

■ Place burgers on rolls and top each with 1 tbsp of the onion topping. Add slices of hot cherry peppers and additional mayonnaise, if desired.

PER SERVING 621 **CAL**; 36 g **FAT** (13 g **SAT**); 30 g **PRO**; 41 g **CARB**; 2 g **FIBER**; 888 mg **SODIUM**; 135 mg **CHOL**

Escarole, Bean and Pork Salad

MAKES 4 servings **PREP** 15 minutes
GRILL 12 minutes

- **1 pork tenderloin (about 1¼ lb)**
- **1 tsp dried Italian seasoning**
- **½ tsp plus ⅛ tsp salt**
- **½ tsp black pepper**
- **1 large bunch escarole, washed and cut into bite-size pieces (about 10 cups)**
- **1 can (15 oz) cannellini beans, drained and rinsed**
- **1 yellow sweet pepper, seeded and diced**
- **2 ribs celery, thinly sliced**
- **¼ cup pitted Kalamata olives, sliced**
- **1 shallot, sliced**
- **3 tbsp champagne vinegar**
- **2 tbsp olive oil**

■ Heat grill to medium-high. Season pork tenderloin with Italian seasoning and ¼ tsp each of the salt and black pepper. Grill about 6 minutes per side, turning as needed to avoid burning, or until internal temperature reaches 140°. Place on a platter and loosely cover with foil.

■ In a large bowl, combine escarole, beans, yellow pepper, celery, olives and shallot. Combine vinegar, olive oil and ⅛ tsp each of the salt and black pepper. Toss dressing with escarole and bean mixture.

■ Thinly slice pork tenderloin. Serve with salad. Season pork and salad with remaining ¼ tsp salt and ⅛ tsp black pepper.

PER SERVING 327 **CAL**; 11 g **FAT** (2 g **SAT**); 31 g **PRO**; 25 g **CARB**; 10 g **FIBER**; 668 mg **SODIUM**; 70 mg **CHOL**

Coffee-Rubbed Steak with Charred Zucchini

MAKES 6 servings **PREP** 15 minutes
GRILL 14 minutes
LET REST 5 minutes **MICROWAVE** 90 seconds

- **2 tbsp espresso ground coffee (decaf if desired)**
- **1 tsp chili powder**
- **1 tsp garlic powder**
- **1¼ tsp salt**
- **1 tsp sugar**

COFFEE-RUBBED STEAK WITH CHARRED ZUCCHINI

½ tsp smoked paprika

¼ tsp plus ⅛ tsp black pepper

1½ lb boneless sirloin steak (at least 1 inch thick)

4 small zucchini, trimmed and quartered lengthwise

1 pkg (10 oz) button mushrooms, trimmed

1 yellow sweet pepper, cut from core into 4 pieces

2 tbsp light balsamic salad dressing

1 pkg (8.5 oz) heat-and-serve white or brown rice

■ Heat grill to medium-high. In a small bowl, combine espresso, chili powder, garlic powder, ¾ tsp of the salt, the sugar, paprika and ¼ tsp of the black pepper. Sprinkle 1 tbsp of the rub over 1 side of steak and press in with your hands. Turn steak over and repeat. (Reserve remaining rub for another use.)

■ Season zucchini with ¼ tsp of the remaining salt and remaining ⅛ tsp black pepper. Thread mushrooms onto 2 skewers. Brush mushrooms and yellow pepper pieces with balsamic dressing. Grill vegetables for 6 minutes, turning once. Grill steak for 6 to 8 minutes, depending on thickness, turning once.

■ Meanwhile, microwave rice for 90 seconds. Remove steak from grill and let rest for 5 minutes. Quarter mushrooms and dice yellow pepper. Toss in a bowl with rice and remaining ¼ tsp salt. Slice steak and serve with zucchini and grilled veggie rice.

PER SERVING 408 CAL; 11 g FAT (3 g SAT); 44 g PRO; 34 g CARB; 3 g FIBER; 704 mg SODIUM; 71 mg CHOL

TURKISH LAMB BURGERS

Turkish Lamb Burgers

MAKES 6 servings **PREP** 20 minutes
GRILL 14 minutes

- 8   medium mushrooms (about 4 oz)
- 1   small red onion, halved
- 1   lb ground lamb
- ¾   lb ground chicken
- 1   tsp chopped fresh oregano
- ¾   tsp ground cumin
- ¾   tsp ground cinnamon
- ¾   tsp salt
- ½   tsp black pepper
- ¼   tsp ground allspice
- ½   cup 2% plain Greek yogurt
- ¼   cup white wine vinegar
- ¼   cup crumbled feta cheese
- ¼   cup fresh mint leaves, chopped
- 2   tbsp olive oil
- 2   tsp sugar
- 1   pkg (5 oz) baby kale
- 1   pkg (5 oz) baby spinach
- 1   medium cucumber, trimmed and thinly sliced
- 1   cup cherry tomatoes, halved
- 6   whole wheat pitas, warmed

■ Heat grill to medium-high. Grate mushrooms and half the onion into a large bowl. Add lamb, chicken, oregano, cumin, cinnamon, ½ tsp of the salt, ¼ tsp of the pepper and the allspice. Mix together well. With wet hands, shape into 6 patties.

■ Prepare dressing: In a medium bowl, whisk yogurt, vinegar, feta, mint, oil, sugar and remaining ¼ tsp each salt and pepper. Slice remaining onion into half-moons.

■ Grill burger patties 12 to 14 minutes, turning halfway through. Toss kale, spinach, sliced onion, cucumber and tomatoes. Place 3 cups salad on each plate and top with a burger patty. Serve each with dressing and warm pita on the side.

PER SERVING 476 **CAL**; 22 g **FAT** (7 g **SAT**); 34 g **PRO**; 37 g **CARB**; 7 g **FIBER**; 724 mg **SODIUM**; 105 mg **CHOL**

ITALIAN GRILLED BURGERS

Italian Grilled Burgers

MAKES 6 to 8 servings **PREP** 15 minutes
GRILL 8 minutes

- 2¾   lb ground round, chuck or sirloin
- 1   tbsp chopped fresh parsley
- 1   small garlic clove, crushed and finely chopped
-   Dash Worcestershire sauce
-   Dash Tabasco sauce
-   Pinch dried Greek oregano
-   Salt and freshly ground black pepper
-   Olive oil
- 2   cups mild Gorgonzola cheese, cut into ½-inch-thick slices or crumbled, or mild blue cheese
- 6   to 8 ciabatta or other bread rolls
- 12   slices cooked pancetta or bacon

■ In a bowl, combine meat, parsley, garlic, Worcestershire, Tabasco and oregano. Season with salt and pepper to taste. Form patties 4 to 5 inches across and 1 inch thick.

■ Heat a grill to its highest setting. Brush, clean and rub grill grate with an oiled towel before starting; this will prevent meat from sticking.

■ Brush burgers with a tiny bit of olive oil and place on hottest part of grill. Grill until burgers are nicely browned, about 4 minutes per side for medium. When burgers are almost done on second side, top with Gorgonzola. Split rolls and place on grill to be toasted. Close lid and cook burgers until cheese is melted (check often so buns do not burn; they should only take about 30 seconds).

■ Remove buns, place on a platter, add a burger to each and top with crispy pancetta.

CHURRASCO AND TOSTONES

■ Remove plantains from oven, smash with the bottom of a glass to flatten and flip over. Brush with remaining 1½ tbsp oil, sprinkle with remaining ¼ tsp salt and bake at 400° for an additional 5 minutes. Serve steak and scallions with salsa and tostones alongside.

PER SERVING 523 **CAL**; 22 g **FAT** (4 g **SAT**); 30 g **PRO**; 59 g **CARB**; 8 g **FIBER**; 804 mg **SODIUM**; 68 mg **CHOL**

BBQ Burgers

MAKES 4 servings **PREP** 15 minutes **GRILL** 12 minutes

1¼	lb 92% lean ground beef
½	cup grated onion
7	tbsp bottled barbecue sauce
2	tbsp grated Parmesan cheese
2	tsp Dijon mustard
½	tsp garlic powder
4	slices sourdough bread (about 1½ oz each)
1	tbsp extra-virgin olive oil
4	small leaves Boston lettuce
4	tbsp French's fried onions
	Mixed green salad with fat-free dressing (optional)

■ Heat grill to medium-high. In a large bowl, combine ground beef, onion, 3 tbsp of the barbecue sauce, the Parmesan, mustard and garlic powder. Gently mix until combined, then shape into 4 patties about the size of the sourdough slices.

■ Brush sourdough on both sides with olive oil. Grill for 2 minutes per side, turning once. Transfer to a platter and top with Boston lettuce leaves.

■ Grill burger patties on oiled grill for 4 minutes. Spritz burgers with nonstick cooking spray and flip over. Grill for an additional 4 minutes or to desired doneness. Transfer to lettuce-topped bread and spoon 1 tbsp barbecue sauce onto each burger. Top with 1 tbsp fried onions and, if desired, serve with a mixed green salad.

PER SERVING 483 **CAL**; 18 g **FAT** (7 g **SAT**); 34 g **PRO**; 47 g **CARB**; 2 g **FIBER**; 773 mg **SODIUM**; 78 mg **CHOL**

Churrasco and Tostones

MAKES 4 servings **PREP** 10 minutes
BAKE at 400° for 20 minutes
GRILL 23 minutes

SALSA

1	pkg (10.5 oz) cherry tomatoes
2	ears corn, husks and silk discarded
2	tbsp lime juice
1½	tsp olive oil
¼	tsp salt
1	to 2 tbsp chopped fresh cilantro (optional)

TOSTONES

1½	lb green plantains
3	tbsp vegetable oil
½	tsp salt

CHURRASCO

1	lb flank steak
½	tsp ancho chile powder
½	tsp salt
½	tsp black pepper
4	bunches scallions, cleaned and trimmed

■ Heat grill to medium-high; heat oven to 400°.

■ **Salsa.** Thread tomatoes onto skewers and spritz with nonstick cooking spray. Grill corn 12 minutes, turning frequently, and grill tomatoes 8 minutes, turning once. Transfer to a cutting board and remove tomatoes from skewers into a bowl. Cut kernels from corn cobs and add to bowl along with lime juice, oil, salt and, if desired, cilantro. Set aside.

■ **Tostones.** Peel plantains and cut into ½- to ¾-inch slices. Toss in a bowl with 1½ tbsp of the oil and ¼ tsp of the salt. Place on a nonstick baking sheet and bake at 400° for 15 minutes.

■ **Churrasco.** Meanwhile, carefully split flank steak in half horizontally as if opening a book, cutting into 2 thin pieces. Slice each piece in half (for a total of 4 pieces). Season with ancho chile powder, salt and pepper. Grill steak to taste, about 5 minutes, turning once, for medium-rare. Transfer to a platter to rest. Add scallions to grill; grill 6 minutes, turning once, until charred.

BBQ BURGERS

FARRO
STEAK
SALAD

Farro Steak Salad

MAKES 4 servings **PREP** 10 minutes
COOK 15 minutes **GRILL** 10 minutes
REST 5 minutes

- 1 cup quick-cooking farro
- 1 lb flatiron steak
- ¾ tsp salt
- ⅜ tsp freshly cracked black pepper
- 3 tbsp balsamic vinegar
- 1 tbsp extra-virgin olive oil
- 1 tsp Dijon mustard
- 1 pkg (5 oz) baby spinach
- 4 medium heirloom tomatoes (combination of red, yellow, orange and green), cut into wedges
- ⅓ cup thinly sliced shallots
- 2 oz blue cheese, crumbled

■ Heat grill or grill pan to medium-high. In a medium pot, combine farro and 3 cups water. Cover and bring to a boil. Reduce to a simmer and cook 15 minutes. Drain.

■ Season steak on both sides with ¼ tsp of the salt and ⅛ tsp of the pepper. Grill over medium-high heat 5 minutes per side. Let rest 5 minutes. Meanwhile, in a large bowl, whisk vinegar, oil, mustard, ¼ tsp of the salt and ⅛ tsp of the pepper.

■ Thinly slice steak against the grain. Toss in bowl with cooked farro, spinach, tomatoes, shallots, blue cheese and remaining ¼ tsp salt and ⅛ tsp pepper.

PER SERVING 480 **CAL**; 16 g **FAT** (6 g **SAT**); 36 g **PRO**; 51 g **CARB**; 10 g **FIBER**; 760 mg **SODIUM**; 90 mg **CHOL**

Grilled Chicken and Peaches on Ciabatta

MAKES 4 servings **PREP** 15 minutes
GRILL 10 minutes

- 4 boneless, skinless chicken breasts (about 5 oz each)
- 1 tbsp olive oil
- ¼ tsp salt
- ⅛ tsp black pepper
- 4 oz Brie, cut into 8 slices
- 2 peaches, halved and pitted

GRILLED CHICKEN AND PEACHES ON CIABATTA

- 4 mini ciabattas (about 3 oz each), sliced horizontally
- 4 tsp Dijon mustard
- 1 cup arugula

■ Heat grill or grill pan to medium-high. Rub chicken on both sides with oil and season with salt and pepper. Grill on medium-high for 5 minutes. Flip chicken and place 2 Brie slices on each breast. Grill another 5 minutes, or until chicken is cooked.

■ Meanwhile, grill peaches 3 minutes per side. Slice. Grill rolls 1 to 2 minutes on cut sides.

■ Spread 1 tsp mustard on the bottom of each ciabatta. Follow with chicken breast, some peach slices, ¼ cup arugula and top half of ciabatta.

PER SERVING 500 **CAL**; 15 g **FAT** (7 g **SAT**); 46 g **PRO**; 46 g **CARB**; 3 g **FIBER**; 910 mg **SODIUM**; 125 mg **CHOL**

MANGO-RASPBERRY GRILLED CHICKEN SALAD

Grilled Citrus Chicken Rice Bowl

MAKES 4 servings **PREP** 20 minutes
MARINATE 2 to 4 hours **GRILL** 16 minutes

- ¼ cup orange juice
- 3 tbsp olive oil
- 2 tbsp lemon juice
- 1 tbsp white wine vinegar
- 1 tsp orange zest
- 1 tsp salt
- ½ tsp sugar
- ¼ tsp black pepper
- 2 scallions, finely chopped
- 1 lb boneless, skinless chicken breasts
- 3 cups cooked brown rice
- 1 cup baby arugula
- 1 cup carrot matchsticks
- ½ cup cucumber matchsticks
- 2 tbsp chopped mint

■ In a medium bowl, whisk together orange juice, olive oil, lemon juice, vinegar, orange zest, ¾ tsp of the salt, the sugar, pepper and scallions.

■ Place chicken in a resealable plastic bag and add 3 tbsp of the citrus dressing. Seal bag and shake to coat chicken with dressing. Marinate in refrigerator for 2 to 4 hours.

■ Heat a gas grill or grill pan to medium-high or the coals in a charcoal grill to medium-hot. Remove chicken from marinade; discard marinade. Grill chicken for 7 to 8 minutes per side or until internal temperature reaches 160°. Slice chicken thinly on the bias.

■ In a large salad bowl, combine rice, arugula, carrot, cucumber and mint. Toss with 4 tbsp of the citrus dressing and season with remaining ¼ tsp salt.

■ Serve rice salad with sliced chicken and drizzle with remaining dressing.

PER SERVING 399 **CAL**; 14 g **FAT** (2 g **SAT**); 27 g **PRO**; 40 g **CARB**; 4 g **FIBER**; 519 mg **SODIUM**; 63 mg **CHOL**

Mango-Raspberry Grilled Chicken Salad

MAKES 5 servings **PREP** 8 minutes
GRILL 12 minutes

DRESSING

- 2 tbsp raspberry balsamic vinegar
- 1 tbsp lemon juice
- 1 tbsp chopped chives
- 1 tsp grainy mustard
- ¾ tsp sugar
- ½ tsp salt
- ⅛ tsp black pepper
- ⅓ cup extra-virgin olive oil

SALAD

- 1 lb boneless chicken breasts
- 1 pkg (5 oz) baby spinach
- 2 cups sliced mango (or 1 whole, pitted, peeled and sliced)
- 1 cup raspberries
- ½ small red onion, sliced
- ¼ cup crumbled goat cheese

■ Heat grill or grill pan to medium-high.

■ **Dressing.** In a bowl, whisk together vinegar, lemon juice, chives, mustard, sugar, salt and pepper. While whisking, add oil in a thin stream.

■ **Salad.** Combine chicken and ¼ cup of the dressing in a glass dish or resealable plastic bag.

■ Remove chicken from marinade and grill, turning once, for 12 minutes or until internal temperature registers 160° on an instant-read thermometer. Cool slightly.

■ Meanwhile, combine spinach, mango, raspberries and onion in a large bowl. Toss with remaining dressing.

■ Slice chicken into bite-size pieces and either toss with salad or fan over top of greens. Sprinkle salad with goat cheese and serve.

PER SERVING 337 **CAL**; 18 g **FAT** (4 g **SAT**); 25 g **PRO**; 20 g **CARB**; 4 g **FIBER**; 406 mg **SODIUM**; 58 mg **CHOL**

GRILLED CITRUS CHICKEN
RICE BOWL

TANDOORI CHICKEN
AND LENTIL SALAD

Tandoori Chicken and Lentil Salad

MAKES 6 servings **PREP** 20 minutes
MARINATE 8 hours or overnight
GRILL 12 minutes

- 6 **boneless, skinless chicken breast halves (about 6 oz each)**
- ¾ **tsp salt**
- 1 **cup plain low-fat yogurt**
- 6 **tbsp fresh lemon juice**
- 1 **tbsp grated ginger**
- 2 **cloves garlic, grated**
- 2 **tsp turmeric**
- 2 **tsp paprika**
- 1 **tsp ground cumin**
- 1 **tsp ground coriander**
- ¼ **tsp cayenne pepper**
- 2 **pkg (9 oz each) Melissa's steamed lentils**
- 1 **medium tomato, seeded and diced**
- 2 **ribs celery, finely diced**
- 2 **medium carrots, peeled and grated**
- ¼ **cup extra-virgin olive oil**
- 3 **tbsp chopped fresh parsley**
- ¼ **tsp black pepper**

■ Make marinade: Season chicken with ½ tsp of the salt. In a medium bowl, whisk yogurt, 3 tbsp of the lemon juice, the ginger, garlic, turmeric, paprika, cumin, coriander and cayenne. Transfer to a glass dish or resealable plastic bag and add chicken, turning to coat. Cover and refrigerate 8 hours or overnight.

■ When ready to eat, heat grill to medium-high. Brush grill grate with oil. Remove chicken from marinade; let excess drip off. Add chicken and grill 10 to 12 minutes, depending on thickness, turning once. Meanwhile, make lentil salad. Open packages and gently break lentils apart. Stir in tomato, celery, carrots, olive oil, parsley and remaining 3 tbsp lemon juice. Season with remaining ¼ tsp salt and the black pepper. Serve with chicken.

PER SERVING 437 **CAL**; 14 g **FAT** (2 g **SAT**); 50 g **PRO**; 27 g **CARB**; 6 g **FIBER**; 618 mg **SODIUM**; 126 mg **CHOL**

MOROCCAN-SPICED SALMON AND ZUCCHINI

Moroccan-Spiced Salmon and Zucchini

MAKES 6 servings **PREP** 10 minutes
STAND 5 minutes **GRILL** 16 minutes

- 1 **cup vegetable broth**
- 1 **box (7.6 oz) wheat couscous**
- 30 **small pitted Mediterranean green olives, halved**
- 8 **pitted dates (Medjool or Deglet Noor), chopped**
- 1½ **tsp ras el hanout Moroccan seasoning (see Tip)**
- 1 **tsp salt**
- 1¾ **lb zucchini, trimmed and cut on the bias into ½- to ¾-inch slices**
- 1 **tbsp olive oil**
- ½ **tsp black pepper**
- 6 **salmon fillets (about 5 oz each)**

■ Heat grill to medium-high. Bring vegetable broth and ½ cup water to a boil in a medium lidded pot. Stir in couscous, olives, dates, ½ tsp of the ras el hanout and ¼ tsp of the salt. Cover, remove from heat and let stand 5 minutes.

■ Place zucchini slices in a large bowl and toss with oil. Thread onto skewers and sprinkle on both sides with ½ tsp of the ras el hanout and ¼ tsp each of the salt and pepper. Grill zucchini 5 minutes; turn over and grill an additional 5 minutes. Transfer to a platter and remove skewers.

■ Season salmon with remaining ½ tsp ras el hanout, ½ tsp salt and ¼ tsp pepper. Spritz with nonstick cooking spray. Grill salmon, skin sides up, 3 minutes. Flip salmon and continue to grill 2 to 3 minutes. Remove to platter with zucchini, leaving salmon skin on the grill.

■ Fluff couscous and transfer to a bowl. Serve alongside salmon and zucchini.

Tip: Ras el hanout is available from McCormick's, Williams-Sonoma and Whole Foods.

PER SERVING 512 **CAL**; 16 g **FAT** (3 g **SAT**); 40 g **PRO**; 53 g **CARB**; 5 g **FIBER**; 760 mg **SODIUM**; 90 mg **CHOL**

Grilled Salmon with White Bean, Sun-Dried Tomato and Spinach Salad

MAKES 6 servings PREP 20 minutes
MARINATE 1 to 2 hours GRILL 8 minutes

MARINADE AND SALMON

⅓ cup extra-virgin olive oil

Salt and freshly ground black pepper to taste

Juice of 1 lemon

Juice of 1 orange

2 tbsp chopped fresh basil

6 1-inch-thick boneless, skinless salmon fillets (about 8 oz each)

BALSAMIC VINAIGRETTE

½ cup balsamic vinegar

1 tsp Dijon mustard

2 cups extra-virgin olive oil

Salt and freshly ground black pepper

2 minced shallots

3 tbsp chopped fresh parsley

3 tbsp chopped fresh basil

SALAD

2 lb baby spinach, cleaned

2 cups cooked cannellini beans

1 roasted red sweet pepper, cut into thin strips

½ cup thinly sliced sun-dried tomatoes

■ **Marinade and Salmon.** In a small bowl, combine olive oil, salt and black pepper to taste, lemon juice, orange juice and basil.

■ Season salmon with salt and black pepper. Brush salmon with marinade 1 to 2 hours before grilling, cover in plastic and refrigerate. Pat salmon dry before grilling to avoid flare-ups.

■ Lightly oil the hot grill and grill salmon over very high heat 3 to 4 minutes per side, until browned but inside is medium rare.

GRILLED SALMON WITH WHITE BEAN, SUN-DRIED TOMATO AND SPINACH SALAD

■ **Balsamic Vinaigrette.** In a medium bowl, combine balsamic vinegar and mustard. Gradually whisk in olive oil, then stir in salt and black pepper to taste, shallots and fresh herbs.

■ **Salad.** In a large bowl, toss spinach with beans, roasted pepper and sun-dried tomatoes. Dress salad with desired amount of balsamic vinaigrette. (You can also serve vinaigrette as a sauce to accompany grilled salmon.)

■ Place salmon, hot off the grill, on top of salad and serve.

Grilled Mahi Mahi with Plum Salsa

MAKES 4 servings   **PREP** 15 minutes
GRILL 9 minutes

4	red and yellow plums, pitted and finely diced
2	tsp sugar
1	tsp lemon juice
½	tsp plus ⅛ tsp salt
1¼	lb mahi mahi or sea bass (four 5-oz fillets)
1	tbsp olive oil
⅛	tsp black pepper
½	cup fresh basil, chopped

■ Heat grill or grill pan to medium-high. In a bowl, combine plums, sugar, lemon juice and ⅛ tsp of the salt.

■ Rub mahi mahi with olive oil and season with remaining ½ tsp salt and the pepper. Grill on medium-high for 5 minutes. Flip and grill another 3 to 4 minutes, until fish is cooked through.

■ Stir basil into salsa; spoon salsa over fish before serving.

PER SERVING 280 **CAL**; 4.5 g **FAT** (1 g **SAT**); 27 g **PRO**; 34 g **CARB**; 6 g **FIBER**; 490 mg **SODIUM**; 105 mg **CHOL**

GRILLED MAHI MAHI WITH PLUM SALSA

CHILI-LIME SWORDFISH AND GRILLED CORN

Grilled Hoisin-Glazed Halibut and Bok Choy

MAKES 4 servings PREP 15 minutes
COOK 7 minutes GRILL 8 minutes

- ¼ cup reduced-sodium vegetable broth
- 2 tbsp reduced-sodium soy sauce
- 2 tbsp hoisin sauce
- 1 tbsp lime juice
- 1 tbsp chopped fresh ginger
- 1 tbsp rice vinegar
- ½ tsp Asian chili paste
- 4 halibut or mahi mahi fillets (about 6 oz each)
- ½ lb baby bok choy, trimmed and separated into pieces
- ⅛ tsp salt
- 6 oz whole wheat or whole grain angel hair pasta or thin spaghetti
- ½ red sweet pepper, cored, seeded and cut into thin strips
- 4 scallions, thinly sliced
- 1 lime, cut into wedges

■ In a small bowl, combine broth, soy sauce, hoisin sauce, lime juice, ginger, rice vinegar and chili paste. Reserve 3 tbsp of the sauce for noodles.

■ Heat a gas or grill pan to medium-high or the coals in a charcoal grill to medium-hot. Lightly oil grill grates. Drizzle sauce on both sides of fish and brush to coat. Grill for 4 minutes on flesh side. Turn; drizzle and brush generously with sauce. Grill 4 minutes on skin side or until fish flakes easily. Drizzle any remaining sauce over top. Remove from grill.

■ While fish is grilling, lightly spritz bok choy with nonstick cooking spray and season with salt. Grill for 3 minutes per side or until lightly charred and tender.

■ Meanwhile, cook pasta following package directions. Drain; stir in red pepper, half the scallions and the reserved 3 tbsp sauce.

■ Serve fish with noodles and bok choy with lime wedges and sprinkle remaining scallions on top.

PER SERVING 394 CAL; 4 g FAT (1 g SAT); 35 g PRO; 53 g CARB; 5 g FIBER; 800 mg SODIUM; 45 mg CHOL

Chili-Lime Swordfish and Grilled Corn

MAKES 4 servings PREP 15 minutes
MARINATE 20 minutes GRILL 10 minutes
COOK 3 minutes

FISH

- 1 cup coconut water
- 1 jalapeño, thinly sliced
- 2 cloves garlic, thinly sliced
- 1 lime (to yield 1 tsp zest and 2 tbsp juice)
- 2 tsp chili powder
- ½ tsp salt
- ¼ tsp black pepper
- 4 5-oz swordfish, mahi mahi or halibut fillets, thawed, if frozen
- 12 oz (about 3 cups) spicy sweet potato fries

CORN

- 4 ears corn, shucked
- 1½ tbsp butter, melted
- 1 tsp lime zest
- 1 tsp lime juice
- Pinch salt

■ **Fish.** In a medium bowl, combine coconut water, jalapeño, garlic, lime zest and juice, chili powder, salt and pepper. Place fish in a resealable plastic bag. Add marinade and refrigerate for 20 minutes.

■ **Corn.** Meanwhile, bake sweet potato fries per package directions. Heat grill to medium. Add corn and grill for 10 minutes, turning occasionally.

■ After corn has cooked for 4 minutes, add fish to grill, reserving marinade. Grill for 6 minutes, turning once. Remove to a platter. Pour marinade into a small saucepan and bring to a boil. Boil for 3 minutes and spoon over fish.

■ In a small bowl, blend butter, lime zest, lime juice and salt. Brush over corn. Serve fish and corn with sweet potato fries.

PER SERVING 451 CAL; 17 g FAT (4 g SAT); 32 g PRO; 49 g CARB; 6 g FIBER; 807 mg SODIUM; 63 mg CHOL

**GRILLED HOISIN-GLAZED
HALIBUT AND BOK CHOY**

TACOS WITH GRILLED
SHRIMP IN ADOBO

Tacos with Grilled Shrimp in Adobo

MAKES 8 to 10 tacos **PREP** 5 minutes
MARINATE 20 minutes to 2 hours
GRILL 4 minutes per batch

- 1 lb medium shrimp (30 to 35 count), peeled and deveined
- ½ tsp salt
- ⅓ cup Adobo Marinade (recipe follows), plus more for drizzling
- Metal or soaked bamboo skewers
- Warm tortillas, sliced avocado, chopped onion, sliced radishes and fresh cilantro

■ Toss shrimp in a large bowl with salt. Add Adobo Marinade and toss.

■ Thread shrimp onto skewers and refrigerate on a tray, covered, for at least 20 minutes or up to 2 hours.

■ Prepare a grill or heat a grill pan. Grill shrimp until just cooked through, about 2 minutes per side.

■ Remove shrimp from skewers and make tacos with the accompaniments, using 3 to 4 shrimp per taco. Drizzle with additional marinade before serving.

Adobo Marinade

MAKES 1½ cups **PREP** 5 minutes
COOK 10 minutes **SOAK** 20 minutes

- 5 large cloves garlic, unpeeled
- 4 large ancho chile peppers, seeded
- ½ tsp cumin seeds
- 5 whole peppercorns
- 1 whole clove
- 1 clove garlic, peeled
- ½ cup water
- 1 tsp cider vinegar
- ¼ tsp dried Mexican oregano
- ½ tsp salt
- ½ tsp sugar

■ Heat a large heavy skillet. Toast garlic cloves, turning once or twice until softened and browned in patches, about 8 minutes. Peel.

■ In same skillet, toast ancho chiles in batches, turning and pressing with tongs until fragrant, pliable and have turned a brighter red, about 1 minute. Transfer to a bowl of cold water and soak to soften, about 20 minutes. Drain.

■ Toast cumin seeds, peppercorns and clove in a small skillet over medium heat, stirring, until fragrant, about 1 minute.

■ Combine spices, drained chiles, toasted garlic, raw garlic, the water, vinegar, oregano, salt and sugar in a blender. Blend until smooth, about 2 minutes, adding more water, 1 tbsp at a time, if necessary to help blend.

Santorini Shrimp Salad

MAKES 4 servings **PREP** 15 minutes
COOK 4 minutes **GRILL** 5 minutes

DRESSING

- ¼ cup red wine vinegar
- 3 tbsp chopped fresh parsley
- 2 tsp honey mustard
- ¼ tsp salt
- ¼ tsp black pepper
- ¼ tsp red pepper flakes
- ⅓ cup olive oil

SALAD

- ½ lb green beans, trimmed
- 1¼ lb cleaned shrimp
- 1 cup cherry tomatoes, halved
- ½ cup (2 oz) feta cheese cubes or crumbles
- 1 bag (5 oz) arugula
- ½ red onion, thinly sliced
- ¼ tsp salt

■ **Dressing.** In a medium bowl, whisk together vinegar, parsley, mustard, salt, black pepper and red pepper flakes. While whisking, add oil in a thin stream. Set aside.

■ **Salad.** Bring a saucepan of water to a boil. Add beans; cook for 3 to 4 minutes. Drain and rinse with water.

■ Place shrimp in a resealable plastic bag or glass dish. Add ¼ cup of the dressing and toss to combine. Marinate at least 10 minutes while heating grill or broiler. Thread shrimp onto skewers or place on broiler pan. Grill or broil for 5 minutes, turning, until cooked through.

■ In a medium bowl, toss green beans, tomatoes and feta cheese with 1 tbsp of the remaining dressing. Place arugula and red onion on a serving platter or in a large bowl. Top with shrimp and season with salt. Drizzle with 2 tbsp dressing and add green bean mixture. Serve remaining dressing on the side, if desired.

PER SERVING 339 **CAL**; 18 g **FAT** (4 g **SAT**); 33 g **PRO**; 12 g **CARB**; 3 g **FIBER**; 634 mg **SODIUM**; 228 mg **CHOL**

SANTORINI SHRIMP SALAD

BLACK RICE,
SHRIMP AND
CHARRED CORN

Black Rice, Shrimp and Charred Corn

MAKES 6 servings **PREP** 20 minutes
COOK 40 minutes **GRILL** 20 minutes

- 1½ **cups uncooked black rice (such as Lundberg)**
- 1½ **lb shrimp, peeled, deveined and tails removed**
- 2 **tbsp extra-virgin olive oil**
- 1 **tsp salt**
- ¼ **tsp cayenne pepper**
- 2 **ears corn, husked**
- ½ **small red onion**
- 1 **avocado, peeled, seeded and halved**
- 3 **tbsp lime juice**
- 6 **tbsp Cotija cheese or queso fresco**

■ Combine rice with 3 cups water, cover and bring to a boil. Reduce to a low simmer and cook 40 minutes. Remove from heat and let stand 10 minutes. Fluff with a fork and transfer to a large bowl.

■ Meanwhile, heat grill or grill pan to medium-high. Toss shrimp with 1 tbsp of the oil, ¼ tsp of the salt and ⅛ tsp of the cayenne.

■ Thread shrimp onto skewers. Grill corn 3 to 5 minutes per side, turning 3 times (12 to 20 minutes total). Grill red onion 3 minutes per side, avocado and shrimp 2 minutes per side.

■ Cut kernels from cobs, dice onion and avocado and remove shrimp from skewers. Toss in bowl with cooked rice. Gently toss with lime juice and remaining 1 tbsp oil, ¾ tsp salt and ⅛ tsp cayenne. Garnish each serving with 1 tbsp cheese.

PER SERVING 420 **CAL**; 14 g **FAT** (3 g **SAT**); 31 g **PRO**; 47 g **CARB**; 6 g **FIBER**; 630 mg **SODIUM**; 190 mg **CHOL**

Thai Green Curry Shrimp

MAKES 4 servings **PREP** 15 minutes
COOK 23 minutes **MARINATE** 15 minutes
GRILL 16 minutes

- 1 **cup jasmine rice**
- 1 **can (13.5 oz) light coconut milk**
- 2 **tbsp plus 1 tsp green curry paste**
- 3 **tbsp fresh lime juice**
- 2 **tsp grated ginger**
- 1¼ **lb cleaned and deveined raw shrimp**
- 1 **tbsp olive oil**
- 3 **red sweet peppers, seeded and cut lengthwise into 4 sections**
- ½ **tsp salt**
- ¼ **tsp black pepper**
- ½ **cup fresh basil leaves, sliced**

■ Cook rice per package directions, about 20 minutes. Set aside and keep warm.

■ In a bowl, whisk coconut milk, 2 tbsp of the curry paste, 2 tbsp of the lime juice and the ginger. Place shrimp in a resealable plastic bag, add coconut milk mixture and marinate 15 minutes. Heat grill to medium-high.

■ In a large bowl, whisk remaining 1 tsp curry paste, remaining 1 tbsp lime juice and the oil. Toss pepper pieces in bowl to coat. Season with ¼ tsp of the salt. Grill pepper pieces 10 minutes, turning frequently. Remove to a cutting board.

■ Thread shrimp onto skewers, reserving marinade. Grill skewers 6 minutes, turning once, until cooked through. Season with remaining ¼ tsp salt and the black pepper. Meanwhile, bring 1 cup of the reserved marinade to a boil (discard remaining marinade). Boil 3 minutes. Slice peppers into thin strips.

■ Spoon rice onto a platter. Top with pepper strips, shrimp and basil. Drizzle a little sauce over platter and serve remaining sauce alongside.

PER SERVING 425 **CAL**; 10 g **FAT** (5 g **SAT**); 33 g **PRO**; 50 g **CARB**; 4 g **FIBER**; 657 mg **SODIUM**; 228 mg **CHOL**

THAI
GREEN CURRY
SHRIMP

TUSCAN GRILLED VEGGIE PLATTER

Tuscan Grilled Veggie Platter

MAKES 6 servings **PREP** 30 minutes
GRILL 10 minutes

- **2** tbsp Chianti vinegar or other red wine vinegar
- **2** tsp sugar
- **1** tsp spicy brown mustard
- **½** tsp salt
- **¼** tsp black pepper
- **5** tbsp extra-virgin olive oil
- **1** tbsp chopped fresh sage
- **1** tbsp chopped fresh parsley
- **2** tbsp chopped fresh basil
- **1** lb asparagus, trimmed
- **1** medium eggplant (about 1 lb), cut into ½-inch slices
- **1** large summer squash (about 8 oz), cut into ½-inch slices
- **1** red sweet pepper, seeded and cut into ½-inch strips
- **8** oz small carrots, halved lengthwise
- **2** large shallots (about 6 oz total), peeled and cut into 8 pieces
- Beans and Orzo (recipe follows)

- In a small bowl, whisk vinegar, sugar, mustard, ¼ tsp of the salt and the black pepper. Gradually whisk in oil; add sage, parsley and basil. Set aside.

- Heat a gas grill to medium-high or the coals in a charcoal grill to medium-hot. Lightly grease grates.

- Brush vegetables with dressing. Grill about 5 minutes per side, until crisp-tender. Brush with additional dressing and turn as needed to prevent burning. Cook in batches, if necessary. (You may want to use a grilling grid for thinner vegetables.)

- Arrange grilled vegetables on a platter. Season with remaining ¼ tsp salt. Serve with Beans and Orzo.

PER SERVING 502 **CAL**; 19 g **FAT** (3 g **SAT**); 16 g **PRO**; 74 g **CARB**; 14 g **FIBER**; 770 mg **SODIUM**; 0 mg **CHOL**

Beans and Orzo Cook 6 oz (1⅓ cups) orzo per package directions. Toss with 1 can (14.5 oz) butter beans, drained and rinsed, 1 tbsp of the dressing, 1 tsp olive oil and 1 tsp grated lemon zest.

Grilled Pizza Margherita

MAKES 12 pizzas **PREP** 30 minutes
STAND 45 minutes **GRILL** 6 minutes

- **4** cups lukewarm water
- **1** tsp fresh yeast
- **1** tbsp molasses
- **3** tbsp kosher salt
- **2** cups extra-virgin olive oil
- **4½** cups all-purpose flour
- **4½** cups bread flour
- **1** cup whole wheat flour
- **1½** cups grated Pecorino Romano cheese
- **1½** cups grated Bel Paese cheese
- **1** cup canned tomato sauce
- **6** tbsp chopped fresh parsley
- **½** cup chopped fresh basil

- In a large mixing bowl, combine water, yeast and molasses. Mix gently until all yeast dissolves. Set mixture aside 5 to 10 minutes, until yeast bubbles and floats to the surface. Stir in salt and 1 cup of the olive oil.

- With mixer on low speed, add all-purpose, bread and whole wheat flours. Mix until flour is absorbed and dough pulls away from side of bowl. Roll dough into a large ball and let stand 5 minutes.

- Cut dough into 12 pieces. Roll pieces into balls and place on an oiled baking sheet. Brush balls lightly with olive oil and cover with plastic wrap.

- If you are using dough right away, let it sit 30 minutes before grilling. If not, it can be stored for up to 1 day in the refrigerator, but it must sit at room temperature for an hour before stretching.

- When dough is ready, prepare a grill to medium-hot (preferably charcoal, but gas works nicely too). Make sure rack is set at least 4 inches from fire.

- For each pizza, on an oiled piece of parchment paper, stretch out a piece of dough using lightly oiled palms of your hands. If dough is sticking to the surface, lift it and drizzle a little more oil on surface. The dough should be a 12-inch circle and paper-thin. The shape of the dough is not as important as its thickness.

- Lift dough with parchment, invert it onto hot spot of grill and peel off paper. Dough will start to rise immediately. After about 2 minutes, carefully lift edge of dough to check color of the underside, which should be an even golden brown.

- Flip dough over and place it on edge of grate or on a cooler spot of grill. Brush cooked side of dough with olive oil. Combine cheeses in a medium bowl. Evenly spread a scant ¼ cup of the combined cheese to very edge of dough. Next, with a tablespoon, dollop tomato sauce on pizza (8 to 10 small spoonfuls)—don't spread sauce over entire surface. Drizzle pizza with 1 tbsp of the olive oil and sprinkle with ½ tbsp of the parsley.

- Carefully slide pizza back to edge of hot section of grill, and rotate until bottom is evenly golden brown. It should take 3 to 4 minutes. Do not put pizza directly over fire; bottom may burn before the cheese melts.

- Garnish with chopped basil.

GRILLED PIZZA
MARGHERITA

GRILLED
QUINOA BOWL

Grilled Quinoa Bowl

MAKES 4 servings **PREP** 15 minutes
COOK 15 minutes **STAND** 5 minutes
GRILL 18 minutes

- 1½ cups red quinoa
- 6 slices bacon (6 oz), diced
- 2 peaches, halved and pitted
- 8 oz red chard
- 2 tbsp white balsamic vinegar
- 1 tbsp extra-virgin olive oil
- 1 tbsp honey
- 1 tsp Dijon mustard
- ¾ tsp salt
- ¼ tsp freshly cracked black pepper

■ In a medium pot, combine quinoa and 3 cups water. Cover and bring to a boil. Reduce to a low simmer and cook 15 minutes. Let stand 5 minutes.

■ Meanwhile, heat a skillet to medium heat. Add bacon and sauté 6 minutes, until crisp. Remove to a paper towel-lined plate with a slotted spoon. Pour 1 tbsp of the bacon fat into a large bowl; discard any remaining fat.

■ Heat a grill or grill pan to medium-high. Toss peaches and chard in bowl with bacon fat. Grill peaches 3 minutes per side and chard 2 minutes per side (in 3 batches). Slice peach halves; chop chard. Return to bowl and toss gently with quinoa and bacon.

■ Whisk vinegar, oil, honey, mustard, salt and pepper. Gently stir into quinoa mixture.

PER SERVING 400 **CAL**; 14 g **FAT** (3 g **SAT**); 13 g **PRO**; 60 g **CARB**; 8 g **FIBER**; 700 mg **SODIUM**; 10 mg **CHOL**

Grilled Ratatouille

MAKES 4 servings **PREP** 35 minutes
MARINATE 30 minutes **GRILL** 14 minutes

- 1 eggplant (about 1 lb), trimmed and cut lengthwise into ½-inch-thick pieces
- 2 medium zucchini, trimmed and cut lengthwise into ½-inch-thick pieces
- 1 red sweet pepper, cut from core into 4 pieces
- 1 orange sweet pepper, cut from core into 4 pieces
- ⅓ cup balsamic vinegar
- 2 tsp honey
- 1 tsp grainy mustard
- ½ tsp plus ⅛ tsp salt
- ¼ tsp black pepper
- ¼ cup extra-virgin olive oil
- 2 large cloves garlic, minced
- 1 cup cherry tomatoes
- 1 can (19 oz) chickpeas, drained and rinsed
- ¼ cup fresh parsley, chopped
- ¼ cup grated ricotta salata cheese

■ Place eggplant, zucchini and sweet peppers in a large resealable plastic bag. In a medium bowl, whisk together vinegar, honey, mustard, ½ tsp of the salt and the black pepper. While whisking, add oil in a thin stream. Stir garlic into marinade and set aside ¼ cup. Add remaining marinade to bag with vegetables. Marinate for 30 minutes.

■ Thread cherry tomatoes onto 1 or 2 skewers. Oil grill grate and heat grill to medium-high. Grill marinated vegetables for 8 to 10 minutes, turning once. You may need to do this in a few batches, depending on the size of your grill. Grill tomato skewers for 4 minutes, turning once.

■ Transfer eggplant, zucchini and peppers to a cutting board. Transfer tomatoes to a serving bowl with chickpeas. Dice eggplant, zucchini and peppers. Add to bowl with reserved marinade, parsley and remaining ⅛ tsp salt. Top with ricotta salata just before serving.

PER SERVING 400 **CAL**; 12 g **FAT** (2 g **SAT**); 14 g **PRO**; 62 g **CARB**; 14 g **FIBER**; 779 mg **SODIUM**; 4 mg **CHOL**

GRILLED RATATOUILLE

HOLIDAY SPELT SALAD,
RECIPE PAGE 238

Side Dishes

Find delicious complements to main dishes with these fresh salads, hearty grains and colorful vegetables.

½ lb oyster mushrooms, separated from stem
½ yellow sweet pepper, sliced
½ red sweet pepper, sliced
1 lb baby spinach
½ tsp salt
¼ tsp black pepper
1 tsp fresh thyme leaves
1 tsp fresh marjoram leaves
Lemon slices, for squeezing

■ Heat oil in a large skillet over medium-high heat. Add garlic and cook 1 minute. Stir in mushrooms and sweet peppers; cook 4 minutes, stirring occasionally.

■ Gradually add spinach and stir until wilted, about 4 minutes. Stir in salt, black pepper, thyme and marjoram. Serve with lemon.

PER SERVING 61 CAL; 3 g FAT (0 g SAT); 2 g PRO; 8 g CARB; 3 g FIBER; 236 mg SODIUM; 0 mg CHOL

Orange-Infused Heirloom Carrots

MAKES 8 servings PREP 10 minutes
COOK 10 minutes

2½ lb heirloom carrots, peeled
2¼ cups orange juice
¼ cup (½ stick) butter or margarine
¼ cup honey
¼ tsp salt
⅛ tsp black pepper
1 tbsp chopped fresh parsley

■ Place carrots in a large skillet with 2 cups of the orange juice and water to cover. Bring to a boil; reduce heat and simmer 5 minutes. Drain.

■ Add butter, honey, remaining ¼ cup orange juice, salt and pepper. Cook over medium-low heat, covered, 5 minutes, stirring occasionally, until carrots are tender and glazed.

■ Place carrots on a serving plate and drizzle with glaze from skillet. Sprinkle with parsley.

PER SERVING 153 CAL; 6 g FAT (4 g SAT); 2 g PRO; 25 g CARB; 3 g FIBER; 149 mg SODIUM; 15 mg CHOL

TALEGGIO SWEET POTATO GRATIN

Taleggio Sweet Potato Gratin

MAKES 8 servings PREP 25 minutes
COOK 5 minutes BAKE at 375° for 90 minutes

1 large leek
2 tbsp butter
4 large peeled sweet potatoes
6 oz Taleggio cheese, cut into small cubes
4 tsp chopped fresh sage
1 tsp chopped fresh thyme
1½ cups heavy cream
1 tsp salt
1 tsp garlic powder
¼ tsp black pepper

■ Slice leek and cook in butter 5 minutes. Cut potatoes into ⅛-inch slices. In a 2-qt baking dish, layer one-third of the sweet potatoes, half the leek slices, 2 oz Taleggio, 2 tsp chopped fresh sage and ½ tsp chopped fresh thyme. Repeat layering. Top with remaining third of the potatoes and Taleggio. In a small saucepan, combine cream, salt, garlic powder and pepper; bring to a simmer. Pour over potatoes and down sides of baking dish. Bake at 375°, covered, for 45 minutes, then uncovered for 45 minutes. Cool 10 minutes before serving.

PER SERVING 337 CAL; 27 g FAT (17 g SAT); 6 g PRO; 19 g CARB; 2 g FIBER; 462 mg SODIUM; 96 mg CHOL

Sautéed Baby Spinach and Oyster Mushrooms

MAKES 8 servings PREP 15 minutes
COOK 9 minutes

2 tbsp extra-virgin olive oil
4 cloves garlic, sliced

SAUTÉED BABY
SPINACH AND
OYSTER
MUSHROOMS

ORANGE-INFUSED
HEIRLOOM CARROTS

FINGERLING POTATOES WITH CHIVE VINAIGRETTE

Fingerling Potatoes with Chive Vinaigrette

MAKES 8 servings **PREP** 15 minutes
ROAST at 400° for 20 minutes

- **1¾ lb fingerling potatoes**
- **4 tbsp extra-virgin olive oil**
- **½ tsp kosher salt plus another ¼ tsp**
- **¼ tsp black pepper plus another ⅛ tsp**
- **2 tbsp white wine vinegar**
- **½ tsp Dijon mustard**
- **3 tbsp chopped fresh chives**

■ Slice potatoes in half lengthwise, then, if necessary, in half crosswise into 3-inch pieces. Toss in 2 tbsp extra-virgin olive oil, ½ tsp salt and ¼ tsp pepper. Roast on a rimmed baking sheet at 400° for 20 minutes. Meanwhile, prepare vinaigrette: In a large bowl, whisk 2 tbsp extra-virgin olive oil, white wine vinegar, mustard, ¼ tsp salt and ⅛ tsp pepper. Stir in chives. Toss hot potatoes in vinaigrette and serve warm.

PER SERVING 140 **CAL**; 7 g **FAT** (1 g **SAT**); 2 g **PRO**; 18 g **CARB**; 2 g **FIBER**; 190 mg **SODIUM**; 0 mg **CHOL**

Sweet-Tart Red Cabbage with Roasted Pears

MAKES 8 servings **PREP** 20 minutes
BAKE at 450° for 25 minutes **COOK** 35 minutes

- **4 firm pears**
- **2 tbsp canola oil**
- **1 tbsp granulated sugar**
- **12 cups sliced red cabbage**
- **⅓ cup white vinegar**
- **¼ cup granulated sugar**
- **¼ cup packed brown sugar**
- **1 sliced onion**
- **½ tsp salt**
- **¼ tsp black pepper**
- **¼ tsp ground ginger**
-   **Pinch of ground cloves**

■ Peel, halve and core pears; place, cut sides down, on a baking sheet. Brush with 1 tbsp canola oil and sprinkle with the 1 tsp sugar. Bake at 450° for 25 minutes, turning after

KALE AND JICAMA SLAW

15 minutes. Toss red cabbage with white vinegar, ¼ cup granulated sugar and brown sugar. In a large skillet cook onion in 1 tbsp canola oil 5 minutes. Add cabbage and ⅓ cup water; cook 25 minutes, covered, stirring occasionally. Season with salt, pepper, ginger and cloves; cook 5 minutes, uncovered. Place pears over cabbage and serve.

PER SERVING 205 **CAL**; 4 g **FAT** (0 g **SAT**); 3 g **PRO**; 43 g **CARB**; 7 g **FIBER**; 185 mg **SODIUM**; 0 mg **CHOL**

Kale and Jicama Slaw

MAKES 8 servings **PREP** 30 minutes

- **⅓ cup lime juice (from 2 large limes)**
- **1 tbsp honey**
- **1 tsp grainy mustard**
- **¾ tsp salt**
- **¼ tsp black pepper**
- **½ cup olive oil**
- **1 bunch kale, tough stems discarded, shredded**
- **½ medium jicama, peeled and cut into matchsticks (3½ cups)**
- **1 medium orange sweet pepper, cored, seeded and cut into thin strips**
- **½ cup sweetened dried cranberries**
- **2 small shallots, thinly sliced (¼ cup)**
- **¼ cup sunflower seeds (optional)**

■ In a medium bowl, combine lime juice, honey, mustard, ½ tsp of the salt and the black pepper. While whisking, gradually add oil.

■ Combine kale, jicama, sweet pepper, cranberries and shallots in a very large bowl or on a large platter. Drizzle with ⅔ cup of the dressing and season with remaining ¼ tsp salt. Toss to combine, adding sunflower seeds, if desired. Serve with remaining dressing alongside.

PER SERVING 220 **CAL**; 14 g **FAT** (2 g **SAT**); 3 g **PRO**; 24 g **CARB**; 5 g **FIBER**; 268 mg **SODIUM**; 0 mg **CHOL**

PEPPER AND CREMINI
MUSHROOM SKEWERS

Pepper and Cremini Mushroom Skewers

MAKES 6 servings **PREP** 20 minutes **GRILL** 20 minutes

- 2 tbsp champagne vinegar
- 1 tsp Dijon mustard
- ⅛ tsp plus ¼ tsp salt
- ¼ tsp black pepper
- 6 tbsp olive oil
- 2 tsp chopped fresh oregano
- 1 tsp chopped fresh thyme
- 6 metal skewers
- 1 lb small sweet peppers
- 1 red onion, peeled and cut into thin wedges
- 8 oz cremini mushrooms, woody stems removed and large ones cut in half

  Fresh oregano and thyme sprigs for garnish

■ In a small bowl, whisk together vinegar, mustard, ⅛ tsp of the salt and ⅛ tsp of the black pepper. Gradually drizzle in oil, whisking constantly until mixture emulsifies; add chopped oregano and thyme. Set aside.

■ Thread skewers, using about 4 peppers, alternating with 4 pieces of onion and 4 mushrooms, for each. Brush generously with dressing.

■ Heat a gas grill to medium-high or the coals in a charcoal grill to medium-hot. Lightly grease grates. Grill skewers for about 5 minutes, turn and brush with additional dressing. Grill for 5 minutes more or until vegetables are crisp-tender.

■ Remove to a serving platter and season with remaining ¼ tsp salt and ⅛ tsp black pepper. Garnish with oregano and thyme sprigs.

PER SERVING 158 **CAL**; 14 g **FAT** (2 g **SAT**); 2 g **PRO**; 8 g **CARB**; 3 g **FIBER**; 172 mg **SODIUM**; 0 mg **CHOL**

Spicy Thai Vegetables

MAKES 6 servings **PREP** 25 minutes
MARINATE 15 minutes **GRILL** 13 minutes

- 3 tbsp reduced-sodium soy sauce
- 2 tbsp canola oil
- 2 tbsp lime juice
- 1 tbsp fish sauce
- 1 tbsp chopped fresh ginger
- 1 tbsp chopped lemongrass
- 2 tsp sugar
- 1 red Thai chile or small serrano chile, seeded and chopped
- 6 baby bok choy (about 1½ lb), sliced in half lengthwise, stem end left intact
- 1 large bunch scallions, trimmed
- 6 red Thai chiles (optional)
- 2 cups red, orange and yellow grape tomatoes
- 4 oz sugar snap peas

  Lime wedges for squeezing

  Hot chili oil (optional)

  Fresh Thai basil (optional)

■ In a mini chopper, combine soy sauce, canola oil, lime juice, fish sauce, ginger, lemongrass, sugar and chopped Thai chile. Whirl to blend. Place in a dish with bok choy, scallions and, if using, whole Thai chiles, Marinate 15 minutes.

■ Heat a gas grill to medium-high or the coals in a charcoal grill to medium-hot. Lightly grease grates.

■ Remove vegetables from marinade; reserve remaining marinade. Grill bok choy for about 4 minutes per side, scallions and chiles (if using) for 2 to 3 minutes per side. Remove to a platter.

■ Place a grilling grid on grill and heat for a few minutes. Grill tomatoes and sugar snap peas on grid for about 5 minutes, turning frequently. Remove to platter with other vegetables; drizzle with reserved marinade. Serve with lime wedges for squeezing and, if desired, hot chili oil. Garnish with Thai basil, if desired.

PER SERVING 96 **CAL**; 5 g **FAT** (0 g **SAT**); 5 g **PRO**; 10 g **CARB**; 3 g **FIBER**; 607 mg **SODIUM**; 0 mg **CHOL**

SPICY THAI VEGETABLES

HONEYED
BEETS WITH
SPICED
WALNUTS

Honeyed Beets with Spiced Walnuts

MAKES 8 servings **PREP** 25 minutes
ROAST at 400° for 45 minutes

- 2 **lb red and golden beets (about 3 bunches)**
- ¼ **cup honey**
- 2 **tbsp olive oil**
- ½ **tsp salt**
- ¼ **tsp black pepper**
- 2 **sprigs fresh thyme plus 1 tsp chopped**
- ¼ **tsp ground coriander**
- ¼ **tsp ground cumin**
- ⅛ **tsp ground ginger**
- ⅔ **cup roughly chopped walnuts**
- 2 **oz Roquefort cheese, crumbled**

■ Heat oven to 400°. Place a large piece of aluminum foil on a rimmed baking sheet. Trim beets and cut into 2-inch chunks. Place on foil and toss with 2 tbsp of the honey, 1 tbsp of the oil, ¼ tsp of the salt and ⅛ tsp of pepper. Place thyme sprigs on top and seal foil around beets. Roast at 400° for 45 minutes. Allow beets to cool slightly before peeling (use gloves to keep hands from staining). Toss with juices from foil.

■ Make spiced nuts: In a small skillet, heat remaining 2 tbsp honey, 1 tbsp oil, ¼ tsp salt and ⅛ tsp pepper, the chopped thyme, coriander, cumin, ginger and 1 tsp water over medium heat. Stir in walnuts until coated. Remove skillet from heat.

■ Top beets with spiced nuts and cheese.

PER SERVING 184 **CAL**; 12 g **FAT** (2 g **SAT**); 4 g **PRO**; 18 g **CARB**; 3 g **FIBER**; 332 mg **SODIUM**; 6 mg **CHOL**

Roasted Cauliflower and Broccoli with Spicy Yogurt Sauce

MAKES 8 servings **PREP** 15 minutes
ROAST at 400° for 25 minutes **COOK** 2 minutes

- 8 **cups cauliflower florets**
- 8 **cups broccoli florets**
- ¼ **cup olive oil**

ROASTED CAULIFLOWER AND BROCCOLI WITH SPICY YOGURT SAUCE

- ½ **tsp plus ⅛ tsp salt**
- ⅛ **tsp black pepper**
- 2 **cloves garlic, sliced**
- ½ **tsp hot paprika**
- ½ **tsp smoked paprika**
- ⅓ **cup plain yogurt**

■ Heat oven to 400°. In a large bowl, toss cauliflower and broccoli with 3 tbsp of the olive oil, ½ tsp of the salt and the pepper. Distribute in 1 layer over 2 rimmed baking sheets. Roast at 400° for 15 minutes. Stir and roast 10 minutes more.

■ Meanwhile, heat remaining 1 tbsp olive oil in a sauté pan over medium heat. Stir in garlic and both paprikas; cook for 2 minutes. Scrape into yogurt and season with remaining ⅛ tsp salt. Drizzle veggies with spicy yogurt sauce.

PER SERVING 116 **CAL**; 7 g **FAT** (1 g **SAT**); 4 g **PRO**; 11 g **CARB**; 4 g **FIBER**; 240 mg **SODIUM**; 1 mg **CHOL**

Assorted Vegetable Platter

MAKES 6 servings **PREP** 30 minutes
GRILL 10 minutes

- 3 **tbsp pomegranate balsamic vinegar**
- 3 **tbsp honey**
- ½ **tsp salt**
- ¼ **tsp black pepper**
- 6 **tbsp canola oil**
- 1 **tbsp chopped fresh sage**
- 1 **tbsp chopped fresh parsley**
- 1 **tsp chopped fresh rosemary**

- 1 **lb asparagus, trimmed**
- 1 **medium eggplant (about 1 lb), cut into ½-inch slices**
- 1 **large summer squash (about 8 oz), cut into ½-inch slices**
- 1 **red sweet pepper, seeded and cut into ½-inch strips**
- 8 **oz baby carrots, halved lengthwise**
- 2 **large shallots (about 6 oz), peeled and cut into 8 pieces**

■ In a small bowl, whisk together vinegar, honey, ¼ tsp of the salt and the black pepper. Gradually whisk in oil; add sage, parsley and rosemary. Set aside.

■ Heat a gas grill to medium-high or the coals in a charcoal grill to medium-hot. Lightly grease grates.

■ Brush vegetables with dressing. Grill for about 5 minutes per side, until crisp-tender. Brush with additional dressing and turn as needed to prevent burning. Cook in batches if necessary. (You may want to use a grilling grid for thinner vegetables.)

■ To serve, arrange on a platter and drizzle with remaining dressing. Season with remaining ¼ tsp salt.

PER SERVING 239 **CAL**; 14 g **FAT** (1 g **SAT**); 5 g **PRO**; 28 g **CARB**; 6 g **FIBER**; 228 mg **SODIUM**; 0 mg **CHOL**

GREEN BEANS WITH CRISPY GARLIC

Green Beans with Crispy Garlic

MAKES 8 servings **PREP** 15 minutes
COOK 8 minutes 30 seconds

- ¼ **cup canola oil**
- 8 **large cloves garlic, thinly sliced**
- 1½ **lb green beans, trimmed and cut on the bias**
- 1 **tsp salt**
- 3 **tbsp rice vinegar**
- 1 **tbsp grated ginger**
- 2 **tbsp sesame seeds**
- 1 **tsp sesame oil**

■ In a small skillet, heat canola oil until shimmering. Fry garlic cloves for 15 to 30 seconds, until golden. (Be careful not to burn.) Remove garlic with a slotted spoon to a paper towel-lined plate. Carefully pour 2 tbsp of the oil into a large skillet and place over medium heat.

■ Add beans, ⅔ cup water and ½ tsp of the salt. Increase heat to medium-high. Bring to a boil and cook 5 to 7 minutes, until liquid evaporates and beans are tender-crisp. Add rice vinegar and ginger; cook 1 minute. Stir in sesame seeds, sesame oil and remaining ½ tsp salt. Transfer to a platter and garnish with crispy garlic.

PER SERVING 67 **CAL**; 4 g **FAT** (1 g **SAT**); 2 g **PRO**; 8 g **CARB**; 3 g **FIBER**; 293 mg **SODIUM**; 0 mg **CHOL**

Sweet Potato Gratin

MAKES 12 servings **PREP** 30 minutes
BAKE at 400° for 55 minutes **COOL** 15 minutes

- 3 **cloves garlic, chopped**
- 1 **tbsp chopped fresh rosemary**
- 1 **tbsp chopped fresh thyme**
- 2 **lb sweet potatoes, peeled and sliced ⅛ inch thick**
- 1 **lb baking potatoes, peeled and sliced ⅛ inch thick**
- 1¼ **tsp salt**
- ¼ **tsp plus ⅛ tsp black pepper**
- 5 **oz Gruyère cheese, grated**
- 1 **cup heavy cream, heated**

■ Heat oven to 400°. In a small bowl, mix together chopped garlic, rosemary and thyme. In a 2-qt baking dish, layer one-third of the sweet potato and baking potato slices, slightly overlapping some of the edges. Sprinkle with ¼ tsp of the salt, ⅛ tsp of the pepper, half the garlic-herb mixture and one-third of the shredded cheese. Repeat layering a second and third time. Mix remaining ½ tsp salt with heavy cream; pour over potatoes.

■ Place baking dish on a rimmed baking sheet. Cover with aluminum foil. Bake at 400° for 30 minutes. Uncover and bake another 25 minutes, until bubbling and top is golden-brown. Cool 15 minutes before serving.

PER SERVING 178 **CAL**; 11 g **FAT** (7 g **SAT**); 5 g **PRO**; 15 g **CARB**; 2 g **FIBER**; 310 mg **SODIUM**; 40 mg **CHOL**

Scalloped Potatoes with Leeks and Manchego Cheese

MAKES 8 servings **PREP** 25 minutes
COOK 5 minutes **BAKE** at 375° for 60 minutes

- 2 **cups half-and-half**
- ⅛ **tsp nutmeg**
- ⅛ **tsp cayenne**
- 3 **lb large baking potatoes, peeled and cut into slices about ⅛ inch thick**
- 2 **tbsp unsalted butter**
- 2 **large leeks, rinsed, halved lengthwise and sliced**
- 3 **scallions, sliced**
- ½ **tsp salt**
- 2 **tbsp flour**
- 3 **cups shredded Manchego cheese**

■ Heat oven to 375°. Lightly coat a 3-qt baking dish with nonstick cooking spray.

■ Combine half-and-half, nutmeg and cayenne in a large pot; add potatoes and bring to a boil. Lower heat and simmer for 5 minutes. Drain potatoes over a large bowl, reserving half-and-half.

■ Meanwhile, melt butter in a large skillet over medium heat; add leeks and scallions. Cook for 5 minutes, stirring occasionally.

■ Layer one-third of the potatoes in prepared baking dish, overlapping as necessary. Sprinkle with ¼ tsp of the salt, 1 tbsp of the flour, half the leek mixture and 1 cup of the cheese. Repeat layering. Top with remaining third of the potatoes and 1 cup cheese.

■ Pour half-and-half over potatoes; tilt dish from side to side to evenly distribute. Cover and bake at 375° for 30 minutes; uncover and bake for an additional 30 minutes or until potatoes are tender and top of casserole is lightly browned.

■ Cool slightly before serving.

PER SERVING 401 **CAL** 20 g **FAT** (12 g **SAT**); 14 g **PRO**; 41 **CARB**; 3 g **FIBER**; 763 mg **SODIUM**; 60 mg **CHOL**

SCALLOPED POTATOES
WITH LEEKS AND
MANCHEGO CHEESE

MAPLE-BACON
BRUSSELS SPROUTS

ROASTED CARROTS
WITH CHESTNUTS AND
GOLDEN RAISINS

CHILE-CHEDDAR MASHED
POTATOES

Chile-Cheddar
Mashed Potatoes

MAKES 8 servings **PREP** 15 minutes
COOK 10 minutes

- 2½ lb baking potatoes, peeled and cut into 1-inch chunks
- 2 large cloves garlic, peeled and halved
- 1 cup 2% milk, heated
- 3 tbsp unsalted butter
- 4 oz sharp white cheddar cheese, shredded
- 1 can (4 oz) diced mild green chiles
- 1 tsp salt

■ Place diced potatoes and garlic in a lidded pot. Fill with cold water until potatoes are covered by 1 inch. Cover pot and bring to a boil. Reduce heat to a simmer and cook 10 minutes, until fork-tender.

■ Drain potatoes and immediately return to pot. Stir in milk and butter; mash until smooth. Stir in cheese, chiles and salt.

PER SERVING 216 **CAL**; 9 g **FAT** (6 g **SAT**); 7 g **PRO**; 27 g **CARB**; 2 g **FIBER**; 451 mg **SODIUM**; 29 mg **CHOL**

Maple-Bacon
Brussels Sprouts

MAKES 8 servings **PREP** 15 minutes
COOK 23 minutes

- 8 oz maple bacon, diced
- 2 lb Brussels sprouts, trimmed and halved
- ½ cup heavy cream
- ¼ cup pure maple syrup
- ¾ tsp salt
- ¼ tsp black pepper

■ Heat a large skillet over medium heat. Cook bacon until crispy, about 8 minutes. Remove with a slotted spoon to a paper towel-lined plate.

■ In the same pan, pour off all but 3 tbsp of the bacon fat (if not enough fat, add canola oil to compensate). Add Brussels sprouts and cook 10 minutes, stirring occasionally. Pour in heavy cream; reduce by half, about 3 minutes. Stir in cooked bacon, maple syrup, salt and pepper. Cook 2 more minutes, until Brussels sprouts are tender and sauce has thickened.

PER SERVING 215 **CAL**; 15 g **FAT** (7 g **SAT**); 7 g **PRO**; 16 g **CARB**; 4 g **FIBER**; 473 mg **SODIUM**; 35 mg **CHOL**

Roasted Carrots
with Chestnuts and
Golden Raisins

MAKES 8 servings **PREP** 10 minutes
ROAST at 400° for 30 minutes

- 2 lb carrots (about ½ to ¾ inch thick), peeled and tops trimmed
- 2 tbsp olive oil
- ½ tsp salt
- ¼ tsp pepper
- 1 cup peeled and roasted chestnuts, roughly chopped
- ½ cup golden raisins
- 1 tbsp honey

■ Heat oven to 400°. On a rimmed baking sheet, toss carrots with olive oil, ¼ tsp of the salt and the pepper. Roast at 400° for 15 minutes. Stir in chestnuts, raisins and honey. Roast another 10 to 15 minutes, until fork-tender. Gently toss carrots with remaining ¼ tsp salt.

PER SERVING 156 **CAL**; 4 g **FAT** (0 g **SAT**); 2 g **PRO**; 30 g **CARB**; 4 g **FIBER**; 235 mg **SODIUM**; 0 mg **CHOL**

CARIBBEAN-STYLE
GRILLED CORN

Beans and Greens with Sherry-Shallot Vinaigrette

MAKES 6 servings **PREP** 10 minutes
COOK 4 minutes

- ½ **lb fresh green beans**
- ½ **lb fresh wax beans**
- 2 **tbsp olive oil**
- 2 **tbsp sherry vinegar**
- 1 **tsp Dijon mustard**
- ½ **tsp salt**
- ¼ **tsp pepper**
- ¼ **cup finely diced shallots**
- 10 **cups roughly chopped escarole**

■ Bring a pot of salted water to a boil. Add beans; return to a boil and cook 3 to 4 minutes, until crisp-tender. Drain beans and run under cold water until cool. Set aside.

■ In a large bowl, whisk together oil, vinegar, mustard, salt and pepper. Stir in shallots. Toss dressing with beans and escarole.

PER SERVING 87 **CAL**; 5 g **FAT** (1 g **SAT**); 3 g **PRO**; 10 g **CARB**; 5 g **FIBER**; 137 mg **SODIUM**; 0 mg **CHOL**

Caribbean-Style Grilled Corn

MAKES 4 servings **PREP** 10 minutes
GRILL 20 minutes

- 4 **ears corn with husks**
- ½ **cup light or regular mayonnaise**
- 1 **tbsp jerk seasoning**
- 1 **cup sweetened coconut flakes**
- 4 **lime wedges**

■ Heat grill or grill pan to medium-high heat. Carefully pull back corn husks, leaving them attached at the base. Remove silk and discard. Recover corn with husks. Grill corn on medium-high heat for 20 minutes, rotating every 5 minutes. (Husks will char.)

■ In a small bowl, combine mayonnaise and jerk seasoning. Pull back husks and liberally spread mayonnaise mixture on grilled corn, about 2 tbsp per ear.

■ Scatter coconut on a large plate. Roll mayonnaise-coated corn in coconut. Serve with lime wedges.

PER SERVING 275 **CAL**; 18 g **FAT** (6 g **SAT**); 5 g **PRO**; 30 g **CARB**; 4 g **FIBER**; 502 mg **SODIUM**; 11 mg **CHOL**

Snap Peas and Radishes

MAKES 4 servings **PREP** 10 minutes
COOK 2 minutes

- 1 **lb snap peas**
- 2 **tbsp olive oil**
- 2 **tbsp tarragon vinegar**
- 1 **to 2 tbsp chopped fresh tarragon**
- ½ **tsp salt**
- 6 **radishes, washed, trimmed and thinly sliced**
-   **Freshly cracked black pepper**

■ Bring a pot of lightly salted water to a boil. Add snap peas; cook 1 to 2 minutes, until crisp-tender. Drain and run under cold water until cool.

■ In a large bowl, whisk together oil, vinegar, tarragon and salt until well combined. Toss snap peas and radishes in dressing. Season with freshly cracked pepper. Serve at room temperature or chilled.

PER SERVING 107 **CAL**; 7 g **FAT** (1 g **SAT**); 4 g **PRO**; 8 g **CARB**; 3 g **FIBER**; 298 mg **SODIUM**; 0 mg **CHOL**

SNAP PEAS AND RADISHES

TRIPLE MELON SALAD

Roasted Tomato Panzanella

MAKES 8 to 12 servings **PREP** 20 minutes
ROAST at 425° for 20 minutes
GRILL OR BROIL 6 minutes

- 3 tbsp white or regular balsamic vinegar
- 3 tbsp olive oil
- 1 tsp Dijon mustard
- ½ tsp salt
- ¼ tsp black pepper
- 2 pkg (10.5 oz each) cherry tomatoes
- 1 pkg (10.5 oz) yellow cherry tomatoes
- 2 cloves garlic, sliced
- 1 loaf (¾ to 1 lb) sourdough oval
- 1 pkg (8 oz) mozzarella pearls (such as BelGioioso) or quartered small fresh mozzarella balls
- 1 cup packed fresh basil leaves, torn

■ Heat oven to 425°. In a small bowl, whisk vinegar, oil, mustard, salt and pepper. Toss tomatoes and garlic with 2 tbsp of the dressing. Spread onto 2 rimmed baking sheets. Roast at 425° for 20 minutes, shaking pans halfway through to turn tomatoes. Cool slightly.

■ Heat grill or grill pan to medium-high; if broiling, increase oven temperature to broil. Slice bread lengthwise into 1-inch planks. Spritz with nonstick cooking spray. Grill or broil bread 2 to 3 minutes. Turn over and grill or broil 2 to 3 minutes more, until toasted. Cut into 1-inch cubes.

■ In a very large bowl, combine bread cubes, tomatoes and sliced garlic, mozzarella and basil. Drizzle with remaining dressing and gently toss. If making ahead, keep all salad components (including dressing) separate until just before serving.

PER SERVING 263 **CAL**; 15 g **FAT** (5 g **SAT**); 7 g **PRO**; 24 g **CARB**; 2 g **FIBER**; 349 mg **SODIUM**; 54 mg **CHOL**

Triple Melon Salad

MAKES 8 servings **PREP** 15 minutes
COOK 3 minutes

- ½ small seedless watermelon, rind removed, diced (4 cups)
- ½ honeydew melon, seeded, rind removed, diced (2 cups)
- ½ cantaloupe, seeded, rind removed, diced (2 cups)
- 3 oz prosciutto, torn or cut into strips
- 3 tbsp packed fresh mint leaves, chopped
- ⅛ tsp salt
  Pinch cayenne pepper

SYRUP

- ⅓ cup sugar
- ¼ cup fresh lime juice
- 2 jalapeños, seeded and minced

■ Combine watermelon, honeydew and cantaloupe in a large bowl. Set aside.

■ **Syrup.** In a medium saucepan, combine sugar, fresh lime juice, jalapeños and 2 tbsp water. Bring to a simmer over medium-high heat and cook for 3 minutes. Remove from heat, strain out jalapeño pieces and cool completely.

■ While syrup cools, add prosciutto, mint, salt and cayenne to melon in bowl. Pour the syrup over salad and stir gently to combine.

PER SERVING 110 **CAL**; 2 g **FAT** (1 g **SAT**); 4 g **PRO**; 23 g **CARB**; 1 g **FIBER**; 312 mg **SODIUM**; 7 mg **CHOL**

ROASTED TOMATO PANZANELLA

ROASTED BRUSSELS
SPROUTS AND
SPINACH SALAD

CHARRED
ASPARAGUS AND
TOMATO SALAD

Roasted Brussels Sprouts and Spinach Salad

MAKES 6 servings **PREP** 15 minutes
ROAST at 400° for 22 minutes

3	tbsp red wine vinegar
1	tsp Dijon mustard
⅛	tsp salt
⅛	tsp black pepper
⅓	cup extra-virgin olive oil
1¼	lb Brussels sprouts, trimmed and cut into quarters
6	scallions, cut into 1-inch pieces
12	cups baby spinach
1	cup red grapes, halved
3	tbsp sunflower seeds
2	tbsp crumbled Gorgonzola cheese
	Additional salt and pepper (optional)

■ In a small bowl, whisk vinegar, mustard, salt and pepper until combined. Gradually whisk in olive oil until thickened.

■ Place Brussels sprouts and scallions on a large baking sheet and toss with 2 tbsp of the dressing. Roast at 400° for 22 minutes, turning once, until tender. Cool slightly.

■ In a large bowl, combine spinach, grapes and sunflower seeds. Toss with 4 tbsp of the remaining dressing. Add Brussels sprouts and scallions.

■ Top with cheese. Serve with remaining dressing and, if desired, additional salt and pepper.

PER SERVING 224 **CAL**; 16 g **FAT** (3 g **SAT**); 6 g **PRO**; 19 g **CARB**; 7 g **FIBER**; 201 mg **SODIUM**; 2 mg **CHOL**

Charred Asparagus and Tomato Salad

MAKES 8 servings **PREP** 10 minutes
COOK 20 minutes

2	tbsp red wine vinegar
1	tsp mustard
⅛	tsp salt
⅛	tsp black pepper
¼	cup extra-virgin olive oil
1	tbsp minced shallots
2	lb asparagus, woody ends trimmed
16	cups mixed spring salad greens
2	cups red and yellow grape tomatoes, halved

■ In a small bowl, whisk vinegar, mustard, salt and pepper. Gradually whisk in oil; stir in shallots. Set aside.

■ Heat a large nonstick skillet over medium-high heat. Add asparagus in 2 batches, and cook 7 to 10 minutes, until nicely darkened on each side. Place in a large bowl and toss with 2 tbsp of the dressing. Set aside.

■ In a large bowl, toss greens and tomatoes with remaining dressing. Arrange asparagus on top and serve.

PER SERVING 114 **CAL**; 7 g **FAT** (1 g **SAT**); 4 g **PRO**; 12 g **CARB**; 6 g **FIBER**; 94 mg **SODIUM**; 0 mg **CHOL**

MIDDLE EASTERN
CHOPPED SALAD
(FATTOUSH)

MIXED LETTUCES WITH PEAR AND BLUE CHEESE

Mixed Lettuces with Pear and Blue Cheese

MAKES 6 servings **PREP** 10 minutes

- 6 **cups mixed baby lettuces**
- 2 **tbsp grapeseed oil**
- 1 **tbsp pomegranate balsamic vinegar**
- ⅛ **tsp salt**
- ⅛ **tsp black pepper**
- 1 **Bosc pear, thinly sliced**
- ½ **cup crumbled blue cheese**

■ Place baby lettuces in a large salad bowl. Toss with oil and vinegar. Season with salt and pepper. Gently fold in pear slices and blue cheese. Serve immediately.

PER SERVING 105 **CAL**; 8 g **FAT** (3 g **SAT**); 3 g **PRO**; 6 g **CARB**; 1 g **FIBER**; 209 mg **SODIUM**; 8 mg **CHOL**

Middle Eastern Chopped Salad (Fattoush)

MAKES 6 servings **PREP** 20 minutes
GRILL 4 minutes

- 2 **large pitas, brushed with olive oil**
- ¼ **cup olive oil**
- 2 **tbsp lemon juice**
- 2 **tsp lemon zest**
- 2 **tbsp white wine vinegar**
- 1 **clove garlic, minced**
- ¾ **tsp salt**
- ¼ **tsp black pepper**
- 6 **cups chopped romaine**
- 3 **cups cherry tomatoes, halved**

SPINACH SALAD WITH DATES AND PINE NUTS

- 1 **large English cucumber, halved and sliced into half-moons**
- 1 **cup sliced scallions**
- 1 **cup fresh parsley, chopped**
- ¾ **cup fresh mint, chopped**

■ Heat grill or grill pan to medium-high heat. Grill pitas for 1 to 2 minutes per side, until lightly charred.

■ In a large bowl, whisk together olive oil, lemon juice, zest, vinegar, garlic, ¼ tsp of the salt and the pepper. Toss dressing with romaine, tomatoes, cucumber, scallions, parsley, mint and remaining ½ tsp salt. Tear cooled pitas into bite-size pieces and toss with rest of salad.

PER SERVING 178 **CAL**; 10 g **FAT** (1 g **SAT**); 4 g **PRO**; 21 g **CARB**; 4 g **FIBER**; 415 mg **SODIUM**; 0 mg **CHOL**

Spinach Salad with Dates and Pine Nuts

MAKES 8 servings **PREP** 15 minutes

- 3 **tbsp balsamic vinegar**
- 3 **tbsp extra-virgin olive oil**
- 1 **tsp Dijon mustard**
- ½ **tsp salt**
- ¼ **tsp black pepper**
- 1 **pkg (10 oz) baby spinach**
- 1 **cup chopped pitted dates**
- ⅓ **cup toasted pine nuts**
- ¼ **cup thinly sliced shallots**

■ In a large bowl, whisk balsamic vinegar, olive oil, mustard, salt and pepper. Toss with spinach, dates, pine nuts and shallots.

PER SERVING 170 **CAL**; 9 g **FAT** (1 g **SAT**); 2 g **PRO**; 23 g **CARB**; 4 g **FIBER**; 220 mg **SODIUM**; 0 mg **CHOL**

ORECCHIETTE WITH
BROCCOLI RABE

Carrot-Fennel Salad

MAKES 8 servings **PREP** 20 minutes

- 3 **tbsp olive oil**
- 3 **tbsp white wine vinegar**
- 2 **tsp Dijon mustard**
- ½ **tsp salt**
- ⅛ **tsp black pepper**
- 1 **large fennel bulb or 2 small bulbs, very thinly sliced**
- 1 **lb carrots, shaved with vegetable peeler**
- ½ **cup shelled, unsalted pistachios**
- ⅓ **cup fresh parsley, chopped**

■ In a large bowl, whisk oil, vinegar, mustard, ¼ tsp of the salt and the pepper. Toss in fennel, carrots, pistachios and parsley. Season with remaining ¼ tsp salt.

PER SERVING 132 **CAL**; 9 g **FAT** (1 g **SAT**); 3 g **PRO**; 12 g **CARB**; 4 g **FIBER**; 251 mg **SODIUM**; 0 mg **CHOL**

Asparagus Orzo Salad

MAKES 12 servings **PREP** 15 minutes
COOK 11 minutes

- 1 **bunch thin asparagus, trimmed and cut into 1-inch pieces**
- 1 **box (16 oz) orzo pasta**
- 1 **cup crumbled feta cheese**
- ⅔ **cup fresh parsley leaves, chopped**
-    **Zest of 1 lemon (about 1 tbsp)**
- ⅓ **cup fresh lemon juice**
- 1 **tbsp plain yogurt or sour cream**
- 1½ **tsp sugar**
- ¾ **tsp salt**
- ¼ **tsp black pepper**
- ½ **cup extra-virgin olive oil**

■ Bring a large pot of lightly salted water to a boil. Blanch asparagus in boiling water for 2 minutes. Remove to a bowl with a slotted spoon and run under cold water to stop cooking. Return water to boiling. Add orzo and cook according to package directions, about 9 minutes. Drain and rinse with cold water.

■ In a large serving bowl, combine orzo, asparagus, feta, parsley and lemon zest. In a medium bowl, whisk lemon juice, yogurt, sugar, ¼ tsp of the salt, the pepper and oil. Set aside ¼ cup of the dressing; add remaining dressing to salad along with remaining ½ tsp salt. Toss to combine; refrigerate until serving.

■ Immediately before serving, toss salad with reserved ¼ cup dressing. Serve chilled or at room temperature.

PER SERVING 268 **CAL**; 13 g **FAT** (3 g **SAT**); 7 g **PRO**; 31 g **CARB**; 2 g **FIBER**; 263 mg **SODIUM**; 12 mg **CHOL**

Orecchiette with Broccoli Rabe

MAKES 8 servings **PREP** 10 minutes
COOK 19 minutes

- 1 **bunch broccoli rabe**
- 1 **box (1 lb) orecchiette pasta**
- 1 **pkg (10 oz) baby bella mushrooms**
- 2 **tbsp unsalted butter**
- 2 **tbsp olive oil**
- 4 **sliced garlic cloves**
- ½ **cup heavy cream**
- ½ **tsp salt**
- 2 **tbsp grated Parmesan**
-    **Freshly ground black pepper**

■ Bring a large pot of lightly salted water to a boil. Trim tough stems from broccoli rabe and cut into 2-inch pieces. Add broccoli rabe to boiling water and cook 1 minute. Scoop out to a bowl and return water to a boil. Add orecchiette pasta and cook 9 minutes. Meanwhile, clean, trim and slice mushrooms. Melt butter with olive oil in a large skillet. Add mushrooms and cook 3 minutes. Add garlic cloves and cook 1 minute. Drain pasta and set aside. Add broccoli rabe to mushrooms in skillet, along with heavy cream. Simmer 5 minutes. Season with salt and stir in orecchiette. Transfer to a serving bowl and toss with Parmesan. Sprinkle with pepper and serve warm.

PER SERVING 335 **CAL**; 13 g **FAT** (6 g **SAT**); 11 g **PRO**; 45 g **CARB**; 4 g **FIBER**; 192 mg **SODIUM**; 29 mg **CHOL**

CARROT-FENNEL SALAD

Warm Farro Salad

MAKES 8 servings **PREP** 20 minutes
COOK 15 minutes

- 1½ **cups quick-cooking farro**
- ¾ **tsp plus another ¼ tsp salt**
- 3 **tbsp red wine vinegar**
- 2 **tbsp chopped fresh parsley**
- 2 **tsp honey Dijon mustard**
- ¼ **tsp pepper**
- ¼ **cup olive oil**
- 2 **pkg (9 oz each) fresh Brussels sprouts, trimmed**
- 4 **oz diced pancetta**
- 2 **minced garlic cloves**
- ⅓ **cup crumbled blue cheese**

■ Combine farro with 5 cups water and ¾ tsp salt. Bring to a boil, cover and reduce heat to medium-low. Simmer 15 minutes, then drain.

■ Meanwhile, make dressing: Whisk red wine vinegar, parsley, mustard, ¼ tsp salt and pepper. Add olive oil in a thin stream, whisking constantly. Peel apart sprouts into individual leaves. Heat a large stainless-steel skillet over medium-high heat. Add pancetta and cook over medium heat 5 minutes, until crisp. Add garlic cloves and Brussels sprout leaves. Cook 2 to 3 minutes, until leaves are bright green. Remove from heat and add drained farro and dressing. Transfer to a serving bowl and toss with blue cheese.

PER SERVING 292 **CAL**; 15 g **FAT** (4 g **SAT**); 10 g **PRO**; 32 g **CARB**; 5 g **FIBER**; 493 mg **SODIUM**; 14 mg **CHOL**

KAMUT WITH BRUSSELS SPROUTS, CARROTS AND CHERRIES

Kamut with Brussels Sprouts, Carrots and Cherries

MAKES 9 cups **SOAK** overnight
PREP 15 minutes **COOK** 40 minutes

1½ **cups kamut**

2 **cups Brussels sprouts (about ½ lb)**

2 **cups shredded carrots**

1 **cup dried cherries**

1 **cup walnuts, toasted and roughly chopped**

⅓ **cup fresh parsley, chopped**

¼ **cup olive oil**

¼ **cup lemon juice**

2 **tbsp honey**

1¼ **tsp salt**

¼ **tsp black pepper**

■ Soak kamut in cold water overnight. Drain. In a medium lidded pot, add kamut and 4½ cups water. Cover and bring to a boil. Reduce heat to low and simmer 30 to 40 minutes, until tender. Drain and cool.

■ Shred Brussels sprouts with a food processor slicing blade or a coarse grater. Mix with kamut, carrots, cherries, walnuts and parsley.

■ In a small bowl, whisk olive oil, lemon juice, honey, salt and pepper. Stir into salad. Serve at room temperature or chilled.

PER CUP 305 **CAL**; 14 g **FAT** (2 g **SAT**); 7 g **PRO**; 43 g **CARB**; 6 g **FIBER**; 347 mg **SODIUM**; 0 mg **CHOL**

WILD RICE, CANTALOUPE AND CUCUMBER SALAD

Wild Rice, Cantaloupe and Cucumber Salad

MAKES 8 servings **PREP** 20 minutes
COOK 40 minutes **STAND** 20 minutes

1½ **cups wild rice blend**

1 **container (5.3 oz) 0% plain Greek yogurt**

½ **cup light mayonnaise**

¼ **cup white balsamic vinegar**

½ **tsp salt**

¼ **tsp black pepper**

3 **cups diced cantaloupe**

2 **cups diced cucumber**

1 **cup finely diced celery**

1 **cup raisins**

½ **cup roasted sunflower seeds**

¼ **cup finely diced shallots**

■ In a lidded pot, combine rice and 3 cups water. Bring to a boil. Reduce to a simmer, cover and cook 40 minutes or per package directions. Let stand 20 minutes.

■ Meanwhile, in a large bowl, whisk yogurt, mayonnaise, vinegar, salt and pepper. When rice is slightly cooled, stir into dressing with cantaloupe, cucumber, celery, raisins, sunflower seeds and shallots. Serve at room temperature or chilled.

PER SERVING 320 **CAL**; 10 g **FAT** (1 g **SAT**); 7 g **PRO**; 54 g **CARB**; 5 g **FIBER**; 300 mg **SODIUM**; 5 mg **CHOL**

ORGANIC BABY LETTUCES AND QUINOA SALAD

Creamy Polenta

MAKES 8 servings **PREP** 5 minutes
COOK 30 minutes

- 2 **tsp salt**
- 2 **cups polenta or corn grits (not instant)**
- 4 **oz soft goat cheese**
- 6 **tbsp unsalted butter**
- 2 **tbsp chopped chives**
- ¼ **tsp black pepper**

■ In a large pot, bring 6 cups water and 1 tsp of the salt to a boil. Slowly whisk in polenta. Reduce to a very low simmer, cover and cook 30 minutes.

■ Stir in goat cheese and butter until melted. Mix in chives, remaining 1 tsp salt and the pepper. Serve immediately.

PER SERVING 244 **CAL**; 12 g **FAT** (7 g **SAT**); 6 g **PRO**; 27 g **CARB**; 2 g **FIBER**; 635 mg **SODIUM**; 29 mg **CHOL**

Holiday Spelt Salad

PHOTO ON PAGE 212

MAKES 8 servings **PREP** 10 minutes
COOK 75 minutes

- 2 **cups spelt**
- 4 **tbsp pomegranate vinegar or balsamic vinegar**
- 3 **tbsp extra-virgin olive oil**
- 1¼ **tsp salt**
- ¼ **tsp black pepper**
- 2 **cups packed arugula**
- 1 **cup pomegranate seeds**
- 4 **oz feta cheese, crumbled**

■ In a large pot, combine spelt and 6 cups water. Bring to a boil. Cover and reduce heat to a low simmer. Cook 65 to 75 minutes, until tender. Drain and rinse under cool water.

■ In a large bowl, whisk vinegar, oil, salt and pepper. Stir in cooked spelt, arugula, pomegranate seeds and feta.

PER SERVING 258 **CAL**; 10 g **FAT** (3 g **SAT**); 8 g **PRO**; 38 g **CARB**; 5 g **FIBER**; 525 mg **SODIUM**; 13 mg **CHOL**

Organic Baby Lettuces and Quinoa Salad

MAKES 6 servings **PREP** 20 minutes

- 3 **tbsp extra-virgin olive oil**
- 1 **tbsp balsamic vinegar**
- 1 **tsp Dijon mustard**
- ¼ **tsp salt**
- ¼ **tsp black pepper**
- 6 **cups mixed baby organic lettuces**
- 1 **cup cooked quinoa, cooled**
- 2 **cups corn kernels (from 2 ears corn)**
- 1 **cup blanched snow peas**
- 2 **cups heirloom cherry tomatoes, halved**
- 1 **avocado, diced**
- ½ **small red onion, thinly sliced**
- ½ **cup shaved Parmesan cheese**

■ Place oil, vinegar, 1 tbsp water, mustard, salt and pepper in a small lidded jar. Shake until combined.

■ In a large salad bowl, combine lettuces, quinoa, corn, snow peas, tomatoes, avocado and onion. Toss with dressing and top with Parmesan. Serve immediately.

PER SERVING 253 **CAL**; 15 g **FAT** (3 g **SAT**); 7 g **PRO**; 26 g **CARB**; 6 g **FIBER**; 312 mg **SODIUM**; 5 mg **CHOL**

CREAMY
POLENTA

RASPBERRY-ALMOND TART,
RECIPE PAGE 256

Desserts

Whether you're looking for just a nibble of something sweet or an indulgent treat, you'll find the perfect ending here.

BLACKBERRY CORN CAKE WITH HONEY WHIPPED CREAM

Honey Cake

MAKES 12 servings **PREP** 20 minutes
BAKE at 350° for 40 minutes **COOL** 15 minutes
COOK 5 minutes **REFRIGERATE** 4 hours

CAKE

- ¾ cup granulated sugar
- ¼ cup packed dark brown sugar
- ¼ cup vegetable oil
- 3 eggs
- 1 cup finely chopped walnuts
- ½ cup Passover cake meal
- ½ cup chopped almonds
- 3 tbsp orange juice
- ½ tsp ground cinnamon
- ⅛ tsp salt

SYRUP

- ⅓ cup granulated sugar
- ⅓ cup orange juice
- ¼ cup honey
- 2 tbsp lemon juice
- ½ cup sliced almonds

■ **Cake.** Heat oven to 350°. Line bottom of an 8-inch cake pan with wax paper. Grease paper and pan.

■ In a large bowl, beat sugars, oil and eggs until smooth. Add walnuts, cake meal, almonds, orange juice, cinnamon and salt. Stir until combined. Spoon into prepared pan.

■ Bake at 350° for 40 minutes, until cake is set. Cool on a wire rack 15 minutes.

■ **Syrup.** In a small saucepan, combine sugar, orange juice, ⅓ cup water, honey and lemon juice. Simmer 5 minutes, stirring frequently, until mixture reduces slightly. Let cool.

■ Using a fork, poke holes in cake and pour syrup over the top. Refrigerate 4 hours. Invert onto platter. Remove wax paper and top with sliced almonds.

PER SERVING 78 **CAL**; 16 g **FAT** (2 g **SAT**); 6 g **PRO**; 32 g **CARB**; 2 g **FIBER**; 48 mg **SODIUM**; 56 mg **CHOL**

Blackberry Corn Cake with Honey Whipped Cream

MAKES 9 servings **PREP** 15 minutes
BAKE at 350° for 45 minutes **COOL** 20 minutes

- 1 cup plus 1 tbsp all-purpose flour
- ¾ cup fine yellow cornmeal
- 2 tsp baking powder
- ½ tsp salt
- ¾ cup granulated sugar
- ⅔ cup milk
- 6 tbsp unsalted butter, melted
- 2 eggs
- 12 oz blackberries
- 1 tbsp turbinado or demerera sugar (optional)
- 1 cup heavy cream
- 2 tbsp honey

■ Heat oven to 350°. Butter and flour a 9 x 9-inch baking pan. In a bowl, mix 1 cup of the flour, the cornmeal, baking powder and salt. In a separate bowl, whisk sugar, milk, butter and eggs. Fold dry mixture into wet mixture until just combined.

■ Toss blackberries with remaining 1 tbsp flour. Gently fold into batter. Transfer to baking pan, using a spatula to smooth the top. Sprinkle with turbinado sugar, if using.

■ Bake at 350° for 40 to 45 minutes, until a toothpick inserted in center of cake comes out clean. Place on a wire rack and immediately run a paring knife around edge of cake. Cool 20 minutes.

■ Whisk heavy cream and honey in a bowl until stiff peaks form. Serve cake warm or at room temperature with whipped cream.

PER SERVING 350 **CAL**; 20 g **FAT** (12 g **SAT**); 5 g **PRO**; 4 g **CARB**; 3 g **FIBER**; 260 mg **SODIUM**; 100 mg **CHOL**

HONEY CAKE

LEMON-THYME CAKE

Lemon-Thyme Cake

MAKES 18 servings **PREP** 15 minutes
BAKE at 350° for 1 hour

- 3 **cups all-purpose flour**
- 1 **tsp baking powder**
- 1 **tsp baking soda**
- ½ **tsp salt**
- 2 **sticks (1 cup) unsalted butter, softened**
- 2 **cups granulated sugar**
- 5 **eggs**
- ¼ **cup plus 2 tbsp lemon juice**
- 2 **tbsp lemon zest**
- 3 **tbsp fresh thyme, roughly chopped, plus sprigs for garnish (optional)**
- 1 **tsp vanilla extract**
- 1 **cup buttermilk**
- 2 **cups confectioners' sugar**
- ¼ **cup heavy cream**

■ Heat oven to 350°. Butter and flour a 12-cup Bundt pan, making sure to cover every crease so the cake will release after it is baked.

■ In a bowl, whisk together flour, baking powder, baking soda and salt. In a separate larger bowl, beat butter and granulated sugar on high speed for 2 to 3 minutes, until fluffy. Beat in eggs, one at a time. Whisk in ¼ cup of the lemon juice, the zest, thyme and vanilla. On low speed, beat in half the flour mixture, then the buttermilk, followed by remaining flour mixture. Pour batter into prepared pan, tapping it on the counter to release air bubbles.

■ Bake at 350° for 50 to 60 minutes, until a toothpick inserted in center of cake comes out clean.

■ Cool in Bundt pan for exactly 10 minutes. Loosen edges with a paring knife, then turn out onto a cake stand or plate, gently shaking to remove. Allow cake to cool completely.

■ In a bowl, beat confectioners' sugar, cream and remaining 2 tbsp lemon juice on low until combined. Drizzle over cake with a spoon. Garnish with thyme sprigs, if desired.

PER SERVING 337 **CAL**; 13 g **FAT** (7 g **SAT**); 5 g **PRO**; 53 g **CARB**; 1 g **FIBER**; 193 mg **SODIUM**; 89 mg **CHOL**

SALTED CARAMEL APPLE CAKE

Salted Caramel Apple Cake

MAKES 12 servings **PREP** 25 minutes
COOK 15 minutes **BAKE** at 350° for 50 minutes

- 6 **tbsp cold butter**
- 1½ **cups packed light brown sugar**
- 1 **tsp sea salt**
- 4 **Gala apples (about 2 lb), cored and peeled, each cut into 8 wedges**
- 1½ **cups all-purpose flour**
- 1 **tbsp pumpkin pie spice**
- 2 **tsp baking powder**
- ¼ **tsp salt**
- ½ **cup (1 stick) butter, softened**
- 2 **eggs**
- 1 **tsp vanilla extract**
- ½ **cup half-and-half**
  Whipped cream (optional)

■ Heat oven to 350°. Butter the bottom of a 10-inch round cake pan with 4 tbsp of the butter. Sprinkle with ½ cup of the brown sugar and the sea salt.

■ Heat remaining 2 tbsp cold butter in a large skillet over medium heat. Add

apples; sauté 13 to 15 minutes, until tender. Cool.

■ In a large bowl, whisk flour, pumpkin pie spice, baking powder and salt. In a second large bowl, beat softened butter and remaining 1 cup brown sugar until smooth. Beat in eggs, one at a time, then vanilla. On low speed, beat flour mixture into butter mixture, alternating with half-and-half. Scrape down sides of bowl; beat for 1 minute.

■ Fan apples over bottom of prepared pan. Spread batter over apples. Bake at 350° for 45 to 50 minutes, until a toothpick inserted in center comes out clean. Cool for 15 minutes.

■ Run a small knife around edge of pan. Place a serving plate on top of pan and turn plate and pan over together. Carefully remove pan. If any apples remain in pan, place on cake.

■ Serve warm or at room temperature with whipped cream, if desired.

PER SERVING 326 **CAL**; 15 g **FAT** (9 g **SAT**); 3 g **PRO**; 45 g **CARB**; 1 g **FIBER**; 305 mg **SODIUM**; 75 mg **CHOL**

S'mores Cake

MAKES 16 servings **PREP** 30 minutes
BAKE at 350° for 35 minutes **COOL** 10 minutes
BROIL 30 seconds

CAKE

- 2⅓ **cups all-purpose flour**
- ½ **cup unsweetened cocoa powder**
- 1 **tsp baking soda**
- ½ **tsp salt**
- 1 **cup (2 sticks) unsalted butter, softened**
- 2 **cups granulated sugar**
- 4 **large eggs**
- 1 **cup milk, mixed with 1 tsp white vinegar**
- 1 **tbsp vanilla extract**

FILLING AND TOPPING

- 1½ **cups confectioners' sugar**
- 1⅓ **cups marshmallow creme**
- ¼ **cup (½ stick) unsalted butter, softened**
- 2 **jars (11.75 oz each) hot fudge topping**
- 2 **graham cracker boards, crushed**
- 1½ **cups mini marshmallows**

■ Heat oven to 350°. Coat three 9-inch round cake pans with nonstick spray for baking.

■ **Cake.** In a medium bowl, whisk together flour, cocoa, baking soda and salt. In a large bowl, with an electric mixer, beat butter until smooth. Add sugar and beat for 2 minutes, until light and fluffy. Beat in eggs, one at a time. On low speed, beat in half the flour mixture, then the milk mixture, followed by remaining flour mixture. Stir in vanilla and divide batter among prepared pans. Bake at 350° for 30 to 35 minutes, or until cake springs back when lightly pressed. Cool in pans on wire racks for 10 minutes. Run a thin knife around edge of pans; turn cakes out of pans and cool completely.

■ **Filling and Topping.** While cake layers cool, combine confectioners' sugar, marshmallow creme, butter and ½ tsp water in a bowl. Beat on low speed until blended and a good spreading consistency.

■ Once cakes have cooled, place 1 cake layer on a plate. Spread top with ⅔ cup of the fudge topping. Sprinkle with 1 tbsp of the crushed graham crackers. Spread a second cake layer with half the marshmallow frosting, then invert onto cake layer on platter. Spread top with ⅔ cup of the fudge topping and carefully spread with remaining marshmallow filling (may look marbled). Sprinkle with 1 tbsp crushed graham crackers. Spread remaining layer with remaining ⅔ cup fudge sauce (do not stack onto cake yet). Sprinkle with remaining crushed graham crackers and top with marshmallows.

■ Arrange oven rack so cake layer can be about 3 to 4 inches from heat source. Heat broiler. Broil marshmallows for 30 seconds, until they just begin to brown. Carefully place layer on cake.

PER SERVING 570 **CAL**; 21 g **FAT** (11 g **SAT**); 7 g **PRO**; 90 g **CARB**; 2 g **FIBER**; 262 mg **SODIUM**; 92 mg **CHOL**

Mini Cupcakes

MAKES 48 servings **PREP** 15 minutes
MICROWAVE 2½ minutes **BAKE** at 350° for 15 minutes **REFRIGERATE** 15 minutes

CUPCAKES

- 2 **oz semisweet chocolate, chopped**
- 1¼ **cups all-purpose flour**
- ¼ **cup unsweetened cocoa powder**
- 2 **tsp baking powder**
- ¼ **tsp salt**
- ¼ **cup (½ stick) unsalted butter, softened**
- ⅔ **cup sugar**
- 2 **large eggs**
- ½ **cup sour cream blended with ½ cup water**
- ½ **tsp vanilla extract**

FROSTING

- 1 **cup heavy cream**
- 8 **oz semisweet chocolate, chopped**
- **Chocolate sprinkles**

MINI CUPCAKES

■ Heat oven to 350°. Line 48 indents of mini muffin pans with paper or foil liners. If you have only 1 or 2 pans, bake batter in batches.

■ **Cupcakes.** Place chocolate in a small glass bowl. Microwave for 45 seconds, stir and microwave for 45 seconds more. Stir until smooth; set aside to cool slightly. In a medium bowl, whisk flour, cocoa, baking powder and salt.

■ With a hand mixer, beat butter until smooth. Beat in sugar until fluffy, then beat in melted chocolate. Beat in eggs, one at a time, beating well after each. On low speed, beat in half the flour mixture, followed by sour cream mixture and remaining flour mixture. Add vanilla.

■ Transfer batter to a large resealable plastic bag and snip off a corner. Pipe into cupcake liners. Bake at 350° for 14 to 15 minutes; cool completely.

■ **Frosting.** While cupcakes are baking, microwave heavy cream for 1 minute, until steaming. Pour over chocolate in a bowl and whisk until smooth. Refrigerate for 15 minutes or until fairly cool. Beat on medium-high speed until thickened and good spreading consistency (about 5 minutes; frosting will be the color of milk chocolate). Transfer to a piping bag fitted with a small star tip and pipe frosting onto mini cupcakes (alternately, spread frosting onto cupcakes). Decorate with chocolate sprinkles.

PER SERVING 88 **CAL**; 5 g **FAT** (3 g **SAT**); 1 g **PRO**; 9 g **CARB**; 1 g **FIBER**; 35 mg **SODIUM**; 20 mg **CHOL**

Mixed-Berry Tiramisu Cake

MAKES 10 servings **PREP** 25 minutes
MICROWAVE 1 minute **REFRIGERATE** overnight

- 1 qt (1 lb) strawberries, hulled and sliced
- 1 cup sugar
- ½ cup liquid egg substitute
- 1 pkg (8 oz) mascarpone cheese
- 1 tsp vanilla extract
- 1 cup heavy cream
- 2 pkg (3 oz each) soft ladyfingers
- 1 pkg (6 oz) raspberries, plus more for garnish
- 1 pkg (6 oz) blueberries, plus more for garnish
- 4 tbsp cocoa powder

■ Place strawberries and ½ cup of the sugar in a medium bowl. Cover with plastic wrap and microwave on high for 1 minute. Stir and let cool.

■ In a large bowl, beat liquid egg substitute and remaining ½ cup sugar until foamy. Add mascarpone and vanilla; beat until smooth. In a separate bowl, whip cream until soft peaks form. Fold cream into mascarpone mixture.

■ Arrange half the ladyfingers in the bottom of a 9-inch square glass baking dish. Combine strawberries, raspberries and blueberries; spoon half the mixture over ladyfingers, followed by half the mascarpone mixture. Sift 1½ tbsp of the cocoa powder over the top. Repeat layering.

■ Cover and refrigerate overnight. To serve, sift remaining 1 tbsp cocoa powder over top and garnish with additional berries.

PER SERVING 365 **CAL**; 21 g **FAT** (11 g **SAT**); 6 g **PRO**; 42 g **CARB**; 3 g **FIBER**; 167 mg **SODIUM**; 97 mg **CHOL**

Banana Split Cake

MAKES 18 servings **PREP** 20 minutes
BAKE at 350° for 40 minutes **COOL** 15 minutes
STAND 10 minutes

- 3½ cups all-purpose flour
- 1½ tsp baking soda
- 1 tsp salt
- 1½ cups sugar
- 1¼ cups (2½ sticks) unsalted butter, softened
- 4 eggs
- 4 medium very ripe bananas, mashed
- 1 tsp vanilla extract
- ½ cup buttermilk
- 12 oz semisweet chocolate, finely chopped
- 1¼ cups heavy cream
- ⅔ cup strawberry preserves
- ⅔ cup pineapple preserves
- ½ cup chopped walnuts
- 3 maraschino cherries

■ Heat oven to 350°. Butter and flour two 8-inch cake pans; line bottom of pans with parchment paper.

■ Whisk together flour, baking soda and salt. In another bowl, beat sugar and butter until fluffy, 2 to 3 minutes. Add eggs to butter mixture one at a time, beating after each. Stir in mashed bananas and vanilla. Beat in half of the flour mixture, followed by the buttermilk and then remaining flour mixture. Pour batter evenly into cake pans. Bake at 350° for 35 to 40 minutes, until a toothpick inserted in the middle of the cake comes out clean. Cool in pans for 15 minutes, then turn onto wire racks and cool.

■ Place chopped chocolate in the bowl of a stand mixer. Bring cream to a low boil, then pour over chocolate; stir until smooth. Place bowl onto stand mixer fitted with whisk attachment. Beat on medium-high speed until fluffy, 5 to 7 minutes; let stand 10 minutes.

■ Trim cakes to flatten tops. Carefully slice each cake in half horizontally, creating 4 layers. Place 1 layer on stand; spread on strawberry preserves. Top with another layer. Spread ⅔ cup of the ganache on top. Stack on another layer. Spread on pineapple preserves. Top with final layer. Ice cake with remaining ganache. Scatter walnuts over the top and place cherries in the center of the cake. (Cake may be easier to slice if refrigerated for 1 hour before serving.)

PER SERVING 516 **CAL**; 28 g **FAT** (16 g **SAT**); 6 g **PRO**; 65 g **CARB**; 3 g **FIBER**; 266 mg **SODIUM**; 103 mg **CHOL**

BANANA SPLIT CAKE

PEAR UPSIDE-DOWN CAKE

Pear Upside-Down Cake

MAKES 16 servings **PREP** 30 minutes
BAKE at 350° for 60 minutes **COOL** 5 minutes

- 2 **tbsp cold unsalted butter**
- ½ **cup packed dark brown sugar**
- 2 **Bartlett pears (about 1 lb), peeled, cored and thinly sliced**
- 2 **cups all-purpose flour**
- 1 **tbsp ground ginger**
- 2 **tsp baking powder**
- ½ **tsp salt**
- ½ **tsp ground cardamom**
- ½ **cup (1 stick) unsalted butter, softened**
- 1 **cup granulated sugar**
- 2 **large eggs**
- 1 **tsp vanilla extract**
- ⅔ **cup milk**
- **Vanilla or brown sugar ice cream (optional)**

■ Heat oven to 350°. Add cold butter to a 10-inch springform pan. Heat in oven until melted, about 3 minutes. Swirl pan to coat bottom with melted butter. Sprinkle with brown sugar.

■ Fan slices of pears over sugar, pointed ends toward center of pan, overlapping slightly. Set aside.

■ In a small bowl, whisk together flour, ginger, baking powder, salt and cardamom. With a stand mixer, beat softened butter in a large bowl until smooth. Add granulated sugar and beat 2 minutes, until creamy. Beat in eggs, one at a time, beating well after each addition. Beat in vanilla.

■ On low speed, beat in flour mixture, alternating with milk, beginning and ending with flour mixture. Spoon batter over pears and spread to pan edge with a spatula. Wrap bottom of pan with foil and bake at 350° for 55 to 60 minutes. Test center of cake with a toothpick; if pick tests clean, remove to a wire rack. Cool 5 minutes.

■ Invert cake onto plate; remove side of pan. Carefully lift off pan bottom and cool cake to room temperature. Serve slightly warm with ice cream, if desired.

PER SERVING 302 **CAL**; 11 g **FAT** (7 g **SAT**); 4 g **PRO**; 48 g **CARB**; 2 g **FIBER**; 186 mg **SODIUM**; 62 mg **CHOL**

MERINGUE-TOPPED LEMON-POPPY SEED CUPCAKES

Meringue-Topped Lemon-Poppy Seed Cupcakes

MAKES 15 cupcakes **PREP** 25 minutes
BAKE at 350° for 21 minutes **BROIL** 45 seconds
REFRIGERATE 1 hour

CUPCAKES

- 1¾ **cups all-purpose flour**
- 1 **tbsp poppy seeds**
- 1½ **tsp baking powder**
- ¼ **tsp salt**
- ½ **cup (1 stick) unsalted butter, softened**
- ¾ **cup sugar**
- 2 **eggs**
- ½ **tsp vanilla extract**
- ½ **tsp lemon extract**
- 2 **tbsp lemon juice**
- 1 **tsp lemon zest**
- ⅔ **cup milk**
- ½ **cup jarred lemon curd**

MERINGUE

- 4 **pasteurized egg whites**
- ¼ **tsp cream of tartar**
- 6 **tbsp sugar**

■ **Cupcakes.** Heat oven to 350°. Line fifteen 2½-inch muffin cups with paper baking cups.

■ In a large bowl, whisk together flour, poppy seeds, baking powder and salt. Set aside. In a second large bowl, beat butter and sugar on medium-high for 2 minutes, until light and fluffy. Gradually add in eggs, one at a time, until just combined. Beat in extracts, lemon juice and zest. On low, beat in flour mixture, alternating with milk, until just combined.

■ Evenly spoon batter into muffin cups, filling each about three-fourths full. Bake at 350° for 20 to 21 minutes or until a wooden pick inserted in the center comes out clean. Remove to a wire rack and cool completely.

■ Fill cupcakes by placing lemon curd in a pastry bag fitted with a medium star piping tip. Press the end of the tip into each cupcake and gently press until top of cupcake starts to rise.

■ **Meringue.** Heat broiler. Place egg whites in a clean bowl and beat on medium-high until foamy. Beat in cream of tartar and gradually add in sugar. Beat until stiff peaks form. Frost cupcakes with meringue. Broil 6 inches from heat for 45 seconds, until tops start to lightly brown. Refrigerate for 1 hour before serving.

PER CUPCAKE 196 **CAL**; 8 g **FAT** (5 g **SAT**); 4 g **PRO**; 30 g **CARB**; 0 g **FIBER**; 118 mg **SODIUM**; 45 mg **CHOL**

PUMPKIN CAKE ROLL

FILLING AND FROSTING

- ¾ **cup canned pumpkin puree**
- 1 **large egg yolk**
- 6 **tbsp granulated sugar**
- 1½ **cups heavy cream**

■ **Cake.** Heat oven to 375°. Coat a 15 x 10 x 1-inch pan with nonstick cooking spray. Line pan with wax paper; coat paper with spray.

■ In a medium bowl, whisk flour, baking powder, pumpkin pie spice and salt.

■ In a large bowl or in a stand mixer, whip eggs at medium speed until slightly thickened, about 2 minutes. On high speed, beat in granulated sugar, 1 tbsp at a time, until thick and lemon-color, about 5 to 7 minutes. On low, beat in pumpkin puree. Fold in flour mixture in 2 batches. Spread evenly in prepared pan.

■ Bake at 375° for 10 to 12 minutes, until cake springs back slightly when pressed. Meanwhile, sift ¼ cup of the confectioners' sugar over a clean kitchen towel. When cake is done, loosen edges and immediately invert onto prepared towel. Remove pan and wax paper. Sift remaining ¼ cup confectioners' sugar over cake. From a short end, roll up cake with towel, jelly-roll fashion. Cool completely on a wire rack for at least an hour.

■ **Filling.** In a small saucepan, whisk pumpkin puree, egg yolk and 3 tbsp of the granulated sugar. Cook for 5 minutes over medium heat, stirring frequently (mixture should reach 160°). Transfer to a medium bowl. Refrigerate for 20 minutes.

■ Once cake is cool, gently unroll. Whip ¼ cup of the heavy cream with 1 tbsp of the remaining granulated sugar to stiff peaks. Fold into filling and spread over cake. Reroll without towel.

■ **Frosting.** Whip remaining 1¼ cups cream with remaining 2 tbsp sugar to stiff peaks. Spread over cake roll. Dust with a little pumpkin pie spice, if desired. Refrigerate until serving.

PER SERVING 271 CAL; 13 g FAT (8 g SAT); 5 g PRO; 35 g CARB; 2 g FIBER; 135 mg SODIUM; 128 mg CHOL

Pumpkin Cake Roll

MAKES 12 servings **PREP** 20 minutes
COOK 5 minutes **BAKE** at 375° for 12 minutes
COOL 1 hour **REFRIGERATE** 20 minutes

CAKE

- 1 **cup all-purpose flour**
- 1½ **tsp baking powder**
- 1 **tsp pumpkin pie spice, plus more for serving (optional)**
- ¼ **tsp salt**
- 4 **eggs, at room temperature**
- ¾ **cup granulated sugar**
- ¾ **cup canned pumpkin puree**
- ½ **cup confectioners' sugar**

French Silk Pie

MAKES 12 servings **PREP** 40 minutes **BAKE** at 450° for 11 minutes **COOL** at least 30 minutes **COOK** 15 minutes **REFRIGERATE** at least 5 hours

1	refrigerated rolled piecrust (from a 14.1 oz pkg)
1¾	cups heavy cream
6	oz semisweet chocolate, chopped
⅓	cup unsalted butter
⅓	cup plus 1 tbsp sugar
2	egg yolks, beaten
	Chocolate curls (optional)

■ Heat oven to 450°. Fit piecrust into a 9-inch pie plate and decoratively flute edge. Pierce all over with a fork.

Bake crust at 450° for 9 to 11 minutes. Cool at least 30 minutes.

■ In a medium heavy saucepan, combine 1 cup of the cream, the chopped chocolate, butter and ⅓ cup of the sugar. Cook over low heat, stirring constantly, until chocolate is melted, about 10 minutes. Remove from heat. Gradually whisk half the hot mixture into beaten egg yolks. Return egg mixture to chocolate mixture in saucepan. Cook over medium-low heat, stirring constantly, until mixture is slightly thickened and begins to bubble, about 5 minutes. Remove from heat. (Mixture may appear slightly curdled.) Stir in ¼ cup of the remaining cream. Place saucepan in a bowl of ice water, stirring occasionally, until mixture stiffens and becomes hard to stir (about 20 minutes). Transfer chocolate mixture to a medium mixing bowl. Let cool.

■ Beat cooled chocolate mixture with an electric mixer on medium to high speed 2 to 3 minutes, until light and fluffy. Spread filling in baked pastry shell. Cover and refrigerate pie at least 5 hours. To serve, whip remaining ½ cup heavy cream with remaining 1 tbsp sugar. Spoon into center of pie. Garnish with chocolate curls, if desired.

PER SERVING 346 **CAL**; 29 g **FAT** (17 g **SAT**); 3 g **PRO**; 23 g **CARB**; 1 g **FIBER**; 110 mg **SODIUM**; 94 mg **CHOL**

APPLE CRUMB PIE

Apple Crumb Pie

MAKES 12 servings **PREP** 20 minutes
BAKE at 425° for 25 minutes and at 375° for
45 minutes **COOL** at least 2 hours

- **1 prepared refrigerated piecrust (from a 14.1 oz pkg)**

CRUMB TOPPING

- **1 cup all-purpose flour**
- **⅓ cup packed light brown sugar**
- **½ tsp ground cinnamon**
- **⅛ tsp salt**
- **Pinch ground cloves**
- **6 tbsp (¾ stick) unsalted butter, cut into pieces and chilled**
- **⅓ cup chopped pecans (optional)**

PIE FILLING

- **2 Golden Delicious apples (¾ to 1 lb total), peeled, cored and thinly sliced**
- **2 Granny Smith apples (¾ to 1 lb total), peeled, cored and thinly sliced**
- **2 cups cranberries, thawed, if frozen**
- **⅔ cup packed light brown sugar**
- **¼ cup all-purpose flour**
- **½ tsp ground cinnamon**
- **¼ tsp salt**
- **Pinch ground cloves**
- **2 tbsp fresh lemon juice**

■ Place a rack in the lowest slot of your oven; place foil on bottom of oven to catch drips. Heat oven to 425°. Fit piecrust into a 9-inch pie plate and decoratively crimp edge. Refrigerate until ready to fill.

■ **Crumb Topping.** Combine flour, brown sugar, cinnamon, salt and cloves in a bowl. Rub in butter with fingertips until crumbly. Stir in nuts, if using.

■ **Pie Filling.** In a large bowl, toss apples, cranberries, brown sugar, flour, cinnamon, salt and cloves. Add lemon juice and toss to coat.

■ Spoon filling into pie shell, mounding slightly in center. Cover with foil and bake at 425° for 20 to 25 minutes.

■ Carefully remove pie from oven; reduce oven to 375° and top pie with crumb topping.

■ Return pie to oven and bake at 375° for 45 minutes, until fruit is tender. Let cool at least 2 hours before slicing and serving.

PER SERVING 368 **CAL**; 19 g **FAT** (9 g **SAT**); 3 g **PRO**; 49 g **CARB**; 4 g **FIBER**; 163 mg **SODIUM**; 31 mg **CHOL**

Strawberry Key Lime Pie

MAKES 12 servings **PREP** 25 minutes
COOK 10 minutes **BAKE** at 375° for 15 minutes and at 350° for 17 minutes
REFRIGERATE 3 hours or overnight

- **½ lb strawberries, hulled and finely diced, plus 6 strawberries, hulled and sliced**
- **½ cup plus 2 tbsp sugar**
- **3 tbsp unsalted butter, cold**
- **2 whole eggs, beaten**
- **18 graham cracker boards**
- **1 stick (½ cup) unsalted butter, melted**
- **5 egg yolks**
- **½ cup Key lime juice**
- **1 can (14 oz) sweetened condensed milk**
- **¾ cup heavy cream**

■ Combine ½ lb diced strawberries, ½ cup of the sugar, the cold butter and whole eggs in a pot over medium heat. Stir constantly until thickened, being careful not to scramble, 8 to 10 minutes. Pour through a fine-mesh strainer and cool. Refrigerate strawberry curd at least 1 hour.

■ Heat oven to 375°. Add graham crackers and 1 tbsp of the sugar to a food processor and process until finely ground. Pour in melted butter and process until well combined. Transfer to a 9-inch pie plate and press into bottom and sides of dish with the bottom of a measuring cup. Bake at 375° for 15 minutes. Cool slightly.

■ Reduce heat to 350°. In a bowl, beat egg yolks, lime juice, condensed milk and strawberry curd until smooth. Pour into pie shell and bake at 350° for 15 to 17 minutes, until set. Cool, then refrigerate at least 2 hours or overnight.

■ Whip heavy cream and remaining 1 tbsp sugar until stiff peaks form. Transfer to a piping bag fitted with a star tip. Pipe a circle around the pie and a few circles in the center. Garnish with sliced strawberries.

PER SERVING 390 **CAL**; 23 g **FAT** (13 g **SAT**); 7 g **PRO**; 43 g **CARB**; 1 g **FIBER**; 105 mg **SODIUM**; 170 mg **CHOL**

STRAWBERRY
KEY LIME PIE

SWEET POTATO PIE

Sweet Potato Pie

MAKES 12 servings **PREP** 20 minutes
MICROWAVE 10 minutes **BAKE** at 425° for
15 minutes and at 350° for 45 minutes
CHILL overnight

- 2 **large sweet potatoes (1¼ lb total), scrubbed**
- 1 **pkg (14.1 oz) refrigerated piecrusts**
- 3 **large eggs**
- ¾ **cup half-and-half**
- ¾ **cup plus 1 tsp sugar**
- 2 **tsp pumpkin pie spice**

■ Heat oven to 425°. Pierce potatoes all over with a fork. Place on a microwave-safe plate and microwave 10 minutes or until tender, turning over halfway through. Peel and mash until completely smooth. Cool slightly.

■ Fit one piecrust into a 9-inch pie plate and form a flat edge. Using a 1-inch acorn- or leaf-shaped cookie cutter, cut out 45 to 50 shapes from second crust; place on a baking sheet and refrigerate until ready to use.

■ Separate 1 egg. In a large bowl, beat cooled sweet potatoes, half-and-half, remaining 2 eggs plus the egg yolk, ¾ cup of the sugar and the pumpkin pie spice. Pour into piecrust.

■ Beat remaining egg white. Brush edge of piecrust with egg white. Overlap pastry shapes around edge, reserving 7 on a small piece of foil. Brush crust edge and extra shapes with egg whites; sprinkle with remaining 1 tsp sugar.

■ Bake pie and extra shapes at 425° for 15 minutes. Remove extra dough shapes from oven and reduce temperature to 350°. Carefully cover edge with foil. Bake at 350° for 40 to 45 minutes.

■ Cool pie completely on a wire rack. Refrigerate overnight or until chilled. Garnish with decorative shapes before serving.

Raspberry-Almond Tart

PHOTO ON PAGE 240

MAKES 12 servings **PREP** 25 minutes
REFRIGERATE 1 hour **BAKE** at 375° for
45 minutes

CRUST

- 1¼ **cups all-purpose flour**
- 1 **stick (½ cup) unsalted butter, cold, cut into cubes**
- 1 **tbsp sugar**
- ¼ **tsp salt**

FILLING

- 5 **tbsp unsalted butter, softened**
- ½ **cup plus 1 tbsp sugar**
- ⅛ **tsp salt**
- ¾ **cup almond flour (such as Bob's Red Mill)**
- 1 **whole egg plus 1 egg white**
- 1 **tbsp all-purpose flour**
- ½ **tsp almond extract**
- 12 **oz raspberries**
- 1 **tsp lemon zest**

■ **Crust.** Combine flour, butter, sugar and salt in a food processor; pulse until mixture resembles coarse crumbs (butter will be the size of peas). Add 3 tbsp ice water and process until just combined. Pour onto a clean counter and form into a disk. Wrap in plastic and refrigerate 1 hour.

■ Heat oven to 375°. Roll dough into a 10½-inch circle on a floured surface. Fit into a 9-inch tart pan with a removable bottom, trimming edge. Refrigerate while making filling.

■ **Filling.** In a food processor, combine butter, ½ cup of the sugar and salt. Process until smooth. Add almond flour, eggs, all-purpose flour and almond extract. Process until smooth.

■ Toss raspberries with remaining 1 tbsp sugar and the lemon zest. Scatter half the berries in bottom of tart shell. Spread almond mixture (frangipane) evenly over top. Scatter remaining berries over frangipane. Bake at 375° for 45 minutes, until lightly browned. Cool on a wire rack.

PER SERVING 250 **CAL**; 17 g **FAT** (8 g **SAT**); 4 g **PRO**; 23 g **CARB**; 3 g **FIBER**; 90 mg **SODIUM**; 50 mg **CHOL**

MILK CHOCOLATE
ICEBOX PIE

Milk Chocolate Icebox Pie

MAKES 8 servings **PREP** 30 minutes
COOK 6 minutes **COOL** 15 minutes
REFRIGERATE overnight

CRUST

1⅔ **cups finely crushed Nabisco Famous wafer cookies (28 cookies)**

6 **tbsp unsalted butter, softened**

1 **tbsp sugar**

Pinch salt

FILLING

3 **Hershey's milk chocolate bars (1.55 oz each)**

4 **large eggs**

⅔ **cup sugar**

2 **tbsp unsweetened cocoa powder**

½ **cup (1 stick) unsalted butter, softened**

⅛ **tsp salt**

1 **container (8 oz) frozen whipped topping, thawed**

■ **Crust.** In a medium bowl stir together cookie crumbs, butter, sugar and salt. Press into bottom and up sides of a 9-inch pie plate (not deep dish). Refrigerate while preparing filling.

■ **Filling.** Chop 2½ of the chocolate bars; set aside. Combine eggs and ⅓ cup of the sugar in a large metal bowl or double boiler. Bring 2 inches of water to a simmer in a large pot or Dutch oven. Place bowl or double boiler over pan without touching water. Cook, beating constantly with a hand mixer, until mixture is a light color and fluffy and registers 160° on an instant-read thermometer, 5 to 6 minutes. Watch carefully; if eggs get too hot, they will scramble.

■ Remove bowl from heat. Whisk in chopped chocolate and cocoa powder until smooth. Set aside to cool for 15 minutes, whisking occasionally.

■ Once egg mixture is cooled, combine remaining ⅓ cup sugar with the butter and salt in a large bowl. Beat on high speed until a very light color, about 2 minutes. On medium, beat in egg mixture, scraping down side of bowl. Fold in half of the whipped topping and spread into prepared crust. Refrigerate overnight.

■ Just before serving, spread center of pie with remaining whipped topping. Use a vegetable peeler to make large curls from reserved ½ chocolate bar or cut into shards and sprinkle over pie.

PER SERVING 551 **CAL**; 35 g **FAT** (21 g **SAT**); 6 g **PRO**; 52 g **CARB**; 2 g **FIBER**; 284 mg **SODIUM**; 166 mg **CHOL**

PLUM AND BLACKBERRY TART

to oven for a few minutes to gently heat fruit and goat cheese. Serve warm or at room temperature.

PER SERVING 142 **CAL**; 5 g **FAT** (3 g **SAT**); 4 g **PRO**; 21 g **CARB**; 2 g **FIBER**; 89 mg **SODIUM**; 7 mg **CHOL**

Blueberry-Thyme Pie

MAKES 12 servings **PREP** 15 minutes
BAKE at 400° for 15 minutes and at 350° for 60 minutes

2	refrigerated ready-to-roll piecrusts
5	cups blueberries
¾	cup plus 1 tbsp sugar
1	tbsp fresh thyme leaves
⅓	cup quick-cooking tapioca
1	tsp lemon zest
2	tbsp lemon juice
1	egg white, lightly beaten

■ Heat oven to 400°. Fit one piecrust into a 9-inch deep-dish pie plate.

■ In a large bowl, toss together blueberries, ¾ cup of the sugar, the thyme, tapioca, lemon zest and juice.

■ Cut remaining crust into 1-inch-wide strips with a pastry or pizza cutter.

■ Spoon blueberry mixture into pie plate. Weave a lattice top, alternating strips of crust. Crimp edges to seal. Brush crust with egg white and sprinkle with remaining 1 tbsp sugar.

■ Bake pie at 400° for 15 minutes. Reduce heat to 350° and continue baking for 55 to 60 minutes or until center is bubbly and crust is golden. Tent sides with foil after 40 minutes so sides do not get too brown.

■ Remove to a wire rack and cool completely.

PER SERVING 248 **CAL**; 10 g **FAT** (4 g **SAT**); 2 g **PRO**; 41 g **CARB**; 2 g **FIBER**; 139 mg **SODIUM**; 7 mg **CHOL**

Plum and Blackberry Tart

MAKES 6 servings **PREP** 15 minutes
BAKE at 400° for 17 minutes

1	sheet puff pastry (from a 17.5-oz pkg)
¼	cup agave nectar
2	tsp fresh thyme or lemon thyme leaves
2	red plums, thinly sliced
2	black plums, thinly sliced
12	blackberries, halved
3	oz goat cheese
3	tbsp milk

■ Heat oven to 400°. Lightly coat a baking sheet with nonstick cooking spray.

■ Unfold pastry sheet on prepared baking sheet. Cut a 1-inch-wide strip from each long side. Brush a 1-inch-wide strip along the 2 long sides with water. Lay a cut strip along each side to form a border. Brush bottom of tart with 2 tbsp of the agave nectar and sprinkle thyme over the bottom. Using a fork, prick pastry all over, about 1 inch apart.

■ Bake at 400° for 16 to 17 minutes or until nicely browned. Transfer baking sheet to a wire rack; let cool. Gently press down center of tart if puffed.

■ Fan plums and blackberries in a decorative pattern over tart. Drizzle remaining 2 tbsp agave nectar over top. Whip goat cheese and milk together and dollop over top. Return

BLUEBERRY-THYME PIE

APPLE GRANOLA PIE

Bourbon Sweet Potato Pie

MAKES 8 servings **PREP** 15 minutes
MICROWAVE 6 minutes **BAKE** at 400° for
15 minutes and at 350° for 45 minutes
BROIL 2 minutes

- 1 **refrigerated piecrust (from a 15-oz pkg)**
- 1 **lb sweet potatoes (about 2 large)**
- 2 **eggs**
- 4 **tbsp unsalted butter, melted**
- ⅔ **cup packed dark brown sugar**
- ¾ **cup heavy cream**
- ¼ **cup plus 1 tbsp bourbon**
- ½ **tsp cinnamon**
- ½ **tsp vanilla extract**
- ¼ **tsp nutmeg**
- 4 **tsp powdered egg whites**
- ¼ **cup granulated sugar**

■ Heat oven to 400°. Roll out piecrust and fit into a 9-inch pie plate. Crimp edges. Place a piece of parchment on crust and fill with pie weights or dried beans. Bake at 400° for 15 minutes. Remove parchment and weights or beans. Reduce heat to 350°.

■ Meanwhile, pierce sweet potatoes a few times with a fork and place on a plate. Microwave for 3 minutes. Turn over and cook another 2 to 3 minutes. Let cool slightly, then carefully slice and scoop flesh out into a large bowl. Beat sweet potatoes, whole eggs, butter, brown sugar, heavy cream, ¼ cup of the bourbon, the cinnamon, vanilla and nutmeg until smooth. Transfer to crust and smooth top. Bake at 350° for 40 to 45 minutes, until firm.

■ In a mixing bowl, combine powdered egg whites and 3 tbsp warm water. Stir gently until dissolved. Beat in remaining 1 tbsp bourbon until frothy. Gradually add granulated sugar and beat with an electric mixer until stiff peaks form, 5 to 7 minutes. Spoon onto warm pie, making sure meringue reaches edge of crust. Broil on high for 1 to 2 minutes, until lightly browned, watching carefully.

PER SERVING 417 **CAL**; 22 g **FAT** (12 g **SAT**); 5 g **PRO**; 46 g **CARB**; 1 g **FIBER**; 160 mg **SODIUM**; 103 mg **CHOL**

Apple Granola Pie

MAKES 8 servings **PREP** 25 minutes
BAKE at 400° for 25 minutes and at 325° for
25 minutes **COOL** 30 minutes

- 1 **refrigerated rolled piecrust (from a 14.1-oz pkg)**

FILLING

- 4 **Granny Smith apples (about 2 lb), peeled, cored and thinly sliced**
- ½ **cup golden raisins**
- ⅓ **cup plus 2 tbsp granulated sugar**
- 2 **tbsp lemon juice**
- ½ **tsp ground cinnamon**
- 2 **tbsp cornstarch**

TOPPING

- ¾ **cup all-purpose flour**
- ½ **cup old-fashioned oats (not quick-cooking)**
- ¼ **cup packed light brown sugar**
- ¼ **tsp ground cinnamon**
  Pinch of salt
- 7 **tbsp cold unsalted butter, cut into small pieces**
- ¼ **cup sliced almonds**

■ Heat oven to 400°. Unroll crust and fit into a standard 9-inch pie plate.

Flute edge as desired and refrigerate while preparing filling and topping.

■ **Filling.** In a large bowl, combine apples, golden raisins, ⅓ cup of the granulated sugar, the lemon juice and ground cinnamon. Toss to coat and let stand for 10 minutes.

■ **Topping.** In a medium bowl, whisk together flour, oats, brown sugar, cinnamon and salt. Cut butter into mixture with a pastry blender or rub between your fingers until crumbly. Stir in sliced almonds.

■ In a small bowl, combine remaining 2 tbsp granulated sugar and the cornstarch. Sprinkle over apple mixture and toss to combine. Pour mixture into crust, mounding slightly in center. Cover with topping and transfer to oven.

■ Bake at 400° for 25 minutes. Cover pie with foil, reduce oven temperature to 325° and continue baking for 20 to 25 minutes, until apples can be easily pierced with a small knife. Cool at least 30 minutes before slicing.

PER SERVING 447 **CAL**; 19 g **FAT** (9 g **SAT**); 4 g **PRO**; 69 g **CARB**; 4 g **FIBER**; 143 mg **SODIUM**; 31 mg **CHOL**

BOURBON SWEET POTATO PIE

MINI
CHOCOLATE
CHEESECAKES

Mini Pain au Chocolat

MAKES 12 servings **PREP** 10 minutes
BAKE at 400° for 18 minutes

- 1 **pkg (17.3 oz) frozen puff pastry, thawed**
- 1 **egg, beaten with 1 tbsp water**
- ¾ **cup (4.5 oz) Ghirardelli bittersweet chocolate morsels**
- 2 **tbsp seedless raspberry jam or orange marmalade**
- 1 **tbsp sugar**

■ Heat oven to 400°. Unfold pastry sheets on a cutting board and cut each into 6 equal pieces. Roll 1 piece out lengthwise to 7 inches. Brush edges with egg wash. Place a scant tbsp chocolate in center of pastry. Top with ½ tsp raspberry jam. Starting on a short side, fold 1 end over chocolate, then fold over other end to resemble an envelope. Place on a baking sheet. Repeat with all pastry pieces, chocolate, and jam. Brush pastries with egg wash; top with sugar.

■ Bake at 400° for 18 minutes or until puffed and golden brown. Cool slightly before serving.

PER SERVING 241 **CAL**; 16 g **FAT** (5 g **SAT**); 4 g **PRO**; 23 g **CARB**; 2 g **FIBER**; 205 mg **SODIUM**; 18 mg **CHOL**

Mini Chocolate Cheesecakes

MAKES 6 mini cakes **PREP** 25 minutes
BAKE at 350° for 30 minutes
MICROWAVE 2½ minutes

CRUST

- 18 **Nabisco Famous chocolate wafers, finely crushed**
- 2 **tbsp unsalted butter, melted**

CHEESECAKES

- 4 **oz semisweet chocolate, chopped**
- 1 **large egg, separated**
- 1 **large egg white**
- ⅓ **cup plus 2 tsp sugar**
- 1½ **pkg cream cheese, softened**
- ⅓ **cup sour cream**
- 1 **tbsp cornstarch**
- ½ **tsp vanilla extract**

MINI PAIN AU CHOCOLAT

TOPPING

- 1 **cup strawberries, chopped**
- ½ **tsp sugar**
- ½ **cup heavy cream**
- 4 **oz semisweet chocolate, chopped**

■ **Crust.** Combine crushed wafers and butter in a bowl. Set aside.

■ **Cheesecakes.** Heat oven to 350°. Line 6 indents of a jumbo muffin tin with jumbo muffin liners.

■ Microwave chocolate 1 minute. Stir until smooth, microwaving more if there are lumps. Set aside to cool slightly. Beat egg white with 2 tsp sugar until stiff peaks form. Set aside.

■ Beat cream cheese until smooth. Add remaining ⅓ cup sugar, the sour cream and cornstarch; beat until sugar is almost dissolved, 2 minutes. Beat in melted chocolate, egg yolk and vanilla until smooth and no white streaks remain, scraping sides of bowl. Fold in beaten egg whites. Divide evenly

among indents in prepared muffin tin, ⅓ to ½ cup batter in each.

■ Top each cheesecake with 3 tbsp of the crumb mixture, patting slightly to adhere. Bake at 350° for 20 to 30 minutes, until puffed and set in the center. Remove from oven and cool 30 minutes in pan on a wire rack. Refrigerate at least 1 hour.

■ Once cheesecakes are cool, remove from pan, invert them and remove liners (some crumbs will fall off). Place on a wire rack set over wax paper.

■ **Topping.** Stir strawberries and sugar. Let stand to blend flavors. Microwave heavy cream 30 seconds. Pour over chopped chocolate and whisk until chocolate is melted and mixture is smooth and shiny. Refrigerate 10 minutes. Spoon over cheesecakes and spread with a small spatula. Top each cake with 1 heaping tbsp of the strawberry topping.

PER ½ MINI CAKE 339 **CAL**; 24 g **FAT** (14 g **SAT**); 4 g **PRO**; 27 g **CARB**; 2 g **FIBER**; 170 mg **SODIUM**; 73 mg **CHOL**

1 tbsp sugar and 1 tbsp water in a pot. Cook over medium heat until berries burst, about 5 minutes. Cool. Refrigerate until using.

■ Remove cakes from pan and peel off liners. Spoon berries on top of each cake and, if desired, garnish with mint leaves.

PER SERVING 310 **CAL**; 20 g **FAT** (11 g **SAT**); 8 g **PRO**; 28 g **CARB**; 2 g **FIBER**; 290 mg **SODIUM**; 75 mg **CHOL**

Berry Cheesecake Pops

MAKES 24 pops **PREP** 20 minutes
BAKE at 350° for 45 minutes
REFRIGERATE overnight
MICROWAVE 2 minutes **FREEZE** 30 minutes
DECORATE 45 minutes

- **2 pkg (8 oz each) cream cheese, softened**
- **⅓ cup sugar**
- **¼ cup mixed berry, strawberry or seedless raspberry preserves**
- **¼ cup sour cream**
- **2 tbsp cornstarch**
- **1 tsp vanilla extract**
- **⅛ tsp salt**
- **2 large eggs**
- **1 bag (12 oz) Wilton White Candy Melts**
- **24 lollipop sticks**
- **⅔ cup cornflake crumbs**
- **2 oz semisweet chocolate, chopped**

■ Heat oven to 350°. Coat an 8-inch square baking dish with nonstick cooking spray.

■ In a large bowl, beat cream cheese, sugar and preserves until smooth. Stir in sour cream, scraping down sides of bowl. Add cornstarch, vanilla and salt. Blend on low speed. Add eggs, one at a time, blending well after each. Pour into prepared pan, spreading level.

■ Bake at 350° for 45 minutes, until set in the center. Cool on a wire rack, then refrigerate overnight.

■ Use a small scoop to shape cheesecake into 1-inch balls (start at center of pan; if possible, don't use browned edges). Roll cheesecake

MINI BERRY GOAT CHEESE CAKES

Mini Berry Goat Cheese Cakes

MAKES 12 servings **PREP** 20 minutes
BAKE at 350° for 15 minutes

- **8 oz gingersnaps**
- **4 tbsp unsalted butter, melted**
- **8 oz goat cheese, at room temperature**
- **8 oz cream cheese, at room temperature**
- **⅔ cup plus 1 tbsp sugar**
- **⅛ tsp salt**
- **2 eggs**
- **1 tsp vanilla extract**
- **1 cup blackberries**
- **1 cup raspberries**
- **1 cup blueberries**
- **Mint leaves, for garnish (optional)**

■ Heat oven to 350°. Add gingersnaps to a food processor; process until finely ground (yields about 1 cup). Pour in melted butter; process until well combined. Insert 12 liners in a standard-size square or round muffin pan. Press 2 tbsp of the ground gingersnaps firmly into each liner.

■ Beat goat cheese and cream cheese with a hand mixer on low until smooth. Add ⅔ cup of the sugar and the salt; beat until combined. Incorporate eggs, one at a time, then add vanilla. Beat on high until smooth, about 2 minutes.

■ Pour evenly into muffin liners. Bake at 350° for 15 minutes, until set. Cool to room temperature, then refrigerate until cold.

■ Meanwhile, combine blackberries, raspberries, blueberries, remaining

BERRY CHEESECAKE POPS

balls between your hands and place on a wax paper-lined baking sheet.

■ Melt white candy in microwave, per package directions, about 1 minute. Dip each stick into melted candy and insert into cake balls. Freeze for 30 minutes.

■ Remelt candy, if needed. Have cornflake crumbs ready in a small bowl. Remove half of the cheesecake

pops from freezer. Dip to coat in white candy, shaking off excess. Dip bottom halves of pops in cornflake crumbs to resemble a crust. Place upright on wax paper.

■ Melt semisweet chocolate in microwave for 1 minute. Stir until smooth and transfer to a small resealable plastic bag. Remove remaining pops from freezer and dip

in white candy to coat. Shake off excess and let dry on wax paper. Snip a small corner from bag of chocolate. While spinning a pop in one hand, drizzle chocolate in a thin spiral. Refrigerate pops until serving.

PER POP 171 CAL; 11 g FAT (8 g SAT); 2 g PRO; 15 g CARB; 0 g FIBER; 97 mg SODIUM; 40 mg CHOL

MAPLE-PEAR
CHEESECAKE PIE

Maple-Pear Cheesecake Pie

MAKES 12 servings **PREP** 25 minutes
COOK 20 minutes **BAKE** at 375° for 30 minutes
REFRIGERATE at least 3 hours

- 12 graham cracker boards (or 1½ cups graham cracker crumbs)
- 4 tbsp unsalted butter, melted
- ¾ cup plus 1 tbsp maple syrup, plus more for drizzling
- 2 to 3 pears, peeled, halved and cored
- 2 pkg (8 oz each) cream cheese, at room temperature
- 1 large egg
- 2 tsp cornstarch
- ⅛ tsp ground cinnamon
- Toasted walnuts (optional)

■ Heat oven to 375°. In a food processor, crush graham crackers until even crumbs are created. Add melted butter and 1 tbsp of the syrup and pulse until blended. Press into a 9-inch pie plate. Set aside.

■ In a large lidded pot, combine ½ cup of the syrup and 2 cups water and bring to a boil over high heat. Reduce heat to medium and add pear halves. Cover and cook 10 minutes.

■ Meanwhile, in a medium bowl, beat cream cheese until smooth. Add remaining ¼ cup syrup, the egg, cornstarch and cinnamon. Spread into prepared crust.

■ Bake cream cheese layer at 375° for 20 minutes.

■ Uncover pears and turn over. Cover and continue to cook 10 minutes more. Remove to a cutting board and cool slightly.

■ Slice pears into thin wedges. Fan into pie over cream cheese filling. Cool to room temperature, then refrigerate at least 3 hours. Drizzle with additional syrup and sprinkle with toasted walnuts, if desired.

PER SERVING 319 **CAL**; 19 g **FAT** (10 g **SAT**); 4 g **PRO**; 36 g **CARB**; 2 g **FIBER**; 251 mg **SODIUM**; 71 mg **CHOL**

Cherry Galette

MAKES 8 servings **PREP** 30 minutes
REFRIGERATE 1 hour
BAKE at 375° for 55 minutes

DOUGH

- 1¼ cups all-purpose flour
- 1 stick (½ cup) cold unsalted butter, cubed
- 1 tbsp sugar
- ¼ tsp salt

FILLING

- 1½ lb sweet cherries, stemmed, pitted and halved
- ⅓ cup granulated sugar
- 1 tbsp cornstarch
- 1 tbsp lemon juice
- ¼ tsp almond extract
- ⅛ tsp salt
- Cream or half-and-half, for brushing
- 2 tbsp turbinado or raw sugar

■ **Dough.** In a food processor, combine flour, butter, sugar and salt. Pulse until butter resembles coarse crumbs (a few larger pieces are okay).

With machine running, stream in 2 tbsp ice water, about 20 seconds. Check to see if dough has come together. If it seems dry, add ice water, 1 tbsp at a time, with machine running, being careful not to make dough too wet. Do not overmix. Transfer dough onto a work surface, form into a disk, wrap in plastic and refrigerate for 1 hour.

■ **Filling.** Heat oven to 375°. In a bowl, combine cherries, sugar, cornstarch, lemon juice, almond extract and salt. Set aside.

■ On a lightly floured surface, roll out chilled dough to a 13-inch circle. Transfer dough to a baking sheet lined with parchment paper. Pour filling into middle of dough, leaving a 2-inch border around edges. Fold edges over filling (galette should be 9 inches wide when complete). Brush border with cream and sprinkle with turbinado sugar. Bake at 375° for 50 to 55 minutes, until crust is golden brown. Cool on a wire rack.

PER SERVING 528 **CAL**; 16 g **FAT** (4 g **SAT**); 29 g **PRO**; 65 g **CARB**; 4 g **FIBER**; 661 mg **SODIUM**; 72 mg **CHOL**

CHERRY GALETTE

COCONUT-MANGO TAPIOCA PUDDING

coconut, ½ cup tapioca, another ¼ cup mango and another 1 heaping tbsp coconut. Cover and refrigerate until cool, at least 2 hours.

PER SERVING 390 CAL; 23 g FAT (20 g SAT); 4 g PRO; 48 g CARB; 4 g FIBER; 80 mg SODIUM; 30 mg CHOL

Banana Pudding

MAKES 8 servings PREP 10 minutes
COOK 5 minutes REFRIGERATE at least 3 hours or overnight

½	cup plus 1 tbsp sugar
3	tbsp cornstarch
3	cups 2% or whole milk
6	egg yolks, beaten
1	tsp vanilla extract
3	tbsp unsalted butter
8	9-oz glass canning jars with lids
48	vanilla wafer cookies
4	bananas, sliced
1	cup heavy cream, chilled

■ Blend ½ cup of the sugar and the cornstarch in a medium pot. Stir in milk. Bring to a simmer, stirring often. Whisk 1 cup of the mixture into beaten egg yolks. Stir egg mixture back into pot. Cook for 4 to 5 minutes, until it reaches 160°, thickens and begins to bubble. Remove from heat; stir in vanilla and butter. Cool completely.

■ In the bottom of each jar, place 3 vanilla wafers. Cover with a layer of bananas. Spoon a scant ¼ cup of the pudding on top of each. Repeat layering. Secure lids; refrigerate at least 3 hours or overnight.

■ Just before serving, combine heavy cream and remaining 1 tbsp sugar in a bowl. Using a hand mixer, whisk until stiff peaks form. Spoon over each dessert.

PER SERVING 523 CAL; 25 g FAT (13 g SAT); 7 g PRO; 76 g CARB; 2 g FIBER; 126 mg SODIUM; 218 mg CHOL

Coconut-Mango Tapioca Pudding

MAKES 6 servings PREP 15 minutes
SOAK overnight COOK 50 minutes
COOL 10 minutes REFRIGERATE at least 2 hours

½	cup large pearl tapioca
2	cups coconut water
1	can (13.5 ounces) coconut milk
1	tsp vanilla extract
⅛	tsp salt
1	egg yolk
⅓	cup sugar
2	ripe mangoes, peeled, pitted and diced (2 cups)
1	cup unsweetened large flake coconut (such as Bob's Red Mill), toasted

■ Soak tapioca in coconut water overnight in a bowl covered with plastic wrap.

■ In a medium lidded pot, combine tapioca-coconut water mixture, coconut milk, vanilla and salt. Cover, bring to a boil, then reduce to a low simmer. Cook, covered, for 40 minutes.

■ In a bowl, whisk egg yolk and sugar. Slowly whisk in half the tapioca; pour contents from bowl into pot. Cook another 10 minutes over low heat, until thickened. Remove from heat and cool 10 minutes.

■ Meanwhile, puree 1 cup of the mango in a blender or food processor. Mix into remaining 1 cup mango.

■ In each of 6 cups, layer ¼ cup mango, followed by 1 heaping tbsp

BANANA
PUDDING

**DARK CHOCOLATE
SOUFFLÉ**

Dark Chocolate Soufflé

MAKES 6 servings **PREP** 10 minutes
BAKE at 375° for 17 minutes

Butter for coating ramekins

¼ **cup granulated sugar, plus extra for coating ramekins**

7 **oz bittersweet dark chocolate, roughly chopped**

¼ **cup heavy cream**

3 **egg yolks**

¼ **tsp vanilla**

6 **egg whites**

Pinch salt

Confectioners' sugar (optional)

■ Heat oven to 375°. Butter and sugar six 6-ounce ramekins. Fill a small pot with 1 inch of water and bring to a simmer. In a metal bowl large enough to rest on the pot, combine chocolate and heavy cream. Stir until melted. Remove from heat and whisk in egg yolks, one at a time, being careful not to scramble. Stir in vanilla.

■ In a large bowl (or a stand mixer fitted with whisk attachment), whisk egg whites on high until soft peaks form. While whisking, add sugar and salt; whisk on high until stiff peaks form.

■ Gently fold chocolate mixture into whipped egg whites until no streaks remain. (Do not overmix or the soufflés won't rise to the maximum level.) Carefully spoon mixture evenly among ramekins. Bake at 375° for 17 minutes or until puffed and a cake tester inserted in the middle comes out clean. Dust with confectioners' sugar, if desired, and serve immediately.

PER SERVING 265 **CAL**; 20 g **FAT** (10 g **SAT**); 8 g **PRO**; 23 g **CARB**; 2 g **FIBER**; 67 mg **SODIUM**; 119 mg **CHOL**

Maple Pudding with Quick Praline

MAKES 6 servings **PREP** 10 minutes
COOK 11 minutes **REFRIGERATE** 4 hours

3 **cups whole milk**

3 **large egg yolks**

3 **tbsp plus 1 tsp cornstarch**

⅔ **cup maple syrup**

½ **tsp maple flavoring**

¼ **tsp salt**

Quick Praline (recipe follows)

■ In a medium bowl, whisk together 1 cup of the milk, the egg yolks and cornstarch.

■ In a medium saucepan, combine remaining 2 cups milk, the maple syrup, maple flavoring and salt. Cook over medium heat until just steaming, about 6 minutes.

■ Whisk about 1½ cups of the hot milk mixture into the egg yolk mixture. Whisk egg-milk mixture back into saucepan. Cook, stirring constantly with a wooden spoon, to a simmer, until thick and large bubbles break the surface, about 5 minutes. Strain into 6 dessert cups or glasses. Place plastic wrap directly on surface of puddings and refrigerate at least 4 hours. Just before serving, remove plastic wrap and sprinkle each

pudding with some of the Quick Praline.

PER SERVING 320 **CAL**; 13 g **FAT** (4 g **SAT**); 6 g **PRO**; 47 g **CARB**; 1 g **FIBER**; 190 mg **SODIUM**; 115 mg **CHOL**

Quick Praline

MAKES 8 servings **PREP** 5 minutes
TOAST at 350° for 10 minutes **COOK** 5 minutes
COOL 30 minutes

■ Spread ⅔ cup pecans on a baking sheet. Toast at 350° for 10 minutes. Line a large baking sheet with nonstick foil.

■ In a small saucepan, combine ½ cup sugar, 2 tbsp water and a pinch of salt. Cook over medium-high heat until bubbly, then cook at a low boil, without stirring, until light amber, about 5 minutes. Stir in pecans until coated and quickly spread onto foil-lined sheet. Cool 30 minutes, then chop into pieces.

MAPLE PUDDING WITH
QUICK PRALINE

MAPLE AND
VANILLA-ROASTED
FRUIT

Maple and Vanilla–Roasted Fruit

MAKES 3 to 4 cups, depending on the type of fruit **PREP** 10 minutes
ROAST at 375° for 50 minutes

- ⅓ cup maple sugar
- 1 vanilla bean
- 1 tsp finely grated lemon zest
- 2 lb seasonal fruit, peeled, halved, cored and/or pitted
- 1 tbsp freshly squeezed lemon juice
- 1 tbsp unsalted butter, cut into small bits

  Ice cream, yogurt or crème fraîche, for serving (optional)

- Position a rack in center of oven and heat oven to 375°.

- Place sugar in a small bowl. With a sharp knife, split vanilla bean in half lengthwise and scrape seeds into sugar (reserve the vanilla pod). Work sugar, vanilla seeds and lemon zest together with your fingertips until sugar is fragrant and moist-looking.

- Arrange fruit in a 9 x 13-inch metal baking dish, cut sides up. Drizzle with lemon juice and sprinkle with sugar. Dot butter bits all over fruit. Add vanilla pod and 2 tbsp water to dish.

- Roast at 375° for 30 minutes, occasionally spooning pan juices over fruit. Turn fruit and continue to roast, basting once or twice, until tender, 15 to 20 minutes more.

- Serve with ice cream, yogurt or crème fraîche, if desired.

Poached Pears with Crème Fraîche

MAKES 4 servings **PREP** 10 minutes
COOK 48 minutes

- 4 firm Bosc pears
- 1½ cups pomegranate juice
- ½ cup port wine
- ½ cup toasted walnuts
- ½ cup crème fraîche
  Mint, for garnish

- Peel pears. Cut a small slice from bottom of each pear so it will stand upright.

POACHED PEARS WITH CRÈME FRAÎCHE

- Place pomegranate juice and port in a large lidded skillet and bring to a boil. Place pears in skillet on their sides. Cover and simmer 40 to 45 minutes, until tender. Turn pears a few times so all sides color evenly.

- Remove pears to serving plates. Cook poaching liquid over high heat 3 minutes, until thick and syrupy.

- Spoon sauce over pears. Garnish with walnuts, crème fraîche and mint.

PER SERVING 392 **CAL**; 21 g **FAT** (8 g **SAT**); 4 g **PRO**; 46 g **CARB**; 6 g **FIBER**; 26 mg **SODIUM**; 40 mg **CHOL**

Summer Berries with Sabayon

MAKES 6 servings **PREP** 15 minutes
COOK 5 minutes

- ¾ cup sweet Marsala or Moscato wine
- ⅓ cup sugar
- 6 egg yolks

- 6 oz blackberries
- 6 oz blueberries
- 6 oz raspberries
- 1 pint strawberries, hulled and diced
- 5 gingersnap cookies, crushed

- For sabayon, fill a small pot with 2 inches of water. Bring to a simmer. In a metal bowl large enough to fit over pot, whisk together wine and sugar. Add egg yolks, whisking constantly over simmering water until mixture is frothy and thickens, about 5 minutes. (Temperature should reach 165°.) Do not scramble yolks.

- In a large bowl, toss together blackberries, blueberries, raspberries and diced strawberries. Distribute among 6 glasses. Spoon sabayon over berries. Garnish with crushed cookies. Serve warm or chilled.

PER SERVING 211 **CAL**; 5 g **FAT** (2 g **SAT**); 4 g **PRO**; 32 g **CARB**; 5 g **FIBER**; 12 mg **SODIUM**; 205 mg **CHOL**

Apple Fritters with Calvados Glaze

MAKES 12 fritters **PREP** 15 minutes
FRY 6 minutes per batch

- **2** **cups all-purpose flour**
- **⅓** **cup granulated sugar**
- **1** **tbsp baking powder**
- **½** **tsp salt**
- **¾** **tsp cinnamon**
- **¼** **tsp nutmeg**
- **2** **Granny Smith apples, peeled, cored and cut into ¼-inch dice**
- **¾** **cup apple cider**
- **2** **eggs, lightly beaten**
- **3** **tbsp butter, melted**
- **1** **tsp vanilla extract**
- **6** **cups vegetable oil**
- **2** **cups confectioners' sugar**
- **2** **tbsp apple cider**
- **2** **tbsp Calvados**

■ In a large bowl, whisk together flour, sugar, baking powder, salt, cinnamon and nutmeg. Fold in diced apples. Stir in cider, eggs, butter and vanilla until combined.

■ Heat oil in a large, heavy-bottomed Dutch oven to 375°.

■ Form 4 fritters, using a ⅓-cup ice cream scoop, and drop into oil. Fry 3 minutes; turn and fry an additional 3 minutes. With a slotted spoon, remove to a cooling rack placed over a baking sheet. Repeat until all fritters are fried.

■ Combine confectioners' sugar, cider and Calvados. While fritters are slightly warm, spread a heaping tbsp of the glaze over each fritter. Serve slightly warm or at room temperature.

PER FRITTER 342 **CAL**; 18 g **FAT** (4 g **SAT**); 3 g **PRO**; 43 g **CARB**; 1 g **FIBER**; 213 mg **SODIUM**; 43 mg **CHOL**

Stone-Fruit Cobbler

MAKES 8 servings **PREP** 25 minutes
BAKE at 400° for 25 minutes

- **2½** **lb peaches, plums and nectarines, peeled and cut into chunks (about 5 cups)**

STONE-FRUIT COBBLER

- **1** **cup plus 3 tbsp sugar**
- **2** **tbsp tapioca**
- **¾** **tsp ground ginger**
- **½** **tsp ground cinnamon**
- **¼** **tsp ground nutmeg**
- **¼** **tsp salt**
- **1** **cup Bisquick**
- **2** **tbsp unsalted butter, melted**
- **⅓** **cup milk**
- **Vanilla ice cream (optional)**

■ Heat oven to 400°. Coat a 6-cup shallow baking dish with nonstick cooking spray.

■ In a large bowl, combine fruit, 1 cup of the sugar, the tapioca, ginger, cinnamon, nutmeg and salt. Spoon into prepared dish.

■ In a medium bowl, whisk together Bisquick, 2 tbsp of the sugar, the butter and milk. Stir until thick batter forms. Dollop heaping tablespoonfuls over fruit. Sprinkle remaining 1 tbsp sugar over top. Bake at 400° for 25 minutes, until fruit is bubbly and topping has browned. Serve warm with vanilla ice cream, if desired.

PER SERVING 220 **CAL**; 6 g **FAT** (3 g **SAT**); 3 g **PRO**; 45 g **CARB**; 2 g **FIBER**; 266 mg **SODIUM**; 9 mg **CHOL**

Batter. In a medium bowl, whisk together flour, baking powder and salt.

In a large bowl, beat butter until smooth. Add sugar; beat until fluffy. Beat in egg and vanilla. On low speed, add flour mixture alternately with milk, beating well after each addition.

Spread half the batter in prepared pan. Cover with blueberries and cherries. Drop remaining batter on top by tablespoonfuls. Cover with topping.

Bake at 350° for 50 to 55 minutes, until golden brown. Remove pan to a wire rack. Run a small offset spatula around side. Cool for 15 minutes. Remove side. Run spatula around center and bottom of pan; place two wide spatulas under cake and gently lift cake from pan bottom. Serve with crème fraîche, if desired.

PER SERVING 271 CAL; 12 g FAT (8 g SAT); 4 g PRO; 38 g CARB; 1 g FIBER; 129 mg SODIUM; 49 mg CHOL

Grilled Peaches with Ricotta, Honey and Pistachios

MAKES 6 servings PREP 10 minutes
GRILL 8 minutes

- 3 peaches, halved and pitted
- 1 cup ricotta cheese
- ¼ cup honey
- ¼ cup roughly chopped pistachios
- 6 mint leaves

Heat grill or grill pan to medium-high. Grill peaches 4 minutes per side, until charred and slightly softened.

Whip ricotta and 2 tbsp of the honey with a hand mixer until well combined. Spoon evenly over peaches, then sprinkle with pistachios and drizzle with remaining 2 tbsp honey. Garnish with mint leaves. Serve warm.

PER SERVING 164 CAL; 8 g FAT (4 g SAT); 6 g PRO; 19 g CARB; 1 g FIBER; 36 mg SODIUM; 21 mg CHOL

Blueberry-Cherry Buckle

MAKES 12 servings PREP 25 minutes
BAKE at 350° for 55 minutes COOL 15 minutes

TOPPING

- ½ cup all-purpose flour
- ¼ cup packed light brown sugar
- ¼ cup granulated sugar
- ½ tsp ground cinnamon
- 4 tbsp cold unsalted butter, cut into pieces

BATTER

- 2 cups all-purpose flour
- 2 tsp baking powder
- ¼ tsp salt
- ½ cup unsalted butter, softened
- ½ cup granulated sugar
- 1 egg
- 1 tsp vanilla extract
- ½ cup milk
- 1 cup blueberries
- 1 cup dark cherries, pitted
   Crème fraîche (optional)

Heat oven to 350°. Butter and flour a 10-inch tube pan with a removable bottom.

Topping. In a small bowl, combine flour, sugars and cinnamon. Cut in butter until crumbly.

GRILLED PEACHES WITH
RICOTTA, HONEY AND
PISTACHIOS

BLACKBERRY-
RHUBARB
COBBLER

Blackberry-Rhubarb Cobbler

MAKES 8 servings **PREP** 15 minutes
BAKE at 350° for 1 hour **LET STAND** 10 minutes

- 4 cups blackberries
- 4 cups sliced rhubarb (1-inch pieces)
- 2 tbsp quick-cooking tapioca
- 1 tbsp lemon juice
- 1 tbsp lemon zest
- ¾ cup granulated sugar
- 1 cup old-fashioned oats
- ¼ cup all-purpose flour
- ½ cup light brown sugar
- 5 tbsp cold butter, cut into small pieces

■ Heat oven to 350°. In a bowl, combine blackberries, rhubarb, tapioca, lemon juice, lemon zest and granulated sugar. In a separate bowl, combine oats, flour and brown sugar. Crumble in cold butter; mix with your hands until it resembles coarse crumbs.

■ Pour fruit mixture into a 2-qt baking dish. Top with oat mixture. Bake at 350° for 1 hour or until topping is browned. Let stand 10 minutes before serving.

PER SERVING 292 CAL; 8 g FAT (5 g SAT); 3 g PRO; 54 g CARB; 6 g FIBER; 10 mg SODIUM; 19 mg CHOL

Blueberry Shortcake

MAKES 6 servings **PREP** 20 minutes
BAKE at 425° for 14 minutes **COOK** 6 minutes

- 1½ cups all-purpose flour
- ½ cup plus 3 tbsp sugar

BLUEBERRY SHORTCAKE

- 2 tsp baking powder
- ¼ tsp salt
- ⅓ cup cold butter, cut into small pieces
- ½ cup cold 2% milk
- ½ tsp almond extract
- 3 cups blueberries
- 1 tbsp fresh lemon juice
- 1 tsp lemon zest
- 1 cup heavy cream
- ½ tsp vanilla extract

■ Heat oven to 425°. Whisk together flour, 2 tbsp of the sugar, the baking powder and salt. With hands, mix butter into flour mixture until coarse crumbs form. Stir in milk and almond extract. Gently gather dough, divide into 6 pieces and place on a baking sheet about 2 inches apart. Bake at 425° for 12 to 14 minutes, or until lightly browned and cooked through.

■ Meanwhile, combine 1⅓ cups of the blueberries, ½ cup of the sugar, the lemon juice and lemon zest in a small pot. Bring to a simmer over medium heat; cook 6 minutes or until blueberries burst and mixture thickens slightly. Stir in remaining ⅔ cup blueberries. Remove from heat and cool slightly.

■ In a medium bowl, beat heavy cream on medium-high speed until foamy. Add vanilla extract and remaining 1 tablespoon sugar and beat until stiff peaks form.

■ Slice shortcakes in half lengthwise. Spoon ¼ cup of the blueberries on top of the bottom half of each shortcake; dollop each with whipped cream. Place top half of shortcake on each and serve.

PER SERVING 464 **CAL**; 26 g **FAT** (16 g **SAT**); 5 g **PRO**; 56 g **CARB**; 3 g **FIBER**; 256 mg **SODIUM**; 82 mg **CHOL**

Blueberry-Strawberry Shortcake

MAKES 10 servings **PREP** 20 minutes **REFRIGERATE** 2 hours **BAKE** at 325° for 30 minutes

- 4 cups all-purpose flour
- ¼ cup sugar, plus extra for sprinkling and to sweeten cream
- ¾ tsp salt
- 1 cup (2 sticks) unsalted butter, very cold
- 1 cup solid vegetable shortening, very cold
- ½ cup buttermilk
- 1 qt strawberries, hulled and sliced
- 1 qt blueberries
- 3 cups heavy cream, whipped

■ In a large mixing bowl, combine flour, ¼ cup sugar and salt. Cut in butter and shortening until mixture resembles coarse sand. Add buttermilk and mix just until dough comes together in a ball. Divide dough evenly into thirds; wrap in plastic and refrigerate 2 to 3 hours.

■ Heat oven to 325°. Roll each piece of dough on lightly floured parchment to a 10-inch circle. Prick with a fork and sprinkle liberally with sugar. Bake at 325° for 30 minutes.

■ To assemble: Set aside a few berries to top finished dessert. Place 1 pastry disk on a serving plate and cover with a third of the remaining berries, followed by a third of the whipped cream. Repeat layering 2 more times; finish with reserved berries.

BLUEBERRY-STRAWBERRY SHORTCAKE

RED VELVET TRIFLE

- Spread batter into prepared pan and bake at 350° for 35 to 40 minutes, until a toothpick inserted in center of cake comes out clean. Cool in pan on a wire rack for 10 minutes, then turn out onto rack and cool completely.

- **Filling and Topping.** In a bowl, beat together Neufchâtel, butter and ¾ cup of the heavy cream until smooth. On low, beat in 2 cups of the confectioners' sugar, the sour cream, milk and ½ tsp of the vanilla extract.

- Trim edges from cake and cut cake into 1½-inch cubes (set aside 1 cube for topping). Place one-third of the cake cubes in a trifle dish or large bowl. Top with half the filling. Repeat layering with cake cubes and remaining filling, then top with remaining one-third of the cake. Beat remaining ¾ cup heavy cream with remaining 2 tbsp confectioners' sugar and ¼ tsp vanilla. Spread over top of trifle. Crumble reserved cake cube over trifle. Cover with plastic and refrigerate overnight.

PER SERVING 522 **CAL**; 31 g **FAT** (19 g **SAT**); 7 g **PRO**; 54 g **CARB**; 1 g **FIBER**; 256 mg **SODIUM**; 134 mg **CHOL**

Chocolate Raspberry Trifle

MAKES 24 servings **PREP** 15 minutes
BAKE at 350° for 35 minutes **COOK** 7 minutes
REFRIGERATE at least 1 hour, then up to overnight

- 1 box (16.25 oz) chocolate cake mix
- 2 large eggs
- ½ cup vegetable oil
- 4 large egg yolks
- ½ cup plus 5 tbsp sugar
- ¼ cup (½ stick) unsalted butter, cut up
- 4 oz bittersweet chocolate, chopped
- 2½ cups heavy cream
- 1 tsp vanilla extract
- 2 pkg (6 oz each) fresh raspberries
  Chocolate curls or cocoa powder, for garnish

- Heat oven to 350°. Coat a 13 x 9 x 2-inch baking pan with

Red Velvet Trifle

MAKES 16 servings **PREP** 30 minutes
BAKE at 350° for 40 minutes **COOL** 10 minutes
REFRIGERATE overnight

CAKE

- 2½ cups all-purpose flour
- ¼ cup unsweetened cocoa powder
- 1 tsp baking soda
- ½ tsp salt
- 2 sticks (1 cup) unsalted butter, softened
- 1½ cups packed light brown sugar
- 3 large eggs
- 1 cup sour cream blended with ¼ cup milk and 1 bottle (1 oz) red food coloring
- 2 tsp vanilla extract

FILLING AND TOPPING

- 1 pkg (8 oz) Neufchâtel cheese, softened
- ½ stick (¼ cup) unsalted butter, softened
- 1½ cups heavy cream
- 2 cups plus 2 tbsp confectioners' sugar
- ½ cup sour cream
- ½ cup milk
- ¾ tsp vanilla extract

- Heat oven to 350°. Coat a 13 x 9 x 2-inch pan with nonstick baking spray with flour.

- **Cake.** In a medium bowl, whisk together flour, cocoa, baking soda and salt. In a large bowl, beat butter until smooth. Beat in brown sugar until light colored and fluffy, 2 minutes. Beat in eggs, one at a time. On low, beat in half the flour mixture. Scrape down side of bowl and beat in sour cream mixture and remaining half of the flour mixture. Stir in vanilla.

CHOCOLATE RASPBERRY TRIFLE

nonstick cooking spray. Line bottom with wax paper; coat paper with spray. Prepare cake mix per package directions with eggs, oil and 1¼ cups water. Bake at 350° for 35 minutes or until cake springs back when pressed. Cool 10 minutes in pan on a wire rack; invert directly onto rack, remove paper and cool completely.

■ While cake cools, in a large metal bowl, combine egg yolks, ½ cup sugar, ¼ cup water and butter. Place bowl over a pot of simmering water. Cook, whisking constantly, until mixture is pale and thickened and

registers 160° on an instant-read thermometer, about 7 minutes. Remove bowl from saucepan and whisk in chocolate until smooth. In a separate bowl, beat 1 cup of the cream with 2 tbsp of the sugar and the vanilla until medium-firm peaks form. Fold whipped cream into chocolate mixture until no white remains. Cover surface directly with plastic and refrigerate at least 1 hour.

■ Once cake has cooled, cut into 1½-inch cubes. Whip remaining 1½ cups cream with remaining 3 tbsp sugar to medium-firm peaks. Begin

layering trifle: Spoon half the cake cubes into a 4-qt glass bowl or dish. Compress slightly. Spread half the chocolate mousse (about 1½ cups) over cake cubes. Top mousse with 1 pkg of the raspberries and half the whipped cream (about 1½ cups). Repeat layering and garnish with chocolate curls or cocoa powder. Serve immediately or refrigerate up to overnight until serving.

PER SERVING 292 **CAL**; 21 g **FAT** (9 g **SAT**); 3 g **PRO**; 27 g **CARB**; 2 g **FIBER**; 146 mg **SODIUM**; 91 mg **CHOL**

EGGNOG ICE CREAM
PARFAITS

FLOURLESS BROWNIE
SUNDAES

MANGO-RASPBERRY
TRIFLE

Flourless Brownie Sundaes

MAKES 6 servings **PREP** 15 minutes
MICROWAVE 45 seconds
BAKE at 350° for 20 minutes

- ¼ cup (½ stick) unsalted butter
- 2 oz unsweetened chocolate, chopped
- ⅔ cup sugar
- 1 egg plus 1 egg yolk
- 1½ tsp vanilla extract
- ¼ cup unsweetened cocoa powder
- ½ cup mini semisweet chocolate chips
- 6 small scoops ice cream
  Chocolate sauce, for drizzling

■ Heat oven to 350°. Coat a jumbo muffin pan with nonstick cooking spray.

■ Combine butter and chocolate in a medium glass bowl. Microwave for 45 seconds, then stir until smooth.

■ Whisk in sugar, then egg and egg yolk. Whisk in vanilla extract and sift cocoa powder over mixture. Fold in cocoa with a rubber spatula; stir in mini chips. Divide among 6 prepared pan indents (¼ cup in each), spreading tops level. Bake at 350° for 15 to 20 minutes, until tops are shiny.

■ Run a knife around edge of cakes; remove from pan. Cool a few minutes on a rack; transfer to plates. Top each with a scoop of ice cream; drizzle with chocolate sauce.

PER SERVING 493 **CAL**; 26 g **FAT** (16 g **SAT**); 7 g **PRO**; 62 g **CARB**; 3 g **FIBER**; 52 mg **SODIUM**; 106 mg **CHOL**

Eggnog Ice Cream Parfaits

MAKES 6 servings **PREP** 10 minutes

- ½ cup heavy cream
- 1 tsp sugar
- ¼ tsp vanilla extract
- 24 gingersnap cookies, crushed
- 3 cups eggnog-flavor ice cream
- 3 cups rum raisin ice cream
  Cinnamon, mint and cherries for garnish

■ In a large bowl, beat heavy cream on medium speed until foamy. Add sugar and vanilla; beat on medium-high until soft peaks form. Refrigerate until serving.

■ In each of six 12-ounce dessert glasses, layer 2 tbsp cookie crumbs, one ½-cup scoop eggnog ice cream, 2 tbsp cookie crumbs and one ½-cup scoop rum raisin ice cream. Garnish with whipped cream, cinnamon, mint and cherries.

PER SERVING 467 **CAL**; 12 g **FAT** (6 g **SAT**); 5 g **PRO**; 55 g **CARB**; 0 g **FIBER**; 102 mg **SODIUM**; 27 mg **CHOL**

Mango-Raspberry Trifle

MAKES 12 servings **PREP** 20 minutes
COOK 6 minutes **COOL** 30 minutes
REFRIGERATE overnight

- 2 pkg (2.75 oz each) vanilla pudding and pie filling (not instant)
- 4 cups 2% milk
- 1 container (6 oz) low-fat mango Greek yogurt
- 6 cups angel food cake cubes (from 10-oz cake)
- 4 ripe mangoes, peeled and cut into ½-inch dice
- 2 containers (6 oz each) raspberries
- 1 cup heavy cream
- 1 tbsp sugar
- ½ tsp vanilla extract
- ⅓ cup toasted sliced almonds

■ Cook pudding with milk according to package directions, 4 to 6 minutes. Cool 30 minutes in refrigerator; stir in yogurt.

■ In a 14- to 16-cup footed glass trifle dish, layer 2 cups of the cake cubes, one-third of the pudding mixture, one-third of the mangoes and one-third of the raspberries. Repeat layering twice. Cover and refrigerate overnight.

■ Whip cream, sugar and vanilla until medium-soft peaks form. Swirl over top of trifle. Top with almonds.

PER SERVING 325 **CAL**; 12 g **FAT** (6 g **SAT**); 7 g **PRO**; 50 g **CARB**; 4 g **FIBER**; 342 mg **SODIUM**; 35 mg **CHOL**

CHOCOLATE-CHERRY
BREAD PUDDING

Chocolate-Cherry
Bread Pudding

MAKES 6 servings **PREP** 25 minutes
SLOW COOK on LOW for 3 hours
COOL 30 minutes

Nonstick cooking spray

½ cup refrigerated or frozen egg product, thawed, or 2 eggs, lightly beaten

¼ cup sugar

¼ tsp almond extract

⅛ tsp salt

1 cup fat-free milk

3 cups dried whole wheat bread cubes*

½ cup chopped bittersweet chocolate (2 oz)

⅓ cup dried tart cherries

1 cup warm water

3 tbsp confectioners' sugar

2 tbsp low-fat Greek yogurt

1 tsp fat-free milk

3 tbsp sliced almonds, toasted (optional)

■ Lightly coat a 1-qt soufflé dish or casserole** with cooking spray. Tear off an 18 x 12-inch piece of heavy foil; cut in half lengthwise. Fold each piece lengthwise into thirds. Crisscross the foil strips and place the dish in the center of the crisscross; set aside.

■ In a medium bowl, combine eggs, sugar, almond extract and salt. Whisk in the 1 cup milk. Gently stir in bread cubes, chocolate and cherries. Pour mixture into prepared dish. Cover dish tightly with foil.

■ Pour the warm water into a 3½- to 5-qt slow cooker. Using the ends of the foil strips, transfer dish to cooker. Leave foil strips under dish.

■ Cover and cook on LOW for 3 to 3½ hours or until a knife inserted in center comes out clean. Using foil strips, carefully remove dish from cooker; discard foil strips. Cool, uncovered, on a wire rack for 30 minutes before serving.

■ Meanwhile, for icing, in a small bowl, combine confectioners' sugar, yogurt and the 1 tsp milk. Drizzle cooled bread pudding with icing. If desired, sprinkle with almonds.

PER SERVING 189 **CAL**; 4 g **FAT** (2 g **SAT**); 6 g **PRO**; 34 g **CARB**; 2 g **FIBER**; 178 mg **SODIUM**; 1 mg **CHOL**

*Tip: For dried bread cubes, preheat oven to 300°. Cut whole wheat bread slices (about 3 oz) into cubes to make 3 cups. Spread cubes in a single layer in a 15 x 10 x 1-inch baking pan. Bake for 10 to 15 minutes or until dried, stirring twice; cool.

**Tip: Before beginning this recipe, check to make sure that the dish or casserole you plan to use fits into your slow cooker.

Blueberry-Pistachio
Ice Cream

MAKES 12 servings **PREP** 10 minutes
COOK 15 minutes **PROCESS** according to manufacturer's instructions
FREEZE at least 2 hours

2 cups blueberries

1 tbsp lemon juice

½ cup plus 1 tbsp sugar

4 egg yolks

2 cups whole milk

1 cup heavy cream

¼ tsp salt

½ tsp vanilla extract

1 cup unsalted chopped pistachios

■ Combine blueberries, lemon juice and 1 tbsp of the sugar in a saucepan over medium heat. Cook 5 to 7 minutes or until berries burst and become a bit syrupy. Cool.

■ In a bowl, whisk egg yolks and ¼ cup of the sugar. Heat milk, cream, salt and remaining ¼ cup sugar in a pot until barely simmering. Remove from heat and slowly whisk into yolk-sugar mixture to temper. Pour back into pot and cook over medium heat. Stir constantly until mixture coats the back of a wooden spoon (170° to 180°), 4 to 8 minutes. Pour through fine-mesh strainer into a new bowl; cool over an ice bath or in refrigerator.

■ Whisk vanilla and blueberries into cooled liquid. Process in an ice cream maker according to manufacturer's directions. Add pistachios during last 5 minutes. Transfer to a lidded container and freeze at least 2 hours.

PER SERVING 210 **CAL**; 15 g **FAT** (6 g **SAT**); 5 g **PRO**; 16 g **CARB**; 2 g **FIBER**; 45 mg **SODIUM**; 95 mg **CHOL**

**PEACH MELBA
ICE CREAM CAKE**

Peach Melba
Ice Cream Cake

MAKES 16 servings **PREP** 20 minutes
COOK 10 minutes **FREEZE** overnight
STAND 10 minutes

- 1 **pkg (10 oz) shortbread cookies, finely crushed**
- ¼ **cup unsalted butter, melted**
- 2 **pkg (6 oz each) raspberries (3 cups)**
- 3 **tbsp sugar**
- 2 **tsp cornstarch**
- 3 **containers (14 oz each) vanilla ice cream, softened slightly**
- 4 **fresh peaches, peeled and cut into ¼-inch slices**
- 3 **tbsp toasted sliced almonds**

■ Place crushed cookies in a large bowl; stir in butter until thoroughly combined. Press mixture into the bottom and partially up the side of a 9-inch springform pan. Refrigerate until ready to fill.

■ Place raspberries, 2 tbsp of the sugar and the cornstarch in a small saucepan. Over medium heat, bring to a gentle simmer; cook 10 minutes, stirring occasionally. Strain and let cool.

■ Stir ⅓ cup of the raspberry puree into softened ice cream and swirl. Spoon into springform pan and level off with a small spatula. Freeze overnight.

■ Remove cake from freezer and let stand at room temperature for 10 minutes. Toss peaches with remaining 1 tbsp sugar; fan over top. Wrap a warm damp towel around side of pan. Run a spatula around edge of cake; carefully remove side of pan.

■ Garnish with toasted almonds and serve with remaining raspberry puree.

PER SERVING 376 **CAL**; 23 g **FAT** (12 g **SAT**); 6 g **PRO**; 38 g **CARB**; 2 g **FIBER**; 136 mg **SODIUM**; 89 mg **CHOL**

Strawberry Frozen
Zabaglione

MAKES 12 servings **PREP** 25 minutes
COOK 15 minutes **FREEZE** 2 hours then overnight

- 1 **qt (1 lb) hulled and sliced strawberries**
- 1 **cup sugar**
- 4 **egg yolks**
- 2 **eggs**
- ¾ **cup Moscato**
- **Red food coloring**
- 1 **cup heavy cream**
- **Additional whipped cream (optional)**
- **Halved strawberries, for garnish (optional)**

■ Coat a 9 x 5 x 2-inch loaf pan with nonstick cooking spray. Line pan with plastic wrap, smoothing any wrinkles.

■ Blend strawberries in a blender until smooth. Pour into a small bowl and stir in ¼ cup of the sugar. Set aside.

■ On top of a double boiler over simmering water, whisk together egg yolks, eggs and remaining ¾ cup sugar. Whisk in Moscato. Continue to whisk until mixture reaches 160° and mounds on top of itself when whisk is lifted, about 15 minutes.

■ Remove top of double boiler and place in an ice-water bath. Whisk egg mixture until cool. Stir in strawberry puree. Place half the mixture in a separate bowl and tint with a few drops of red food coloring.

■ Beat cream in a bowl until soft peaks form. Fold half the whipped cream into red portion and half into untinted portion in the other bowl.

■ Spread red mixture into prepared pan; freeze for 2 hours. Spoon untinted mixture on top of frozen layer. Cover and freeze overnight.

■ To unmold and serve, briefly dip loaf pan into warm water. Invert onto serving plate and shake gently. Remove pan and plastic wrap. Garnish with whipped cream and halved strawberries, if desired.

PER SERVING 197 **CAL**; 13 g **FAT** (8 g **SAT**); 3 g **PRO**; 16 g **CARB**; 1 g **FIBER**; 27 mg **SODIUM**; 144 mg **CHOL**

**STRAWBERRY
FROZEN ZABAGLIONE**

OREO BROWNIES

Oreo Brownies

MAKES 9 brownies **PREP** 10 minutes
COOK 5 minutes **BAKE** at 325° for 30 minutes

- ¾ cup (1½ sticks) unsalted butter
- 6 oz unsweetened chocolate, coarsely chopped
- 1½ cups sifted all-purpose flour
- ¾ tsp baking powder
- ½ tsp salt
- 4 large eggs
- 2 cups sugar
- 1 tsp vanilla extract
- 1 cup coarsely chopped Oreo cookies

■ Heat oven to 325°. Line a 9 x 9-inch baking pan with foil. Coat foil with nonstick cooking spray.

■ In a small heavy saucepan, heat butter and chocolate over low heat, stirring constantly, until chocolate is melted and smooth, about 5 minutes. Set aside to cool. In a small bowl, stir flour, baking powder and salt. Set aside.

■ In a large mixing bowl, beat eggs and sugar with an electric mixer on high speed 5 minutes or until lemon color and fluffy, occasionally scraping sides of bowl. Add cooled chocolate mixture and vanilla. Beat on low speed until combined. Add flour mixture. Beat on low speed until combined, scraping sides of bowl. Stir in ½ cup of the Oreo pieces. Spread batter into prepared pan and scatter remaining cookie pieces on top.

■ Bake at 325° for 30 minutes or until brownie appears set. Cool in pan on a wire rack. Once cool, use foil to lift brownie from pan. Cut into 9 squares.

PER BROWNIE 313 **CAL**; 17 g **FAT** (9 g **SAT**); 4 g **PRO**; 41 g **CARB**; 2 g **FIBER**; 143 mg **SODIUM**; 75 mg **CHOL**

Chocolate Chip Oatmeal Raisin Treats

MAKES 40 servings **PREP** 15 minutes
STAND 10 minutes **REFRIGERATE** 30 minutes

- 1 cup pitted Medjool dates, tightly packed (see Tip)
- 1¾ cups old-fashioned rolled oats

CHOCOLATE CHIP OATMEAL RAISIN TREATS

- ¾ cup raisins
- ⅓ cup bittersweet chocolate chips (60% to 70% cacao)
- 1 generous tbsp natural peanut, almond or sunflower seed butter
- 1 tsp chia seeds
- ½ tsp ground cinnamon
- ¾ tsp pure vanilla extract
- ⅛ tsp fine sea salt

■ Place dates in a medium bowl. Fill bowl with hot water to cover dates by about an inch. Let stand 10 minutes. Drain.

■ Combine all ingredients in the bowl of a food processor. Process continuously until mixture comes together, forming a dough of sorts. You want the oats to be pretty much completely broken down, with a few bits of raisins and little chips of chocolate still visible.

■ Using a teaspoon-size scoop, portion out small pieces of dough, using your hands to roll them into balls about 1 inch in diameter. Place balls on a cookie sheet. Refrigerate until firm, about 30 minutes. Once chilled, transfer to an airtight container to store in the fridge for up to 10 days.

Tip: The dates should be nice and tacky here, more like a delicious edible "glue" than a soft fruit puree, so you should soak them less than you would if you were making baked goods. Medjool dates work best in this recipe because they're extra sticky, but Deglet Noor dates work too—they may require about 10 minutes more soaking time.

CHOCOLATE-
COCONUT BARS

Chocolate-Coconut Bars

MAKES 24 bars **PREP** 25 minutes
BAKE at 350° for 45 minutes
MICROWAVE 1½ minutes

CRUST

- 1 box (9 oz) Nabisco Famous chocolate wafer cookies
- 6 tbsp unsalted butter, melted
- 1 tsp vanilla extract

BAR BATTER

- 2 cups all-purpose flour
- 1 tsp baking soda
- 1 tsp salt
- 1 stick (½ cup) unsalted butter, softened
- 1 can (15 oz) cream of coconut
- 2 large eggs
- 2 cups (one 11-oz bag) semisweet chocolate chips
- 1¾ cups sweetened flake coconut
- 1 cup walnuts, chopped

■ Heat oven to 350°.

■ **Crust.** Place wafer cookies in a food processor and pulse on and off until finely crushed. Drizzle with melted butter and vanilla and process until crumbs begin to stick together. Pour into a 15 x 10 x 1-inch jellyroll pan and press evenly into bottom. Refrigerate while making bar batter.

■ **Bar Batter.** In a medium bowl, whisk flour, baking soda and salt. In a large bowl, with an electric mixer, beat softened butter and cream of coconut until smooth. Beat in eggs on medium speed. On low, beat in flour mixture. Fold in 1½ cups of the chocolate chips, 1 cup of the coconut and the walnuts. Pour over crust in pan, spreading to edges. Bake at 350° for 35 minutes, until puffed, golden and set. Cool in pan on a wire rack.

■ Chop remaining ¾ cup coconut and bake at 350° for 10 minutes, until golden.

■ Place remaining ½ cup chocolate chips in a glass bowl. Microwave 45 seconds and stir. Microwave an additional 45 seconds and stir until smooth. Transfer to a piping bag or small resealable plastic bag. Snip off a small corner and drizzle over cooled cake. Sprinkle with toasted coconut. Let set, then cut into 24 bars.

PER BAR 386 CAL; 22 g FAT (13 g SAT); 5 g PRO; 45 g CARB; 3 g FIBER; 258 mg SODIUM; 38 mg CHOL

Apple Hazelnut Blondies

MAKES 12 blondies PREP 20 minutes
BAKE at 350° for 10 minutes (nuts) and 30 minutes (blondies) COOL 32 minutes

BLONDIES

- 1 cup hazelnuts
- ¾ cup granulated sugar
- ¾ cup packed light brown sugar
- ½ cup (1 stick) butter, melted
- 2 eggs, lightly beaten
- 1 tsp vanilla extract
- 2 cups all-purpose flour
- 2 tsp baking powder
- ¼ tsp salt
- 2 Fuji apples, peeled, cored and chopped (about 2 cups)

MAPLE ICING

- 1 pkg (8 oz) cream cheese, softened
- 1 cup confectioners' sugar
- 2 tbsp maple syrup
- ¾ tsp vanilla extract

■ **Blondies.** Heat oven to 350°. Coat a 12-cavity brownie pan (such as Wilton Brownie Bar Pan) with nonstick cooking spray.

■ Place nuts on a rimmed baking sheet. Bake at 350° for 10 minutes. Cool slightly and rub nuts with fingers to remove skin. Chop nuts and reserve.

■ Meanwhile, in a large bowl, combine sugars, butter, eggs and vanilla. Whisk together flour, baking powder and salt; stir into sugar-and-butter mixture until dry ingredients are just moistened. Fold in chopped apples and ¾ cup of the chopped nuts.

■ Spoon batter into prepared brownie pan, about ⅓ cup into each cavity. Bake at 350° for 30 minutes or until a toothpick inserted into center comes out clean. Cool on a wire rack for 30 minutes; turn out onto rack to cool completely.

■ **Maple Icing.** In a large bowl, beat cream cheese until smooth. Gradually beat in sugar; add maple syrup and vanilla and beat until smooth.

■ Frost each blondie with a generous 2 tbsp of icing. Sprinkle with remaining ¼ cup chopped hazelnuts.

PER BLONDIE 423 CAL; 21 g FAT (10 g SAT); 6 g PRO; 56 g CARB; 2 g FIBER; 190 mg SODIUM; 76 mg CHOL

APPLE HAZELNUT BLONDIES

PB CHOCOLATE CHUNK COOKIES

Picnic-Perfect Brownies

MAKES 16 brownies **PREP** 15 minutes
BAKE at 350° for 22 minutes
MICROWAVE 1 minute

BROWNIES
- ½ cup all-purpose flour
- ½ cup unsweetened cocoa powder
- ¼ tsp salt
- ¼ tsp baking powder
- ¾ cup sugar
- ¼ cup vegetable oil
- 2 eggs
- 1 tsp vanilla extract
- 1 tsp coffee extract
- ½ cup coarsely chopped walnuts
- ½ cup butterscotch baking chips

DRIZZLE
- ¼ cup semisweet chocolate baking chips
- 2 tsp vegetable oil
- ¼ cup butterscotch baking chips

■ **Brownies.** Heat oven to 350°. Coat an 8 x 8-inch baking pan with nonstick cooking spray.

■ In a medium bowl, whisk together flour, cocoa, salt and baking powder. Set aside. In a large bowl, combine sugar, oil, eggs and extracts. Stir in flour mixture until just moistened. Fold in walnuts and butterscotch chips. Spoon into prepared baking pan.

■ Bake at 350° for 22 minutes or until a toothpick inserted in center comes out clean. Cool completely.

■ **Drizzle.** Place chocolate chips and 1 tsp of the oil in a small bowl. Microwave on high 1 minute. Stir until melted. Place in a small resealable plastic bag and make a tiny snip in one corner. Pipe over cooled brownies. Repeat with butterscotch chips and remaining 1 tsp oil. Cut into 16 brownies.

PER BROWNIE 185 **CAL**; 11 g **FAT** (4 g **SAT**); 2 g **PRO**; 20 g **CARB**; 1 g **FIBER**; 64 mg **SODIUM**; 26 mg **CHOL**

PB Chocolate Chunk Cookies

MAKES 28 cookies **PREP** 15 minutes
BAKE at 350° for 18 minutes per batch

- 2 cups all-purpose flour
- ½ tsp salt
- ½ tsp baking soda
- ¼ tsp baking powder
- ½ cup (1 stick) unsalted butter, softened
- ½ cup creamy peanut butter
- ¾ cup packed dark brown sugar
- ½ cup granulated sugar
- 2 large eggs
- 1 tbsp vanilla extract
- 1 bag (11 oz) semisweet chocolate chunks
- 1 cup dry-roasted peanuts, chopped

■ Heat oven to 350°. In a medium bowl, blend flour, salt, baking soda and baking powder. Set aside.

■ Cream together butter and peanut butter until smooth. Add both sugars and beat until fluffy, about 2 minutes. Beat in eggs, one at a time. On low speed, beat in vanilla.

■ Add flour mixture and beat on low speed until combined. Stir in chocolate chunks and peanuts. Drop by scant ¼ cupfuls onto baking sheets. Bake at 350° for 18 minutes per batch. Cool on wire racks.

PER COOKIE 229 **CAL**; 12 g **FAT** (5 g **SAT**); 5 g **PRO**; 26 g **CARB**; 2 g **FIBER**; 97 mg **SODIUM**; 24 mg **CHOL**

Tip: These are delicious served warm. If desired, microwave on a paper towel for 15 seconds.

PICNIC-PERFECT
BROWNIES

CHOCOLATE-CARAMEL
BROWNIE STACKS

Chocolate-Caramel Brownie Stacks

MAKES 16 servings **PREP** 15 minutes
MICROWAVE 1 minute 50 seconds
BAKE at 325° for 35 minutes
STAND 5 minutes **REFRIGERATE** 2 hours

- 1½ **cups all-purpose flour**
- ½ **cup unsweetened cocoa powder**
- ¾ **tsp baking soda**
- ½ **tsp salt**
- ¾ **cup (1½ sticks) unsalted butter**
- 3 **oz semisweet chocolate, broken up**
- 1¼ **cups sugar**
- 3 **large eggs**
- 2 **tsp vanilla extract**
- 4 **oz (½ pkg) cream cheese, softened**
- ⅓ **cup caramel sauce, plus more for drizzling**
- ½ **tsp unflavored gelatin**
- 1½ **cups heavy cream**
   Chocolate sauce
   Caramel popcorn

■ Heat oven to 325°. Line a 9 x 9 x 2-inch baking pan with foil.

■ Whisk flour, cocoa, baking soda and salt. Combine butter and chocolate in a large glass bowl. Microwave in three 30-second increments, stirring until smooth.

■ Whisk in sugar and flour mixture, then eggs and vanilla. Spread into prepared pan.

■ Bake at 325° for 35 minutes or until pick inserted in center comes out clean. Cool in pan for 10 minutes; use foil to lift from pan to a wire rack. Cool completely.

■ With a serrated knife, slice in half horizontally. Line pan with plastic wrap and insert top layer, cut side up, in pan.

■ In a medium bowl, beat cream cheese and caramel sauce. Sprinkle gelatin over 2 tbsp water in a small glass bowl and let stand 5 minutes. Microwave 15 to 20 seconds, until dissolved. Beat into cream cheese mixture. Whip 1 cup of the heavy cream to stiff peaks. Fold into cream

cheese mixture. Spread onto brownie layer in pan and top with remaining layer, cut side down. Refrigerate 2 hours.

■ Whisk remaining ½ cup cream to stiff peaks. Use plastic to lift stacked brownie from pan. With serrated knife, cut into squares. Top each square with a dollop of whipped cream, some of the caramel sauce, chocolate sauce and caramel popcorn. Serve immediately.

PER SERVING 400 **CAL**; 23 g **FAT** (13 g **SAT**); 5 g **PRO**; 46 g **CARB**; 1 g **FIBER**; 211 mg **SODIUM**; 101 mg **CHOL**

Maple-Raisin Oatmeal Cookies

MAKES 36 cookies **PREP** 15 minutes
BAKE at 350° for 14 minutes

- ¾ **cup all-purpose flour**
- ½ **tsp baking soda**
- ¼ **tsp salt**
- ½ **cup (1 stick) unsalted butter, softened**
- ½ **cup packed light brown sugar**
- ¼ **cup plus 3 tbsp pure maple syrup**
- 1 **egg**
- 1½ **cups quick-cooking oats**
- ½ **cup raisins**
- 1 **cup confectioners' sugar**

■ Heat oven to 350°. In a bowl, whisk together flour, baking soda and salt. In another bowl, beat butter, sugar and ¼ cup of the maple syrup for 3 minutes. Beat in egg until just combined. Pour in flour and beat on low until just combined. Stir in oats and raisins.

■ Drop scant tablespoon-size rounds of batter onto baking sheets, spacing about 2 inches apart. Bake at 350° for 12 to 14 minutes, until golden. Remove to a wire rack to cool completely.

■ In a bowl, beat confectioners' sugar, remaining 3 tbsp maple syrup and 1 tbsp water on low until well combined. Drizzle over cooled cookies.

PER COOKIE 88 **CAL**; 3 g **FAT** (2 g **SAT**); 1 g **PRO**; 15 g **CARB**; 0 g **FIBER**; 38 mg **SODIUM**; 13 mg **CHOL**

MAPLE-RAISIN OATMEAL COOKIES

INDEX

CARROT-FENNEL SALAD,
PAGE 235